KAMLOOPS

An Angler's Study of the Kamloops Trout

Steve Raymond

Third Edition, 1994

KAMLOOPS

An Angler's Study of the Kamloops Trout

Steve Raymond

Frank Amato
PORTLAND

Author's father netting a trout from Hihium Lake, about 1940.

In memory of my father,
LT. COL. FREDERICK R. RAYMOND
He loved the Kamloops trout and its native country and taught his son to do likewise

PHOTO CREDITS:
All photos by Steve and Joan Raymond except the following:
Brian Chan/Gordon Honey: Front/Back cover, Title page
Brian Chan: 9, 70-71, 89,93
Dr. R.J. Bendzak: 33, 100
J. Schollmeyer: 57 #4, 63, 66-67, 69, 87
Steve Probasco: 78-79, 83, 98-99, 126

Steve Raymond
Third Edition, 1994

Frank Amato Publications
P.O. Box 82112 • Portland, Oregon 97282

Book Design: Kristi Workman

Printed in Hong Kong
Softbound ISBN: 1-878175-73-4 • Hardbound ISBN: 1-878175-74-2

CONTENTS

Preface   6

1: A Brief History   8
2: Life History   26
3: Managing the Resource   38
4: The Food of Kamloops Trout   54
5: Fly Patterns   68
6: Tackle and Technique   86
7: Favorite Waters   100

Maps   132

Bibliography   140
Index   142

PREFACE

In the late 1960s, when I started work on the original edition of this book, I had little notion it would survive as long or in as many forms as it has. The original, published in 1971, was followed by a completely revised and expanded edition in 1980; the softcover version of that edition has since gone through several printings. Now we have this new edition, again completely revised and updated and published in a much different format. Like an old trout returning to spawn yet one more time, the book seems to have remarkable endurance.

Such longevity is, I think, due to the angling community's continuing fascination for the Kamloops trout. Since the 1930s, when tales of spectacular fishing for huge fighting trout in the Kamloops region of British Columbia began to make their way around the world, there has been steadily growing interest among anglers in the lore and legend of the mighty Kamloops. Today that interest is evident in the huge numbers of fishermen and fisherwomen who annually flock to the province to test their skills in its numerous lakes. That they are not often disappointed is a tribute not only to the strength and stamina of the Kamloops trout, but also to the courage and vision of the men and women who have managed the fishery over the years and kept it viable.

Yet much has changed in the quarter century since publication of the first edition of this book. The British Columbia Interior, once mostly wilderness, is rapidly becoming urbanized, and transportation improvements have opened the area to onslaughts of visitors in staggering numbers. Along with these changes have come the heavy impacts of industrial and housing development, mining, logging and agriculture, all placing more pressures and demands on the Kamloops trout waters. Some lakes have been ruined beyond repair, but many remain and there are increasingly effective efforts to preserve them.

The advancing sophistication of British Columbia fly fishers is another significant change. Thirty years ago it was unusual to see another fly fisher who really knew what he or she was doing; now B.C. fly fishers are as good as any in the world, and in their refinement of specialized techniques for fishing chironomid imitations they are probably the best in the world. With greater sophistication has also come greater appreciation for the value of the resource, and today B.C.'s organized fly-fishing groups are among the province's most effective forces for conservation.

These changes and many others are chronicled in the pages of this new edition. More lakes also have been added to the list of "favorite waters"—about 200 in all, nearly twice as many as in the earlier editions—and the list of fly patterns has been revised and updated to reflect modern usage. The discussion of management and research techniques also has been brought up to date, and important trends, such as establishment of more private fish-for-fee waters, are documented.

But the biggest change is in the format of the book. The physical size has been greatly expanded and the text streamlined to open up space for many more photographs. So this edition, more than any of its predecessors, offers readers a true graphic vision of the Kamloops trout and its native country.

A few housekeeping notes: Since Canada is on the metric system, I have given measurements of distance, depth and elevation in both metric and traditional English units so that readers can take their choice. I have not done the same for measurements of fish because the common venacular among anglers is still to express weight in pounds and length in inches (I suspect this is because it is psychologically more satisfying to say that a fish weighed 5 pounds than 2.2 kilos).

The secondary roads (or worse) that provide access to most Interior lakes are now changing so rapidly it is almost impossible to keep up, so the maps in this edition show only the primary routes that are unlikely to change. It's best to inquire locally for the latest information on access.

As in the other editions, I am solely responsible for the opinions and conclusions expressed in this one, and these do not necessarily reflect the views of any other individuals or agencies.

Any book of this kind requires a great deal of assistance in preparation, and I would like to express my deep appreciation to many individuals who helped in large or small ways. One who helped in a large way was Brian Chan, small lakes biologist for the Thompson-Nicola region, who was extremely generous in sharing information and in reading portions of the manuscript and suggesting changes. His own book, *Flyfishing Strategies for Stillwaters*, is highly recommended to anglers.

Others who deserve thanks include Peter McVey of Corbett Lake Country Inn (and many other ventures), Bill Roddy of Chataway Lakes and Dan Geary of the Douglas Lake Ranch and its private fisheries. To Frank Amato goes credit for the idea of the format for this new edition.

Many people also rendered generous assistance in preparation of the earlier editions of this book, and since portions of those editions survive in this one, I would like to renew my thanks to them. They include Lee Straight, George Stringer, Alan Pratt and Dr. Bill McMahon. The first edition would not have been possible without the encouragement and help of the late Enos Bradner and Letcher Lambuth, and I would like to honor their memories by again acknowledging their assistance.

Along with every other Kamloops trout angler, I owe a debt to those patient and persevering scientists whose research over the years has uncovered so much information about the habits and life history of the Kamloops. Much of this information has been applied to management of the fishery, with obvious and lasting benefits. Without the work of people like Charles Mottley, Peter Larkin, Stuart Smith, Kanji Tsumura and so many others, there would not be nearly as many Kamloops trout to fish for as there are today—nor would there

be nearly as much to write about. And it is in writing about the Kamloops trout that I owe a special, personal debt to these people, most of whom I know only from having read their work in the pages of scientific journals.

There is a wealth of information about the Kamloops trout in such journals, but most is not readily accessible to the casual angler. Thus I am especially grateful for permission to use some of that information in this book: To the Fisheries Research Board of Canada for permission to quote from its *Journal* and the Journal's predecessors, the *Bulletin of the Biological Board of Canada* and the *Progress Reports of the Pacific Biological Station;* to the American Fisheries Society for permission to quote from its *Transactions*, and to the Canadian Department of Fisheries for permission to quote from the *Canadian Fish Culturist.*

In connection with this edition I am greatly indebted to Kanji Tsumura, head of the small lakes research program of the Research and Development Section of the B.C. Fisheries Branch at the University of British Columbia, Vancouver, for permission to quote from his reports and publications. Tsumura and his colleagues are continuing the tradition of leading-edge fisheries research in British Columbia.

To my wife, Joan; daughter, Stephanie, and son, Randy, my very special thanks for their continuing warm understanding, support and assistance.

Finally, my sincere appreciation to all the anglers with whom I have shared the waters of the Kamloops trout. With them I feel a bond of common experience that cannot easily be understood by those who have not shared in it. The fellowship of angling is one of its greatest rewards, and through the Kamloops trout I have made many good friends. As before, I hope both the fishing and the friendships will long endure.

—Steve Raymond
October, 1993

1: A Brief History

Bill Nation poses with a trout taken by one of his clients. *June 10th, 1935.*

The uncertain warmth of an early spring afternoon melts mounds of old snow hidden in the pine thickets, sending run-off to fuel the headwater springs. The springs give birth to streams that hurry down the wooded slopes and spill into frozen lakes, carving small openings in the ice. A breeze forces the openings wider, spreading cracks across the rotting ice until it splinters into shards that are swiftly swept away. At last, after the long stillness of winter, the lakes are free again to feel the touch and movement of the wind.

Even as the ice retreats, mature Kamloops trout are drawn to the inlet streams by some mysterious instinct not yet fully understood by humans. In ones and twos at first the trout enter the streams, pressing forward against the icy flow. As spring days pass and the last snow is flushed from the hills, the streams grow warmer, and the trout—large, hook-jawed males, precocious smaller males and great dark females burdened with spawn—begin the run in earnest, driving themselves forward with a sudden urgency to fulfill their life's purpose.

While the trout press forward to their spawning, the changing season also stirs something in the blood of anglers. From desktop and dinner table their eyes suddenly gaze into the distance while their minds fill with memories of seasons past—visions of fluttering sedges and rising trout, of days when the fish took eagerly and ran far across the shoals,

filling the afternoon air with the sound of a fly reel under ultimate stress. Old cane rods are taken out after a winter's rest and handled lovingly again and the mothball fragrance of fur and feathers pervades the house as new flies are dressed and stored in plastic boxes and metal fly books. Out come the tattered maps with circled names, names like Peterhope and Plateau, Broken Hook and Hardcastle, and the mind races with furious plans for the dawning season. Then, from nearly every compass point, anglers begin their own migration to the Kamloops trout waters of British Columbia to match their skills against one of the great game fish of the world.

The story of the Kamloops trout and those who fish for it begins during the last glacial period, about 20,000 years ago. Most of what is now British Columbia then lay beneath vast glaciers, mighty tentacles of ice that carved great canyons and left enormous piles of rubble as they retreated slowly to the north. Runoff from the vanishing glaciers sought outlets to the sea, filling the freshly cut canyons, spilling over to dig new channels and battering its way stubbornly to final release in the ocean.

The watercourses thus formed gradually assumed the rough shape of the watersheds we know today, and as these newborn rivers flooded out of the heart of the province, fish and wildlife began following them upstream to their sources. Among them were runs of salmon and steelhead that probed restlessly as far as the young rivers would let them go, planting the seeds of new generations in the glacial gravel of the river bottoms. Years later their progeny would return to spawn in the same places, completing the miraculous migratory cycle that slowly built the runs to mighty hosts.

Yet not all the offspring of these colonizing runs joined in migrations to the sea. Among each new generation of steelhead were some that remained behind to become residents of the rivers of their birth or lakes fed by those rivers. Others became landlocked when rivers changed course or geologic upheavals blocked their exits to the sea. Living, growing and breeding entirely in the fresh waters of the interior, these fish evolved to become the Kamloops trout.

Somewhere from the mists of prehistory came tribes of Indians who settled among the pine forests, lakes and rivers of the young country. They trapped and speared the Kamloops trout on their spawning beds and dried them on crude wooden racks for food, just as they did with the salmon and steelhead in their seasons. Yet there were never enough Indians, nor were their fishing methods efficient enough, to keep the Kamloops trout from thriving in the waters of its natural range, and it was still at peak abundance when white men arrived in the interior a little more than 180 years ago.

One of the first white settlements grew up where the North and South Thompson Rivers converge in a broad, grassy valley surrounded by timbered ridges that are a part of what geologists now call the Southern Interior Plateau. There, in 1812, Fort Kamloops was built, and in time the name Kamloops also was given to the nearby lake where the Thompson's mighty flow widens to a huge expanse of water.

The residents of Fort Kamloops soon learned that Kamloops Lake was the home of a race of silvery trout, some very large, and they began to fish for them. For many years the fish they caught did not even have a formal name; it was not until 1892 that samples of trout from Kamloops Lake were sent to the renowned biologist Dr. David Starr Jordan of Stanford University for identification. T. W. Lambert, author of *Fishing in British Columbia,* one of the earliest published accounts of angling in the province, recorded the event:

"For several years two Americans came every season to Savona's Ferry (on Kamloops Lake) to fish, and, becoming impressed with the beauty of the so-called silver trout, they sent a specimen to Professor Starr Jordan, of the Leland Stanford University of San Francisco. The first specimen did not arrive in good condition and another specimen was sent, in the preparation of which I personally assisted. It was a fish of about 1 1/2 lb. in weight, a very beautiful specimen and a most typical example of the silver trout. Professor Jordan described this fish as a new species, under the name of *Salmo kamloopsii."*

In making his identification, Jordan noted the trout bore a strong resemblance to the familiar rainbow trout and steelhead of the Western United States. But he also noted differences, chiefly in the number of scale rows on the new trout, which was much higher than on the familiar rainbow trout, *Salmo gairdneri.* In Jordan's time such relatively small differences were considered sufficient for a new species, and Jordan decided that was what he had. He chose the name *Salmo kamloopsii* in honor of the lake from which the sample trout had come.

The distribution of *Salmo kamloopsii* was limited to Shuswap, Adams, Kamloops, Okanagan, Kootenay and a few other lakes in Southern British Columbia; natural barriers had kept it from reaching most of the hundreds of small lakes on the Southern Interior Plateau. However, the few large lakes where the Kamloops trout existed naturally were more than enough to handle the small amount of angling pressure in the early days. People were more interested in fur, gold, timber and other sources of wealth than fish, and the often harsh realities of frontier life left little time for fishing anyway except when the catch was needed for survival. Transportation throughout the province, riven by great mountain ranges and deep canyons, was difficult and slow and the population remained small. Yet those who had the time and the means to fish for sport sometimes found angling the like of which may never have been seen anywhere else on earth.

Dr. Lambert was such a man. A surgeon in the employ of the Canadian Pacific Railway Company, his duties left time to explore the angling possibilities of the region and he related the results of these explorations in his little book, published posthumously in 1907. Many remarkable catches are described in this volume, but one far exceeds any of the others; indeed, it may rank as the greatest fishing story of all. In Dr. Lambert's words:

"About twenty-three miles from Kamloops there is a lake known as Fish Lake, in which the fishing is so extraordinary as to border on the regions of romance, though locally it is considered a matter of course. For lake fishing, in point of numbers, it is impossible that this piece of water could be beaten; it is like a battue in shooting, the number to be caught is only limited by the skill and endurance of the angler; indeed, little skill is needed, for anyone can catch fish there, though a good fisherman will catch the most . . .

"From time to time half-breeds and cowboys came into Kamloops with stories of big catches of trout made with a willow bough and a piece of string with a fly tied to it; sometimes 300 or 400 fish would be brought down which had been caught in this way.

"This stimulated the sporting instinct of the inhabitants, and a few visits were paid to the lake and good catches were made, but the fishermen who went there were of a very amateur kind. In the summer of 1897 an American proposed to me that we should go up and try what good tackle could do; in fact, he proposed that we should go up and try to make a record.

"We went up in the first week of August, and the result far surpassed our wildest imagination. We fished three full days, and brought back 1,500 trout, which weighed 700 lb., cleaned and salted. The first day we caught 350, for some time was wasted in finding the best places. The second day a start was made at 5 a.m., and we fished till long after dark, about 9:30 p.m., catching 650; the third day we caught about 500 . . .

"Flies were abundant, and the fish were ravenous for both real and artificial; they almost seemed to fight for our flies as soon as they touched the water. Even when almost every feather had been torn off they would take the bare hook. We fished with three flies, and often had three fish on at one time . . . Our fish were cleaned and salted each day by some Indians, so that none were wasted, and no fish were returned to the water except the very smallest.

"We had estimated our catch on the best day to be over 700 fish; but owing to exhaustion and the necessity of cooking our supper, after being seventeen hours on the water, we did not feel equal to removing our fish from the boat, and during the night a raid was made on them by mink, which are very plentiful round this lake. Though it was impossible to say how many had been carried off, 650 was the exact total of fish counted on the following morning. If allowance is made for a rest for lunch, and time taken off for altering and repairing flies and tackle, it will be easily seen that this number of fish caught by two rods in one day on the fly constitutes a record which would be very hard to beat on this lake or any other. The best I was ever able to do again, with another rod, was a little over 300 . . ."

It is hardly surprising Lambert could never equal his remarkable record on Fish Lake, now known as Lac le Jeune. No lake could long withstand catches of that magnitude, and such grand harvests soon tempted men whose motives were not related to sporting instincts. Biologist J. R. Dymond reported that commercial fishermen were able to make "as much as $500 in a single month trolling for Kamloops trout, which were sold at 27 cents a pound."

Trolling also was the preferred method of most sport fishermen, and it was well suited to the large, deep lakes where Kamloops trout were native. Francis C. Whitehouse, another early British Columbia angling writer, described fishing for Kamloops trout with long greenheart trolling rods secured to the boat with six-foot lengths of rope so they would not be lost if a heavy trout should strike while the angler was busy with the oars. Two rods normally were fished from each boat and each rod was fitted with a heavy reel and 600 feet of line. Lures were attached to leaders made of wire or gut.

The rapid growth of sport and commercial harvests soon caused serious depletion of the Kamloops trout populations of various lakes until it became obvious some form of regulations were needed to preserve the fishery. This led to establishment of a provincial game commission in 1905, and Arthur Bryan Williams, an Irishman by birth and a fly fisherman by disposition, was appointed first commissioner. Williams would hold the post many years and under his administration the commission drafted the first regulations to protect the Kamloops trout and took steps to increase its distribution.

One of the first steps occurred in 1908 when fry hatched from eggs obtained from Kamloops trout spawning in a tributary of Shuswap Lake were planted in two previously barren lakes northeast of Kamloops—Paul and Pinantan. Both lakes had abundant insect life, freshwater scuds and plankton and in this respect were typical of hundreds of small lakes scattered across the Southern Interior Plateau.

The first plant of 5,000 fry went into Paul Lake. The little fish fed eagerly on the great untouched stocks of food and quickly grew fat and strong, and soon word went out among local anglers that Paul Lake was a place to try. As the first fish matured they also found the tributary creeks flowing into Paul Lake and spawned in them, and soon new generations of trout were foraging in the rich shallows of the lake.

In 1922 a hatchery was built to take advantage of the Paul Lake spawning run. Eggs were collected from mature trout and hatched into fry for planting in other lakes. In 1924 a good road was punched through to Paul Lake, making it more readily accessible to anglers.

Another hatchery was built at Gerrard on the Lardeau River above Kootenay Lake in 1914 and eggs were stripped from the huge Kootenay Lake trout when they reached their spawning grounds in the river. Yet another was established on Pennask Lake in the high country between Merritt and Kelowna. From these sources dozens of previously fishless lakes received their first trout. Like those in Paul Lake, these fish usually grew rapidly and provided spectacular fishing within a few years of stocking.

In addition to the government's stocking program, many unofficial and often unrecorded plantings were made by local anglers. Often these were the work of one or two fishermen who would trap a few fry in a creek and carry them in a bucket of water to some virgin lake for release.

Of all the waters that received their first trout in this way, Knouff Lake probably is the outstanding example. A beautiful,

island-dotted lake in rolling timbered hills northeast of Kamloops, Knouff was blessed with broad shoals and weedbeds and enormous sedge hatches in the spring. If ever a lake was ripe and waiting to receive trout, Knouff seemed to be it, so Len Phillips, a local resident, decided to give it the trout it lacked.

Phillips and his son trapped 10 mature trout in the stream between Paul and Pinantan Lakes and placed them in a barrel filled with water. It took them five days to haul the barrel to Knouff Lake, stopping at streams and springs along the way to change the water. One trout died en route, but the nine survivors were liberated in Knouff Lake on May 20, 1917.

For three years the lake was left undisturbed. Then, on May 20, 1920, exactly three years after the first fish were released, it was opened for fishing. According to one account, 28 anglers travelled to the lake, unsure what they would find or whether they would find anything at all. What they found was angling of a kind to stagger the imagination: One trout of 17 1/2 pounds was landed that day, and several of more than 15 pounds were caught.

Within a few years Knouff Lake became known as one of the world's greatest dry-fly waters. It supported incredible hatches of "traveling sedges," large, clumsy insects that fluttered for long distances across the surface after hatching, bringing even the largest trout up to feed. For more than a decade,

"The end of a dream." This Victorian mansion, built about the time the Kamloops trout received its name, still stands in the community of Nicola at the west end of Nicola Lake, B.C.

Knouff Lake offered superlative fishing; at its peak in 1930 a 17 1/4-pound Kamloops trout was taken there on a dry fly, and 8- and 10-pound fish were common.

It was largely the fame of Knouff Lake that first drew significant numbers of anglers from outside British Columbia to sample the province's Kamloops trout waters. As the fishery's popularity grew, stocking efforts continued to expand it, even though little was yet known of the life history of the Kamloops trout and even less about its relationship to its environment. It was soon clear, however, that the Kamloops trout was becoming a resource of growing value and importance to the province, and the government finally acknowl-

edged it needed to know more about these fish to manage them properly. In 1925 Dr. J. R. Dymond was asked to begin an investigation of the Kamloops trout and other game fish of British Columbia. Two years later he was joined in this work by Dr. Charles M. Mottley, a scientific assistant for the Biological Board of Canada.

In 1931 Mottley began a five-year study of the Kamloops trout in Paul Lake. He was an innovative scientist whose work pushed forward the frontiers of fisheries knowledge and filled in most of the gaps in what was then known about the life cycle of the Kamloops trout. Mottley also developed the first stocking formula based on the carrying capacity of lakes and tried to set the record straight about where the Kamloops belonged on the trout family tree.

Noting that Jordan had based his identification of the Kamloops trout as a separate species primarily on its higher number of scale rows, Mottley set out to find whether that was due to heredity or some difference in the environments of the Kamloops and rainbow trout. He conducted an ingenious experiment to determine the answer: "The eggs from a single female Kamloops trout, fertilized by the milt from a single male, were divided into two lots, one of which was raised at the ordinary hatchery temperature at Nelson, B.C., the other being kept for five weeks following the eyed-egg

Bill Nation, famous Kamloops trout fishing guide and fly tier, as he appeared in an advertisement for his guiding service in 1935.

stage at a temperature about 9 degrees F. higher. The fish were reared to a size of three inches, when they were killed and scale counts were made on a sample of 100 from each lot. Those raised at the higher temperature had an average of five rows less than those raised at the ordinary hatchery temperature. This experiment led to the conclusion that the number of scale rows could be modified by changing the temperature at the time of early development."

In other words, Mottley had shown that the difference in the number of scale rows between Kamloops and rainbow trout was due to environmental factors—the lower water temperatures of the spawning tributaries of the Interior lakes—rather than heredity. His experiment proved that the Kamloops was genetically identical with *Salmo gairdneri,* the rainbow trout, and he reclassified the Kamloops as a rainbow variety which he named *Salmo gairdneri kamloops.*

The matter of classification was of little interest outside the scientific community, but it did reveal one important thing: The Kamloops trout could not be exported and still retain its characteristic appearance, growth and behavior; these were due to the circumstances of its native environment, and where those circumstances were lacking the Kamloops would be indistinguishable from any other variety of rainbow trout.

This lesson was not to be learned quickly. For many years after Mottley's experiments, attempts were made to plant Kamloops trout in the coastal waters of British Columbia and several Western states where both the climate and environment were much different from the B.C. Interior. With few exceptions, notably Pend Oreille Lake in Northern Idaho, these attempts met with failure. Anglers outside the province gradually began to understand they would have to go to British Columbia to fish for Kamloops trout; the trout could not be brought to them.

The introduction of Kamloops trout to the smaller, shallower Interior lakes made it readily available to fly fishers, and it quickly proved itself a willing fly-rod fish, responding avidly to wet flies and rising well to floating imitations. Knouff Lake clinched its reputation in this regard, and the rapidly growing Kamloops trout sport fishery and increasing tourist trade it brought became the basis for a new industry. Resorts were built to accommodate visiting anglers and local anglers hired themselves out as guides.

One of the first resorts was built at Paul Lake. Others soon followed on Pinantan, Knouff, Lac le Jeune and other waters. In 1927, James D. Dole of the Dole pineapple family began construction of a lodge on Pennask Lake which was to house the famous Pennask Lake Fishing Club, a private fishing lodge whose membership included Canadian and American businessmen. The lodge opened in 1929 and in the years that followed many well-known visitors inscribed their names in its guest register, including Queen Elizabeth II.

Among the early Kamloops trout guides, the name of Bill Nation stands far above the rest. Arthur William Nation was born in Bristol, England, on June 29, 1881, but spent much of his adult life in the Kamloops country, and for many years his name was synonymous with the Kamloops trout.

Nation was a lean man with a Hoover haircut and a hawkish nose on which he balanced a pair of steel-rimmed spectacles. He began his career as a Kamloops trout guide on Little River, but when Echo Lodge was built on Paul Lake Nation made it his headquarters. From Echo Lodge he guided anglers on Paul Lake and dozens of other waters. His knowledge, gained from lengthy observation of the Kamloops trout, remained unsurpassed for many years, and his legacy is a series of fly patterns that bear his name: Nation's Fancy, Nation's Special, Nation's Silvertip and others, of which we will see more later.

A day with Bill Nation usually began with a leisurely breakfast at Echo Lodge, after which the soft-spoken guide would consult the barometer. Through some special formula known only to him, the barometer would determine where the day's fishing would be spent, or whether it was even worth fishing at all. When a lake had been selected, Nation would hand out flies to his client and they would set off together. Talking incessantly, Nation would row the boat and watch for rises, telling his client where to cast and how to retrieve, and he seldom failed to find fish or show his clients how to catch them.

When the day's fishing was done, the party would return to the lodge where Nation would dress the catch. If the customer wanted fresh fish sent home, Nation would pack them carefully, stuffing them with moss so the fish were in the round, then place them in boxes among layers of moss covered with ice. The boxes were taken to Kamloops for dispatch by railway express.

Another relic from the past, Murray Church, built in 1878, also still stands in the community of Nicola.

Nation fished until the last week of his life. His last customer, in October 1940, was Dr. Bill McMahon of Seattle.

"I arrived in Kamloops in the evening and went out to Paul Lake," McMahon recalls. "Nation met us there that evening. I had borrowed two bamboo rods and Nation went through my tackle after we'd had dinner. As I remember, it was dusk or dark when he stepped outside. He strung up the rods and took one and laid out the line in the air, just feeling it in the dark. 'Yes, this balances well,' he said, and then tried the other one and said they were satisfactory.

"So the next day we started fishing with Bill. My guide was a big Scotsman named Alec. He was one that Bill pressed into service when he had occasion to. He, too, was a very knowledgeable fisherman, but not of the caliber of Bill Nation." Nation himself accompanied McMahon's wife.

"It was a ritual with Bill. There was none of the hurly-burly early morning things. You had your breakfast and then he consulted the barometer. And it was a very considered judgment on the barometer because it determined where you would fish. And under certain circumstances, unfortunately, even though I had only 10 days to fish, he would say: 'Can't fish today.'

"I think there were two such days, and of course I was just screaming to go fishing, so on these days he would troll. He'd go out into the lake with these spoons, multiple long things, if you insisted on fishing. I guess they were baited with worms or something, so he wasn't a purist, but I think that was almost like a form of a little chastisement if you were going to be so stupid as to insist on fishing on a day like this. The gods and the fates did not ordain that you fish on those days; the barometer was off.

"I didn't know the formula, but we would go from the high lakes— Peterhope and some of the others—to Paul Lake itself and all the varying stages in between. We fished Lac le Jeune which was then noted for the fact that there were more fish in the air at one time on that lake than one had ever seen in his life. You'd look over the lake and the lake was alive with big, rising, lunging, leaping rainbows.

"My wife had never, never in her life, held a fly rod in her hand. She actually fished, she threw a fly the first day under his tutelage.

"We always had fine fishing with Bill. He knew he was dying and I think he purposely picked different areas each day, even though the barometer might have said so. He wanted to show us his country and more or less relive his own life.

"He had been in the hospital in Kamloops and the diagnosis was well known (cancer of the esophagus), but he had then left the hospital and come back to Paul just a couple of weeks before we arrived there. And, as we learned, we were the last people that he fished with.

"I left a rod, one of the rods that I had borrowed, so I wrote to Bill after we got home. There was a bit of a delay and then I received a letter from the lady who managed the lodge telling me that Bill had died. She was so sorry, but they had just gathered together all of his tackle and sold it to get some money to take care of his funeral expenses. He didn't have much to show for his lifetime of effort.

"So I've always felt kind of happy that maybe I did help a bit, and I got another rod to replace the one I had left there."

Bill Nation's death ended an era in the history of Kamloops trout fishing. He was tireless in his efforts to improve the fish and the fishing in his beloved lakes and he introduced the Kamloops trout to many anglers who would later write about it or carry word of it to the far corners of the earth. He died a pauper, but few others have lived a life as rich as his, and his name will forever be a part of the lore and legend of the Kamloops trout.

If Nation is the best remembered of the early Kamloops fishermen, he was by no means the only one. Others— Colonel Ashton, Colonel Flint, Colonel Carey, Dr. Lloyd Day and Tommy Brayshaw among them—also made lasting contributions. Their names also remain part of the tradition of Kamloops trout fishing, and tales of their exploits are still shared over campfires.

The decade of the 1930s was the golden age of Kamloops trout fishing. Anglers fortunate enough to visit the Kamloops trout lakes during those difficult years of economic depression often found incredible fishing in waters that were just coming into their prime, with fish of 8 or 10 pounds not uncommon.

The Kamloops trout soon earned for itself a reputation for being something apart from other trout. It fought with unparalleled strength and stamina and a reckless violence not found in other trout, and anglers discovered it was a fish to test their skill to new limits. When hooked, the first response of a bright, well-conditioned Kamloops trout is likely to be a long, swift run that pulls great lengths of line from the reel, followed by a series of violent leaps; then the performance is repeated. Slow to tire, the Kamloops may sulk or sound or run straight at the angler, a sudden tactic that has brought many battles to an early conclusion in favor of the trout.

One who discovered the Kamloops trout's capacity for speed and violence was the British angler W. A. Adamson. In his book, *The Enterprising Angler,* Adamson described an early trip to Hihium Lake where he hooked a 7-pound Kamloops that stripped nearly all the backing from his reel. Fearing he would lose the fish and perhaps his fly line and backing as well, Adamson jumped from his boat into the water and followed the fish on foot across a shallow shoal; the trout finally was subdued and Adamson regained his drifting boat. In three hours' fishing, he caught more than 30 trout from 2 1/2 to 7 pounds, an adventure that was not at all unusual at the time.

By the late 1930s improved transportation had made it possible for more anglers to reach the Interior lakes. The journey up the Fraser Canyon remained an exhausting, frightening trip by auto, but the railroads made it relatively quick and easy to reach the fishing grounds and more roads were being built to previously inaccessible lakes. New resorts also were going up, and as economic times turned slowly for the better, the business of sport fishing became increasingly important to the local economy.

Typical of the resorts was one built at Big Bar Lake north of Clinton, with log cabins and a central lodge. In 1935 the resort advertised "Special rates to Business Girls during July and August." One who was not a "business girl" could stay at the lodge for $4 a week or rent a cabin for $7 a week. The cabins had wood-burning stoves and outdoor plumbing and offered a more primitive lifestyle than many anglers would accept today, but it was a good life, perhaps made better by the fact that its pleasures did not come so easily.

The largest trout ever taken on hook and line may have been a Kamloops caught by a troller in Jewel Lake in 1932. Various weights ranging up to 56 pounds have been given for this fish, but its weight never was recorded officially so it never has been recognized as a world's record—although published photographs of the fish show a monster trout that indeed could have weighed as much as 56 pounds. Some observers have questioned whether the fish actually was caught trolling; the late Tommy Brayshaw commented sardonically that it more likely was caught "with a manure fork."

Jewel lake produced another giant trout in 1933, a fish that weighed 48 pounds three days after it was taken. Because it was not weighed reliably when caught, this fish also never has been acknowledged as a record. But a 51-pounder taken from the same lake in the mid-1940s was weighed and authenticated as the winner of a local fishing derby. However, *Field & Stream* magazine, then recognized as the arbiter of world records, refused to accept the fish as a record because it did not receive a notarized affidavit attesting to the weight of the trout and the circumstances of the catch.

Fisheries officers stripping spawning trout from Kootenay Lake recorded one of 52 pounds in 1930. And Premier Lake, near Cranbrook, yielded a trout of 35 1/2 pounds in 1933.

Bryan Williams recorded the catch of a Kamloops trout of 18 3/4 pounds on a wet fly, and there probably have been larger fish taken that went unreported. The apparent dry-fly record is a 25-pound, 2-ounce Kamloops trout taken on a No. 8 Royal Coachman at Balfour on the West Arm of Kootenay Lake in September 1977. The angler, Tom Durkop, fought the fish 2 1/2 hours and landed it only after another angler towed his boat out of the path of an oncoming ferry boat.

Such giant fish are always the exception rather than the rule, however, and that was true even during the glory days of the 1930s. Still, the lakes were generous with their yield of trout from 2 pounds up, and so were rivers connecting lakes that held Kamloops trout, especially those hosting runs of sockeye salmon. Best of all was the Little River, a swift 2 1/2-mile

This was one day's catch for four rods at Hihium Lake in 1940. By modern standards, such a catch would be considered outright slaughter, but the 50 trout shown in this photo were 30 less than the daily limit for four anglers in 1940.

stretch of water between Big and Little Shuswap lakes where Kamloops trout gathered in the spring to feed on sockeye alevins emerging from the gravel. Lee Richardson, in his book *Lee Richardson's B. C.,* recorded a conversation with Bryan Williams about a day when Williams landed eight trout ranging from 4 to nearly 13 pounds in four hours fishing on Little River. Williams called it his most memorable day of angling, prompting Richardson to recall some exciting Little River moments of his own. He wrote:

"Within minutes the mergansers and gulls telegraphed the approach of another school (of fry), and I began false casting in anticipation of their arrival. This time, amidst the welter of silver and crimson, I managed to hook a 4-pounder . . . Eventually we brought it to net in the calm of the lake." Another school of fry appeared, "and as the fingerlings came through the slot with trout all around, I managed to pin a 7-pounder that took us far into the lake and deep into the backing before it could be brought to net.

"Two more schools ran the gauntlet before the run came to an end, and from each we took one fish. There was time for only one, possibly two, casts before the young sockeyes were gone and the trout with them; yet it was my finest hour in angling." That was a typical reaction to the wild excitement that prevailed when the river was filled with big Kamloops trout slashing through schools of fry.

A stonefly hatch preceding the sockeye emergence also provided exciting spring angling in the Little River, and some fishermen favored autumn days when spawning sockeye crowded the river and Kamloops trout gathered to feast on loose eggs swept down by the current from the spawning redds.

Little River and the mouth of the nearby Adams River were in a class by themselves, but other streams—even some without sockeye runs—also produced spectacular fishing. The Canim and Kootenay both produced many notable catches; Whitehouse, for example, wrote of taking as many as 15 trout up to 3 pounds in a day's fishing on the Kootenay.

But the golden days of Kamloops trout fishing were numbered, and by the end of the 1930s it was becoming obvious that many of the better trout waters had passed their prime. Much of the decline was due to natural causes. Many lakes with inlet streams where trout could spawn became overpopulated and their once-abundant food stocks were whittled down quickly. Sedges were especially vulnerable to foraging trout, and sedge populations in some waters were reduced nearly to the point of extinction. Trout in these lakes grew thinner even as they became more numerous, and lakes that had produced immense fish in the years immediately after they were first stocked instead began producing many small, poorly conditioned trout.

In other lakes where only limited spawning could take place trout populations remained more or less in balance with food stocks, and these waters continued to produce large fish. This often led to the mistaken conclusion by anglers that these lakes were capable of producing big fish under any circumstances, and no matter how many trout were planted in them they would all grow up to imposing size. So fishermen demanded that more trout be stocked in these waters, and provincial authorities responded by stocking some lakes heavily—with the inevitable result that food stocks and the average size of trout both declined rapidly.

Knouff Lake was among the first to fall victim. With only limited spawning water, especially in dry years, the lake had been able to support a natural balance of abundant food supplies and good numbers of large fish. Even the big traveling sedges that made Knouff a Mecca for dry-fly fishermen continued hatching in large numbers.

Tommy Brayshaw was a regular visitor to Knouff Lake from 1928 to 1933, a period in which the trout population was wholly sustained by natural spawning and the lake was never stocked. In his angling diary he recorded the average size of fish caught in the 1933 season was 5 pounds, 2 ounces.

"Then," Brayshaw wrote, "the Kamloops club brought pressure to bear on the new (resort) owner and some 150,000 fry, or fingerlings, I do not know which, were introduced. The following year I went there and was shown a trout of 1 lb. 6 oz. as a 'fine fish.' I fished for an hour or two, catching a number of half-pounders, and then I packed up and left.

"There was a first-class lake ruined by overstocking, but there was another factor in its downfall that I do not think has ever been brought out, and that was that an old chap at the south end of the lake put in a saw mill and raised the level of the lake some two or three feet, giving the small fish access to the shallows where the sedge used to hatch in the millions; I believe these young fish cleaned out the sedge."

The impacts of additional stocking and raising the water level were disastrous. The decline in average size of the trout was immediate and drastic, and within a single year, or two at most, the traveling sedges had all but disappeared. A fishery perhaps unique in all the world had been destroyed, and Knouff was only one of a number of productive lakes ruined by similar examples of ignorance or carelessness.

Other forces also were beginning to take a toll on some of the best lakes. British Columbia's growing human population added its weight to the increasing angling pressure, and mining and agricultural development polluted some lakes. Irrigation practices hurt other waters, although these losses were probably more than offset by new irrigation impoundments that became excellent fisheries in their own right.

By the end of the 1930s there were still many virgin waters in the British Columbia Interior waiting to receive their first trout. But many of the popular lakes that had given the Kamloops trout its reputation and formed the basis for the sport-fishing economy were clearly in need of help. A large-scale effort was needed to restore the fishery, but Canada and most of the rest of the world were at war within a year or two, a war that took all the men, money and material the nation could produce. There was no money to pay for fisheries research or management, and the populace was largely preoccupied with other matters anyway. The fishery was left to fend for itself, and things got worse instead of better.

Paul Lake had been under careful management since Mottley's studies there, but sometime around 1945 the redside shiner was introduced into the watershed, probably by an ignorant angler using shiners for bait. By 1948 there were millions of shiners in Paul Lake, competing with Kamloops trout for the lake's limited food resources. Whatever forage value the smaller shiners may have had for trout was more than offset by their consumption of the lake's natural food supply; the trout population declined rapidly in size and numbers.

Soon redside shiners began to turn up in other lakes. Already faced with inadequate management, increasing angling pressure and the abuse and pollution that are inevitable byproducts of industrial development, the Kamloops trout now was forced to cope with a new, efficient and rapidly multiplying competitor. The fishery continued to suffer.

But as the world began slowly to return to normal pursuits after the war, men and money to manage the fishery gradually became available once again. The provincial government established a Fisheries Research Group to study sport fisheries problems and decide what management practices would be necessary to restore the Kamloops lakes to full production. The group was specifically directed to examine the relationship between the productivity of lakes and the quality and quantity of sport fish they could produce.

The flow of research papers, shut off for the better part of a decade, began again. Kamloops trout waters were surveyed to determine their productivity and fish-growing potential. Biologists began studying the shiners in Paul Lake and their impact on the trout. Other studies examined the spawning habits of Kamloops trout and the relative merits of wild and domestic strains of trout. As results of these studies were published, they were applied in management.

Lakes containing shiners or other scrap fish were poisoned and re-planted with trout. A new and more exact stocking formula was devised, one calculated to achieve a close balance between trout populations and food supplies. Stocking of barren lakes resumed and new angling frontiers began to open even as old waters returned to production. The great days of the '30s would never return—there were now too many fishermen for that—but superb angling in virgin waters was again available to those willing to make the effort to find it.

The rebirth of the fishery also led to a boom in the sport-fishing industry. Resorts flourished and many new ones were built. Continual improvements to the Fraser Canyon highway and other arterial routes made the Interior lakes more readily

Big Bar Lake, where an early trout-fishing resort catered to "business girls."

accessible. New names, like Roche, Lundbom, Leighton and Tunkwa, were added to the list of famous waters at the same time old names like Paul and Pinantan were being restored as angling destinations.

For more than a decade the fishery grew and prospered, and as some lakes peaked and started into decline, others came along to take their place. In the cyclical history of the Kamloops trout fishery, the post-war era produced remarkable fishing, and if it was never quite as spectacular as it had been during the '30s, it was still a memorable time.

Yet once again the days of plenty were numbered. Rapid economic and industrial growth together with a burgeoning population of anglers began placing more pressure on the fishery than it could support. Economic growth meant greater affluence and more leisure time for many people in the Northwest, and large numbers chose to spend it fishing for Kamloops trout. Much of their added wealth also was spent for this purpose, including purchase of recreational vehicles that soon began crowding backwoods roads leading to campsites on countless lakes.

People came to the Kamloops trout lakes in greater numbers and stayed longer than ever before, testing the resource to unprecedented limits. Many were newcomers to the outdoors, with little appreciation for or understanding of it, and in

Battling a Kamloops trout on Roche Lake. The angler is the late Harry Ludwig.

their ignorance unwittingly caused great harm to the ecological balance of dozens of lakes. They cut trees around the shorelines to fuel their campfires and wore away the grass, exposing underlying soil to erosion. They ran off-road vehicles up and down the hillsides, digging deep ruts in the soil, removing ground cover and causing more erosion, and the noise of their machines chased away wildlife that once was abundant around the margins of the lakes.

They even came in winter, on noisy snowmobiles that gave them access to frozen lakes where they cut holes in the ice and caught ripe trout that would have spawned in the spring, exterminating whole year classes of fish in some lakes. When they left, their garbage often remained behind on the ice, waiting to pollute the water when the ice melted in the spring. Many lakes suffered severely from this year-round onslaught.

All this was bad enough, but the attitude of the provincial government made matters even worse. Indifference toward fisheries and wildlife was the most anyone could expect from the conservative government that held power during all but a few years from the '60s to the '90s; more often, the attitude was one of outright hostility. The government's policy was one of ruthless exploitation of the timber, water and mineral resources of the province, with no thought for the impact on fish and wildlife populations or the habitats necessary to sustain them.

Dams, strip mines and enormous logging clearcuts scarred the province from one end to the other, creating sweeping ecological changes of the most brutal kind and causing incalculable damage to fish and wildlife. The Kamloops trout waters did not escape these depredations.

One example was the strip mining of the lake-dotted Highland Valley between Kamloops and Merritt. Mining for copper and other minerals had been going on in the valley for many years, but never on a scale even remotely comparable to the enormous strip mines that began operating in the mid-1970s. The mining companies paid the province $250,000 in mitigation fees for the land and water they would take, and in 1975 that seemed like a lot of money. It paid for construction of an artificial spawning channel at Logan Lake, and that's what the people of British Columbia got out of the deal. In exchange they gave up thousands of acres of land and water and all the fish and wildlife they supported.

Today Highland Valley Copper, a consortium of four mining companies, operates the second largest open-pit mine in the world, removing approximately 275,000 metric tons of rock and soil a day. Whole mountains have been leveled, and the awesome scars could probably be seen from the moon. Three pipelines carry slurry to a tailing pond on the valley floor; the pond is 13 kilometers (about 8 miles) long. About 1,200 people are employed at the mine.

Four trout lakes have been swallowed up by the mine. Big and Little Divide Lakes and Quiltanton Lake were first to go. Most recent was 24-Mile Lake, which held Kamloops trout as large as 17 pounds when it was closed in 1988. The loss of fisheries and wildlife habitat has been staggering, and although Highland Valley Copper is legally obligated to reclaim the land, there is obviously no way to replace mountains and lakes or the fish and wildlife that once inhabited them.

Many lakes not directly affected by the mine have suffered increased pressure from the added population of a mining "company town" built on a steep hillside at Logan Lake. It would have been difficult to find a more inappropriate place to build a new town, and a vigilant and responsible provincial government almost certainly would have prevented it.

The government, however, was busy with other priorities. One was to cut funds for fisheries and wildlife management; research, management and enforcement programs all were slashed. Another was to make sure the B.C. Forest Service had plenty of money to build new logging roads. Many of these roads provided access to lakes that formerly had been almost inaccessible, assuring the rapid slaughter of trout populations and premature destruction of what otherwise might have been the future of the resource. The new roads also added to the proliferation of private cabins around many Interior lakes, adding pollution and esthetic blight.

Roads were even built to a number of waters served by private fishing camps. Not surprisingly, some camp operators were forced out of business as a result. Others, who had worked hard to preserve the quality of fishing in lakes around their camps, saw their efforts destroyed and their businesses hurt.

Damaging as they were, the forest access roads were a minor threat compared with the $1 billion Coquihalla Highway project. After decades of political wrangling and years of work, the highway was finished in the spring of 1986, offering a freeway connection from Hope to Merritt—a massive concrete dagger thrusting into the very heart of the Kamloops trout country. An extension of the highway from Merritt to Kamloops opened a year later.

The new highway sliced hours off travel time to the Interior, changing the entire transportation pattern of the province. Now people could leave downtown Vancouver late Friday afternoon and be camped at the side of an Interior lake before nightfall, and many were quick to take advantage of the opportunity. Another huge highway project, the so-called "Okanagan Connector" or "Peachland Cutoff" was completed in 1990, providing a direct link between Merritt and Kelowna. The cumulative effect of these projects was another quantum increase in pressure on the Kamloops trout lakes.

The pressure was too much for some lakes in the Merritt area. Among them were Lundbom and Marquart, both famous for huge trout. In addition to being one of the most scenic lakes in the area, Lundbom also was home to one of the finest traveling sedge hatches in the province. Both lakes always had suffered from being too close to Merritt, and too easily accessible, but somehow they still managed to survive—until completion of the new highways.

Now there is a major intersection on the Okanagan Connector with signs pointing to a new 50-mile-an-hour gravel road leading to both lakes, and on most summer days they draw more visitors than the municipal swimming pool in downtown Merritt. Hundreds of vehicles crowd around them, stereos blaring, while high-powered outboards race back and forth across the oil-stained surfaces and off-road vehicles streak the hillsides with ruts. Both lakes have been destroyed as serious trout fisheries, and Lundbom has suffered the added insult of being invaded by shiners, probably introduced by ice fishermen illegally using them as bait. The wonderful fishing that once existed in these lakes is now only a fading memory in the minds of those who were fortunate enough to experience it.

Other lakes have suffered fates almost as bad. A staggering annual total of more than 25,000 days of fishing effort has been recorded on Roche Lake; Paul Lake has become a virtual suburb of Kamloops—itself now a major city—and enough cabins have sprouted on the shores of Glimpse Lake to qualify as a small town.

As these and other lakes in the Merritt-Kamloops area were overrun with people, many anglers began taking advantage of the new highways to head farther north to lakes around Little Fort, and now many of these are threatened by big increases in angling pressure.

The resulting overall decline in fishing quality has prompted a trend toward private waters, a new phenomenon in a province with a long history of public fishing. Sensing economic opportunity, owners of the huge Douglas Lake Ranch east of Merritt have begun charging anglers up to $100 a day to fish

Spawning Rainbow Trout
Do NOT Disturb
Fish or Rockwork

Province of British Columbia   Ministry of Environment Fish & Wildlife Branch

This artificial spawning channel at Logan Lake is what the people of British Columbia got in return for the land and water devoured by the Highland Valley Mine.

some of the lakes on their property. Minnie and Stoney lakes are the best-known waters so far affected by this change, which may portend a future in which good fishing will be available only to those with means to pay for it.

As if all this weren't enough, the Kamloops trout also has suffered the indignity of losing its scientific identity. In June 1988 the American Society of Ichthyologists and Herpetologists accepted research findings that the trouts of the North Pacific Basin are more closely related to Pacific salmon (*Oncorhynchus*) than true trouts (*Salmo*). They voted to change the classification of the rainbow trout, including the Kamloops and all other varieties, from *Salmo gairdneri* to *Oncorhynchus mykiss,* a clunky, tongue-twisting appellation if ever there was one.

In an effort to keep up with all the changes of the past two or three decades, fisheries managers have steadily reduced catch limits and imposed more restrictions on angling methods and tackle. These measures have undoubtedly helped preserve trout populations but they have not been able to stem the rapid loss of habitat. Only a fundamental shift in public opinion and government policy can achieve that.

Nevertheless, the new regulations do offer at least short-term benefits for anglers. The classification of some waters as catch-and release or "trophy" fisheries, with restrictions on tackle and bag limits, and other lakes as fly-fishing-only waters will assure protection of trout populations in these lakes for a while. Fly fishers obviously benefit most from these restrictions, but traditionally they contribute proportionally more than the rest of the angling community to protect and conserve the fishery, so such benefits are deserved.

The number of fly fishers who angle for Kamloops trout also has increased rapidly, much faster than the overall increase in anglers. Twenty years ago there were only two small fly-fishing clubs in British Columbia; now there are at least 11, and all participate in projects designed to enhance or preserve fisheries.

Fly fishers have not been alone in these efforts. Operators of private fishing camps and resorts have formed the B.C. Fishing Camp Operators and Outfitters Association with the dual purpose of lobbying for reasonable business regulations and better fisheries and forestry management. From a small beginning in the Kamloops-Merritt area, the association has grown to more than 130 members spanning most of the province.

In response to the influence of these and other conservation-minded groups and the public at large, the B.C. Forest Service has belatedly adopted a policy of consensus public planning for roads and timber harvests. Better late than never, the agency also has adopted lakeshore timber-harvesting guidelines to minimize impacts of logging on fisheries and esthetics. Another program, called Parks & Wilderness for the '90s, is aimed at identifying areas with unique features and protecting them from logging or development. Some trout lakes in unlogged areas may be preserved through this program.

These changes should assure at least some lakes still inac-

cessible by road will stay that way. Meanwhile, to give credit where it is due, the B.C. Forest Service has done a fine job of creating recreation sites and camping areas on lakes where roads already exist. These sites represent a great recreational asset to the people of the province.

The rising influence of conservation groups and the new policies of the B.C. Forest Service are both hopeful signs, but money for fisheries management remains woefully inadequate. As an example, after deducting salaries, travel expenses and vehicle costs, the 1993 budget for managing small lakes in the Thompson-Nicola Region was only $29,000—hardly enough for one or two lakes, let alone the hundreds in the region.

The problem is that revenues from fishing licenses go to the provincial general fund, where they get siphoned off for purposes unrelated (and sometimes inimical) to fisheries management. A separate surcharge on angling licenses has raised money for habitat conservation, such as lake aeration and rehabilitation projects, but those funds are only a drop in the bucket compared to what is needed.

So the recent history of the Kamloops trout has been one of mostly steady decline following periods of peak abundance. In this respect it is not much different from other famous fisheries around the world, but in British Columbia as elsewhere the pace of change seems to be constantly accelerating, hastening the rate of decline. True, some recent changes are positive and hopeful, but most have come too late to mitigate damage already done to the Kamloops trout and its native country.

In saying this, however, I should point out that my perspective is that of an angler who has fished nearly half a century in British Columbia, witnessing its change from a sparsely populated and largely unsettled country to a populous modern industrial state, with all the good and bad things such a transition usually entails. To another person, especially one coming into the country for the first time, it may yet seem fresh and new and relatively unspoiled, with vast potential still to be realized. In fact that is at least partly true, and despite all that has gone wrong, the limits of the resource are still far from being reached.

Even today there are still many lakes where heavy trout rise eagerly to fluttering sedges, where pines still stand in ragged ranks and the silence is broken only by the soft sigh of the wind and the lonely call of a loon. They may no longer be virgin waters, awaiting the first touch of an angler's fly, but they retain much of the flavor and character of the past, and they represent the present and future of the Kamloops trout fishery.

Which brings us to the ultimate purpose of this book: To acquaint the reader with all the magnificent qualities of the Kamloops trout and its surroundings, with its angling history and heritage and with all the subtle interrelationships that make it the splendid game fish that it is. By so doing it is hoped the reader will join the ranks of those dedicated to preservation of the Kamloops trout and its habitat. For these things are worth saving, not only for ourselves, but so future generations of anglers also will have the chance to come and test their skills against the special challenge that only Kamloops trout can give.

Courtney Lake glimmers in the distance, looking south from near Corbett Lake.

2: Life History

False Solomon's Seal in bloom. *Facing page:* "Great thunderheads roll past in the afternoon sky . . . "

The Kamloops trout begins existence as a tiny spark of life buried in the cold, dark gravel of a stream bottom. Typically it is a stream fed by a small spring and swollen by the icy waters of melting snow. The eggs are deposited in nests scooped out by the female parent, fertilized by the male and then covered with a layer of coarse, protective gravel. Water, bearing life-sustaining oxygen, filters through the gravel to the developing embryos.

By the end of May the spawning run is finished and the eggs, with their precious cargo of developing life, are left alone. The earth, overburdened with water from the melted snows and spring rains, gives up its moisture readily, and the spawning tributaries rise and sometimes spill over their banks, their swift currents carrying down last year's decaying leaves and all the tiny flotsam of the forests.

Sometimes there is too much water and the force of it digs new channels, leaving buried eggs to die in the old ones, or the loose gravel of the spawning redds may be swept away, carrying the precious eggs along with it. Sometimes, where loggers have cut away surrounding timber, the exposed soil melts under rain and is carried to the streams to settle as silt, blocking the passage of oxygen-bearing water and suffocating the developing embryos. Even if they escape this fate, the logged-off land may give up its water so quickly the streams will go dry before their time, and the embryos will be left to rot beneath sun-baked gravel.

But when all the floods and freshets have passed, and the streams unaffected by logging have settled back to normal depth and flow, some eggs will yet live in them. The water then is clear and warm, and all around in the forest are signs of new growth. Shoots of green lengthen lodgepole limbtips, wild strawberries show the first small traces of the sweet fruit they will later bear, skunk cabbages unfold their waxy leaves and yellow blooms in the bogs and swarms of hatching insects flicker in the twilight. The spring sun dries out the land and warms the lakes and great thunderheads roll quickly past in the afternoon sky, flashing and rumbling and bursting briefly with rain that makes the world fresh and gleaming until the sun returns to dry it out again.

The days grow longer as they pass, and the bright golden-red eggs buried in the gravel show the twin dark spots of a new pair of yet-unseeing eyes. As days become weeks, the developing shapes of tiny tadpole forms become visible through the eggs' translucent shells. All the while the stream continues to drop and its water temperature to rise, and as these things happen the embryos grow faster. In some seasonal streams the embryos face a race against time to hatch while there is yet enough water to sustain them. For some the race is lost, the

A grove of aspen, lush and green in early spring.

stream dries up and they die on the very threshold of life. But in streams with stable flows most embryos survive until tiny trout-like creatures emerge, as yet unfinished works with enormous black eyes and reddish yolks.

Some spawning streams flow out of lakes or from one lake into another, and in them the embryos develop faster in water warmed before it left the parent lake. These eggs always are the first to hatch, and the emergent trout, or alevins, are given a head start in the competition that will determine which of the year's young will survive. The emergent alevins are only 10 or 12 millimeters long, still lacking scales and bearing little evidence of the fins or tails they will later grow. In shape they still resemble a tadpole, except for the yolk that remains attached to provide them with nourishment through their first few days of life.

The alevins remain concealed in the gravel where they hatched, slowly absorbing their yolk sacs, gaining strength and growing. After three weeks at most the yolk is gone and the tiny trout have reached a length of about 20 millimeters. Now they must leave the relative safety of the gravel to search for food in the open stream.

By hundreds they come forth, wriggling up through the gravel crevices into the full flow of the current. Immediately they begin feeding, and immediately they are fed upon, becoming prey for watchful kingfishers, patient herons and sometimes larger members of their own kind. Few will survive these and the other tests that now begin.

By day the young trout—no longer alevins but fry—school up in the center of the stream, shifting back and forth but never moving far, casting occasional glints of reflected light from their tiny turning sides. At night the schools edge nervously toward the banks. There, apparently in response to some instinct triggered by temperature and the absence of light, the schools split up and some fry slip downstream, beginning their migration to the lake that lies below. When daylight returns they head back to the center of the stream and resume feeding, holding steadily in the current, a swarming host of little trout pausing in the first step of their life's journey.

While the fry of inlet streams are beginning their downstream migration, their counterparts in outlet streams are staying put in the pools where they hatched. There they forage on the stream's microscopic life, holding, feeding and growing in the warmer and more stable flow of the outlet, storing up energy until it is time for them to start the more difficult journey upstream to the lake. Finally, in the warm days of July or August when stream temperatures are at their peak, some secret signal reaches the little trout and they begin to move. Unlike the fry of inlet streams they move mostly in the middle of the day when the temperature is highest and light is strongest. Traveling by day and resting at night, their schools move haltingly against the flow until at last they pass out of the current into the calm of the lake. A second upstream migration may follow in September, but after that movement subsides to a few frantic stragglers.

Even when the last migrant has finished its journey there are still fry left in the streams; among the thousands that hatch both in inlet and outlet streams there are always some that do not respond to nature's signals, that do not migrate, but stay behind through the heat of summer, the change of fall and the bitterness of winter.

The fry—both migrant and non-migrant—find a limited diet in the small streams. Fry of inlet streams subsist mostly on tiny insects, while those in outlet streams may enjoy a more substantial diet of plankters and scuds washed down from the lake. Competition is fierce in either case, and there is not enough food to long sustain even the few trout that remain after the migrations are over. Starvation and death await the losers of the competition.

In the lakes they fare better. By late August most young-of-the-year fry have grown to a length of an inch or better. Now they begin to show their first scales, a series of thin, parchment-like plates arranged in overlapping fashion like shakes on a roof. As each scale grows, fresh material is added in concentric rings to its outer edge. When growth is rapid, as it usually is during summer, the rings are thick and widely spaced; when it is slow, as it will be in winter, the rings and the spaces between them are thinner. The fish's life is docu-

mented in these rings, and biologists trained to read scales can determine a trout's age just like the age of a tree may be told by counting its rings. Scales also reveal whether the trout that grew them migrated immediately after hatching or spent its first winter in its native stream.

Not many trout are able to do that and survive. Only streams fed by lakes or relatively warm springs remain free-flowing through the winter, and even in these trout may face the threat of ice jams that scour the streambottoms. If they do survive the winter, trout that failed to migrate in their first summer of life probably will do so in their second, entering the lake as fingerlings much smaller than their brethren that migrated the year before.

By their second year those early migrants are more than four inches long, handsome little fish with bright silver sides broken by prominent parr marks—dark bluish bars—that they will wear at least through the summer and perhaps into the following year. They range freely through the rich weedy pastures along the shorelines or over shoals and flats in search of food, consuming *Daphnia,* the water flea; copepods, aquatic insects, scuds and terrestrial insects blown onto the surface.

Even here they are vulnerable to a host of predators. Ospreys, eagles, herons, loons, kingfishers and mergansers all find them and eat them, and though predation among Kamloops trout is somewhat rare, they may sometimes fall victim to a larger, hungry member of their own kind. Some lakes also harbor other fish that take a toll of young trout. Disease and the stress of competition are more insidious threats, but the results are just as deadly. Through ruthless selection, nature uses all these measures to weed out first the fry, then the fingerlings, until at last only those trout most fitted for survival—the quickest and most wary, the strongest and the best—still survive.

By the time it has grown to 10 or 12 inches, the Kamloops trout begins foraging in deeper water and starts entering the angler's catch, though many fishermen release such small trout in the hope of finding bigger game. At this stage the Kamloops trout is a small model of the great fish it will later be. The parr marks have disappeared and the fish wears a coat of bright nickel or bronze, depending on whether it lives in a clear-water lake or one with dark, amber-colored water. In either case it is a strong and active fish, swift in its feeding and determined in its fight against the angler.

Given a favorable environment, the Kamloops trout may grow to a length of 12 to 15 inches and weigh a pound or more after two full years of lake feeding. The rate of growth and ultimate size attained are limited only by the richness of the environment, or lack of it, and the time it takes the trout to reach sexual maturity.

In May and June Kamloops trout feed on the surface for hatching midges, mayflies, sedges and the emerging nymphs of dragonflies and damselflies. This is the time when all the teeming life of the lake reaches a peak of feeding, breeding and movement, and it is the best time of all for the fly fisher. But the orgy of surface feeding tapers off quickly as hatches

"The nights bear a hint of Arctic chill and the aspens flame with color . . . "

diminish in July; then the trout go deep, and beneath the sun-warmed waters of late July and August they forage mostly for scuds, snails and leeches.

Summer in the Kamloops trout country is apt to be very warm. Day after day the sun climbs to its zenith in an empty sky and sucks the freshness from the meadows and forests. Squadrons of sunflowers on the slopes turn their faces obediently to follow the sun's track across the sky, and the rich green grass of spring soon turns yellow-dry. The warm surface air, heated to a hundred degrees Fahrenheit or more, shimmers with heat waves, and dragonflies and yellowjackets buzz lazily over the steamy, gunmetal surfaces of the lower lakes. Lightning strikes trigger fiery explosions in the dry pine forests and fires clot the sky with dirty smoke that obscures the sun like fog and holds the heat like a blanket.

In some lakes, particularly smaller ones, the hot, still summer days cause thermal stratification, the water separating into layers of different temperature and oxygen saturation. Sometimes warm water and reduced oxygen cause trout to become lethargic and feed little, if at all. Their growth rate, rapid during spring, comes swiftly to a halt, and an expert reading the scales of these fish will recognize the "summer check" of growth.

August's heat gives way to September's shorter days and a change of weather. Strong winds begin to stir and cool the lakes, breaking up the thermal layers, and trout return to the shallows to feed. Again they seek aquatic insects, feeding on their subsurface forms, but now terrestrials like the flying ant are added to their diet, and trout rise eagerly when the ants fly on warm September afternoons.

The long, lingering Indian summer days of late September are among the best times to fish for Kamloops trout. The trout are fat and strong then, and they feed eagerly to store up strength for the coming winter and the rigors of spawning that will follow. The nights bear a hint of Arctic chill and the aspens flame with color, then softly die away to become faint glowing coals and disappear. The daytime air is often hot and still, poised for the first blast of impending winter; finally it comes, a sudden violent gust, sweeping hard gray clouds across the pinetops, blowing the first big spattering drops of cold rain.

Soon the rain gives way to the first fall of snow, and smaller trout, caught in a last feverish urge to feed, rise vainly to the snowflakes as they spiral gently to the surface and disappear. The flakes are large and wet and soon cover the ground, then disappear almost as quickly as they came—just a rehearsal for the storms that will soon begin in earnest.

Now the days are short, the high-country nights are crackling cold, and in the mornings the lakes are rimmed with thin layers of ice around their shores. At length a snowfall comes that does not melt and the hills gleam whitely with it in the soft winter light. More snow falls, then still more, driven by a bitter wind that forms deep drifts along the ridgetops and in the valleys between them. At last the lingering suspense of autumn is over and the beautiful white agony of winter has begun.

The trout continue feeding until the last possible moment, but each morning the ice reaches farther from the shore, closing off more open water. Finally, on a long, clear night when the air is still and the sky is lit with the frozen light of countless stars, icy tentacles reach out to touch and join, covering the surface with a frozen layer of fantastic crystal patterns. Now the lakes are shut off from the open air, locked into themselves for the long months of winter.

Beneath the ice the water temperature hovers barely above freezing. The trouts' metabolism falls with the temperature and they move around little and feed even less. Their lives and the lives of all the other creatures in the lake are reduced to a slower pace, with life, energy and strength all carefully conserved. If the trout feed at all it is by foraging slowly on bottom organisms, present now in much smaller numbers than before, and scuds remain their primary source of food.

Because their life has become sluggish and slow their need for oxygen is less, and it is well that this is so. Snow covering the surface ice of smaller, sheltered lakes may shut out light for long periods so no photosynthesis can take place. Yet there is no end to organic decay; it continues beneath the ice, though also at a slower rate, and consumes much of the oxygen remaining in the water. Sometimes there is not enough left to sustain life, and trout begin to die. Each year, unless the winter is unusually short and mild, some lakes are "winter-killed" in this subtle, secret way, and the spring thaw reveals them barren of the trout that frolicked in their shallows the year before.

But if nature is kind, the trout will survive the season. Winter never lets go easily, though, and its retreat is perceptible only in a gradual lengthening of days and the slow melt of drifted snow on south-facing slopes. Snow continues to fall, but more and more often it is mixed with rain, and sometimes a pale sun breaks through the scudding clouds to shine on snow-laden forest limbs, which begin dripping away the weight that holds them down. As the days lengthen and warm and the wind begins to lose its bitter edge, patches of ice begin melting on the lake surfaces, forming puddles over the frozen layers that still lie beneath. Then, after all these tentative signs, the fullness of spring comes with a sudden great rush, and sun and wind together triumph quickly over snow and ice, dissolving the accumulation of months in the span of days.

Released at last from their icy prison, mature trout answer the urgent summons to find the inlet streams and begin their spawning runs. Those not yet ready to spawn resume feeding with a vigor that will not be seen again till fall, and once more the lakes and their tributary streams are filled with life and movement.

As spring blossoms and insect hatches move toward their peak abundance, the trout fall again into their familiar rhythm of feeding. First they seek the nymphs and pupae of maturing insects, then the adults as they hatch on the surface. If there are other species of fish in the lake, the trout sooner or later also turn to them as a food source. Generally a Kamloops trout is at least two years old and 15 or 16 inches long before it begins to prey upon other fish, but there are exceptions and trout as small as 10 inches have been found with fish in their stomachs.

The victims of these predations usually are shiners, kokanee, suckers or other forage-sized species, introduced naturally or artificially. In the rivers or large lakes through which sockeye salmon smolts must pass, large Kamloops trout feed eagerly on their schools, driving the little fish to the surface in frantic bursts of spray.

By its third year, a

Hihium Lake, locked in winter's icy grip.

inches are seen often in the spawning runs. In some populations, maturation comes late and the trout may be five years old before they spawn for the first time. Individuals of at least one strain, the Gerrard or Lardeau strain that spawns in the Lardeau River, sometimes do not mature until they are six or seven years old.

By the time it is ready to spawn the Kamloops trout has known the rich feeding of several summers and the lean months of several winters. The exact

typical maiden Kamloops trout is a thing of real beauty, with strength and grace apparent in every curve of its streamlined shape. Kamloops trout in clear-water lakes typically are deep blue-green with a fine spray of black spots along their backs, a color scheme that provides camouflage from predators above. The dark color gives way to a bright nickel finish on the flanks and a snow-white belly underneath. The caudal fin is blue-gray and spotted heavily, with the spots following the lines of the fin rays. The pectoral and ventral fins are pale lavender and the tips of the ventral and anal fins are edged in cream. Trout in lakes with dark or amber-colored water tend to be more heavily spotted, with bronze-colored flanks.

Gradual changes in color and form begin to take place as the Kamloops trout reaches sexual maturity and approaches its first spawning. The maturing male develops a long, deep head and its upper maxillary becomes thick and hard. Its body also thickens and it begins to display the familiar male badge of a pronounced hook, or kype, on the tip of its lower jaw. The female also shows evidence of the changes that are taking place within it, growing thick in the body and sometimes developing a small protuberance on the lower jaw.

In both sexes a faint, iridescent rose tint begins spreading along the lateral line, visible at first only when light strikes it at the proper angle. As the trout ripens this subtle stripe broadens to a bold carmine sash along its sides, its gill plates turn first crimson, then deep purple, and its once clean white belly darkens to a dirty gray.

The changes associated with first spawning generally come to the Kamloops trout at an age of three or four years. Males often mature a year or two before females, a characteristic of all salmon and trout. Some precocious males may spawn at the age of two years, and mature male trout of only six or seven

mechanism that causes it suddenly to break out of its careful pattern and return almost unerringly to its natal stream is not yet fully understood. Accepted theory is that the changes brought about by sexual maturation trigger an instinct within the trout to seek out the characteristic odor of its birth stream. Each stream has its own unique scent, a combination of the chemical constituents of its water, and it is believed this odor is "imprinted" on trout before they migrate from the stream. To the trout it means nothing until sexual maturation suddenly impels it to use its keen olfactory sense to seek the source of a familiar scent.

It is a good theory and one that goes farther than any other to explain the miracle of the spawning run, but it does not account fully for all the observed variations in migratory behavior. One difficulty is that the homing mechanism, however it works, is not perfect; the return of spawning fish to their home streams is never 100 percent, and always there are a few individuals that stray to other streams. In some cases, trout hatched in outlet streams may even stray to an inlet to spawn, and vice versa. Some Kamloops trout lakes have both inlet and outlet streams and spawning runs to both are common. Apparently there is no genetic difference between these runs; trout from a single source stocked in previously barren lakes have quickly established runs to both inlet and outlet streams.

The first ripe trout seek the outlet streams even before the ice is off. Their journey to spawning is relatively easy compared to that of the inlet spawners because they are able to move downstream with the current. Outlet spawners dig their nests and deposit their eggs in water that is extremely cold; only later, after the sun has warmed the lake, will the stream temperature rise enough to accelerate development of the

buried embryos. Because they begin so much earlier, outlet spawning runs may be nearly over by the time inlet runs are just beginning.

The start of the inlet spawning runs seems much more dependent on weather. If the spring thaw is late, the run may be delayed; usually the ice is breaking up or gone altogether and inlet temperatures are rising rapidly before the first ripe trout appear offshore. As inlet temperatures rise, the first fish move tentatively upstream. Their migration takes place during the warmest part of the day, and they seek sheltered places to rest when darkness falls and the temperature plummets. A sudden frosty night may retard the migration temporarily and

a quick thunderstorm also often brings a temporary halt.

Males and females enter the stream together, although in some years one sex greatly outnumbers the other. Always a portion of the run consists of small, precocious males, nature's way of assuring there will be at least some male fish to fertilize the precious eggs. The trout choose runs with a stable flow and comfortable velocity of current over beds of coarse gravel to make their redds. Very large trout, such as those that spawn below Trout Lake in the Lardeau River, are capable of turning over stones six or seven inches in diameter in their nest-digging activities.

Male fish pair up with females, usually in ratios of one to five

A loon takes off from her nest, driving herself forward with windmilling wings.

males for every female. The female begins digging the nest, scooping out a hollow in the gravel with broad thrusts of its powerful tail. Several times it settles into the nest as if to test its size, then resumes digging until the nest finally meets approval. The digging goes on around the clock, with the big females tearing and ripping their tails on the sharp stones, pausing briefly to rest, then resuming their urgent task. The males, meanwhile, fight one another for position. Large males chase their smaller rivals, slamming and biting and pursuing them in furious rushes across the gravel bars and through the pools. The larger the number of males attending a single female, the fiercer the combat, and there is no quarter.

When the nest is ready, the female settles into it and the victorious male, scarred from its struggles, settles alongside. Then, with her mouth stretched wide in exertion, the female shudders convulsively and spills her eggs onto the gravel; simultaneously the male, its mouth also spread in a huge, straining yawn, covers them with milt. The female sheds about a thousand eggs for each pound of weight.

At the last moment smaller males dart in again, trying desperately to get in on the act, but the dominant male turns quickly to defend the nest with all its remaining strength. The female moves on quickly to dig another nest upstream and her fresh digging dislodges gravel that settles over the fertilized eggs in the nest she has just left behind, forming a loose protective layer that shields the eggs from light and hungry predators.

This cycle is repeated until the fish are spent. Even then, the male stays on, guarding the nests long after the female has left to seek quiet water in which to rest before starting the downstream journey back to the lake, or perhaps to die. The male, after guarding the nests for a time, moves on in search of another female, fighting and spawning until its sperm is gone and its strength nearly used up.

For many trout, spawning is the last act of life. They do not all die, as do Pacific salmon, but some expend the last ounce of energy on which life depends. Lacking strength to hold position in the flow they are carried away and swept into the shallows, there to gasp out their last remaining life on a gravel bar. Often they are found and taken by hungry lynx or bear, which also take their share of trout still in the act of spawning, and the banks of high-country tributaries are frequently littered with the remains of trout slain by these animals.

Natural spawning mortality is always highest among older, larger fish, especially males because of their furious combat. But many small, precocious males survive to spawn again. The death rate is highest when a large spawning run overcrowds the redds and increases competition among the males. Conversely, when there are only a few spawners there is less competition and the survival rate is higher. Under those circumstances as many as half the ripe fish entering the stream at the beginning of the run may still be alive at the end of it.

The spent survivors, known as kelts, show little evidence of their former elegance and grace. They are thinner, still dark, and some display white spots of fungus growth. Their fins are ragged and worn, their bellies scarred and bruised. The females have lost a quarter of their weight and the males nearly as much, partly from shedding eggs or milt and partly from exertion.

Spent fish in outlet streams face the difficult task of returning to the lake against the current when it is often at its height. They swim upstream during the warmest hours of the day and rest at night, resuming their struggle when the sun returns. Their counterparts in inlet streams have an easier task, heading downstream with the current. They do so in stages, easing backward, then pausing to rest in quiet water, then easing down farther until they finally reach the lake that is their destination.

The duration of the spawning run depends upon its size. When the run is very large intense combat weakens the male trout quickly and shortens their stay over the spawning redds. When the run is small and competition less, trout spend more time on the redds, sometimes stretching their stay to six or seven weeks.

Surviving kelts feed voraciously in the lakes, trying to regain strength. They are especially vulnerable to anglers at this stage, but a fresh kelt is always a disappointment, too weak to provide much sport and seldom pleasing in appearance. The

energy it spends trying to escape also may be the last it has, so even if a kelt is released it may not survive. If an angler, in ignorance of what he has caught, kills a kelt and tries to eat it he will find its flesh soft, white and tasteless.

If a kelt survives the summer after spawning it will gradually regain some of its former beauty and luster. It may also reach its former weight, but usually will not grow much beyond it unless the lake is exceptionally rich or forage fish are abundant. It is a common misconception that after recovering from spawning, trout will continue growing and reach a larger size; in most cases this is not true.

A few Kamloops trout may live as long as six or seven years—sometimes even longer in the case of the Gerrard strain—and spawn two or three times. They are a small minority, however, having survived flood or drought, the rigors of spawning and the deadly predations of birds, animals, other fish and man. They will have been parent to several thousand offspring, at most of which a few hundred will survive, and they will have drawn strength and nourishment from other creatures of the lake—the tiny, teeming animals of the plankton, the large, conspicuous nymphs of damselflies and dragonflies, the awkward pupae of sedges and midges, the ubiquitous scuds and sinuous leeches, perhaps even other fish.

You may see such trout at twilight, great old fish wise to the ways of anglers, rolling in the shadows for fluttering sedges. By daylight they will be gone, prowling the depths in search of scuds or forage fish. These are fish that have met all the tests that man and nature can contrive and they have survived, and in the world of the Kamloops trout, that is all that matters.

Yet for each of these fish the vigor and strength, the quickness and keenness that have brought it so far must inevitably begin to fail. The trout's eyesight weakens, and as it does the quick, unerring thrust to capture an insect or a tiny fish becomes less certain. Now the old fish must use more energy in feeding than it can recover from its prey, and it begins losing strength and weight. The deterioration is gradual but sure, until finally it becomes an effort for the trout just to keep its now-emaciated body in trim and it knows that it must rest. It seeks a shallow place, perhaps the edge of a weed-covered shoal where sheltering deep water is close at hand, and settles into the soft vegetation. There it remains, its gills working slowly, sustaining a tired life a little longer.

The impatient scavengers of the lake do not wait for the trout to die. Snails begin tearing at its flesh while the trout's heart still beats, and other scavengers gather to await their turn. The end comes slowly and without dignity until some final point is reached, the gills open and close for the last time, and the stout heart is finally still.

Even in death the trout makes a final contribution to the life of the lake, its decaying carcass fueling the food chain that eventually will reach its own offspring and help sustain them. Thus the cycle of the Kamloops trout completes itself, and is renewed.

A pair of large Kamloops trout on their spawning redd.

3: Managing the Resource

T he Kamloops trout is one of nature's most perfect works, the product of a union between the water and the land, the result of countless eons of evolution and upheaval, of endless experimentation and change. Its strength comes from minerals leached secretly from the soil of the surrounding hillsides by melting snow and spring rains, and its life is shaped by the cycle of the seasons. It is tied to the land as firmly as the roots of the lodgepole pines that shelter its spawning streams, and it is an integral part of a complex but fragile ecological scheme that includes other fish, insects, plants, animals and humans.

Since the first humans set foot in British Columbia their activities have profoundly affected the Kamloops trout and its environment. The number of people was small at first and the resource was easily able to absorb the demands they placed upon it, but as the human population grew its demands on the fishery kept pace. By the beginning of the 20th century it was evident those demands had reached the point where measures were necessary to protect and expand the resource.

That realization led to the first government-sponsored management programs. They began with simple measures designed to solve simple problems, but with the passage of time both the problems and solutions grew steadily more complex and difficult. To keep pace with these changes, the science of fisheries management gradually evolved into a wide range of highly sophisticated programs designed to deal with compli-

Colorful lichens cling to a rock surface. *Facing Page:* Typical of the spectacular scenery on the Southern Interior Plateau are these colorful sandstone formations known as "Hoodoos" in the Deadman Creek valley.

cated social, economic, environmental and biological issues.

The agency responsible for these programs has been known by several different names and has occupied several different niches in the provincial government hierarchy throughout its history; today it is called the Fisheries Branch of the Ministry of Environment, Lands and Parks.

The Resource

Effective fisheries management must begin with a basic understanding of the resource to be managed. In the case of the Kamloops trout, that means knowing something about the ecology of British Columbia, including the geology, climate and other natural features of the province, especially the limnological region known as the Southern Interior Plateau— the heart of Kamloops trout country.

Wedged between the Coast Range and the Columbia Mountains at the southern end of the province, the Southern Interior Plateau is a high range of gently rolling hills resting on a bed of sedimentary and volcanic rock, covered with a layer of glacial silt. Here and there the hills are sliced by deep river valleys or canyons, but in most places they rise to elevations of 3,000 to 6,000 feet. After ages of erosion and change the hills have a deceptively gentle appearance; only in the tortured rock of the canyon walls is the evidence of past upheavals plainly visible.

Willard Lake near Ashcroft is a typical example of the hundreds of lakes that lie in glacial folds or cirques on the Southern Interior Plateau.

The Southern Interior Plateau rests in the rain shadow of the Coastal Range and thus is spared the heavy rainfall of the coastal valleys. March and April usually are the driest months, but late spring brings rain and June is the wettest month. Runoff from snowmelt and spring rain collects in glacial folds and cirques and the plateau has many lakes. Most are small; some are too shallow or too alkaline to support fish of any kind, and some do not even exist year-round. Many are partly or completely artificial, constructed for irrigation purposes. Some are large and deep enough to challenge the stoutest boat and most knowledgeable boatman.

The majority of these lakes provide good to ideal habitat for trout. Most are surrounded by soft, soluble soils that allow runoff to penetrate and gather nutrients critical to the aquatic food chain. High elevation provides favorable temperatures and contributes to a rapid evaporation rate, a combination that turns many lakes into "nutrient traps" capable of supporting abundant populations of aquatic life.

Biologists have measured the productivity of these lakes in terms of total dissolved solids (TDS). Most lakes of the Southern Interior Plateau have a TDS of more than 200 parts per million, relatively high for lakes (the ocean, by comparison, has a TDS of 33,000 to 37,000 parts per million). Dissolved solids include the chemical building blocks necessary to support aquatic life, and waters with a high TDS usually produce more plankton, more algae and fixed plants, more insects, crustaceans and other forms of trout food, and ultimately, more and larger trout.

The TDS figure may fluctuate in response to changes in the evaporation rate, photosynthesis or amount of runoff. Pulses of aquatic life or heavy algae blooms also remove dissolved solids from the water for varying lengths of time, but usually these are recycled through waste products or the decaying remains of plants and animals. The runoff after every hard rain also helps replenish the supply.

Calcium is the most important chemical building block leached from the soil. It is needed by nearly all aquatic plants, crustaceans use it to build their outer skeletons, and snails make their shells from it. It also neutralizes acidity from accumulated organic material on the bottoms of some lakes. The marl bottoms characteristic of many Kamloops trout lakes are products of the high calcium content of the water, the marl coming from certain types of calcium-dependent algae. The *Chara* weed common to most of these lakes often is coated with crusts of marl, and its common name—stonewort—is derived from these rock-like deposits.

Lakes with high alkalinity (pH) and rich in dissolved solids and aquatic life usually are designated eutrophic. In a typical eutrophic lake, dead organisms and waste products from living creatures accumulate on the bottom faster than the rate of decay. This means some nutrients are lost forever from the food chain, bound up in undecayed matter, so the lake must receive additional nutrients from outside sources to maintain its productivity.

Eutrophic lakes tend to be shallow so that a large percentage of their bottom is exposed to the sunlight necessary for photosynthesis. They also have a tendency toward thermal stratification and bottom stagnation during summer and may be prone to summer kill. The combination of high productivity, shallow depth, high oxygen depletion rates from decaying organic matter and extended periods of ice cover in winter also makes many of them vulnerable to winter kill.

Certain fauna are characteristic of eutrophic lakes. In addition to trout and the usual complement of aquatic insects, these include red chironomid larvae, known as "bloodworms," and the fascinating transparent larvae of *Chaoborus,* the so-called "phantom midge."

The tremendous fallout of dead organisms and wastes in shallow eutrophic lakes may accelerate their life cycle. Because sediment accumulates faster than decay can remove it, the lake gradually fills with it. Tules, rushes and other plants crowd in from the margins until eventually the lake shrinks to become a shallow pond; ultimately it will become a meadow. This process may take centuries, but in some lakes it happens rapidly enough that drastic changes are visible within the span of a human lifetime.

The other broad classification of lakes is oligotrophic. These lakes have lower pH, fewer dissolved solids and smaller populations of plant and animal life. They are less likely to show evidence of bottom stagnation during summer months because they have less decaying sediment to extract oxygen from the water, and they are less vulnerable to either summer or winter kill. Colorless midge larvae are characteristic in them, and they rarely have heavy algae blooms.

Decomposition of organic material or waste is about equal to deposition of sediments in oligotrophic lakes, so they do not fill up with layers of organic material; usually this means they have a longer lifespan than eutrophic waters. Oligotrophic waters tend to be deeper to begin with, often lying in steep-walled canyons or deep, narrow folds in the earth, hence less of their bottom area is exposed to the sunlight necessary for photosynthesis—another inhibitor of productivity. They usually have high flushing rates, which also reduces productivity. Large lakes tend to be oligotrophic because their concentration of dissolved solids is more dilute than lakes with smaller volumes of water.

The productivity of Kamloops trout lakes also is influenced by the plants growing around their shores. Grasses are the most common plants at lower elevations. Others include isolated stands of aspen, cottonwood and scrub willow that spring up where water collects in folds on the lower hillsides. Farther up the hillsides is the timberline, usually between 2,000 and 3,000 feet on north-facing slopes and higher on slopes facing south. Lower-elevation forests typically consist of pine, fir and larch in open stands with little undergrowth; the lodgepole pine predominates at higher elevations, with a scattering of spruce and alpine fir and dense undergrowth.

The root structures of all these plants hold snowmelt and rainwater, releasing it slowly to fuel the springs that feed the lakes and their tributary streams. When timber is cut or the land is cleared for mining or other purposes, runoff is accelerated and becomes warm and weighted with silt, making tributaries unsuitable for spawning and causing turbidity in lakes. Intensive cattle grazing may have the same effect.

Vegetation surrounding lakes also provides sheltering and resting places for adult mayflies and sedges and essential habitat for terrestrial insects such as the flying ant. Removal of trees and brush from a lakeshore may disrupt the mating cycles of sedges and mayflies and eliminate ant flights altogether.

Many fish, animals and birds share the Kamloops trout's domain. Some are predators while others serve as prey. The list of predators is long and it has been estimated that 90 to 95 percent of the fry of Kamloops trout may fall victim to their deadly activities.

Birds and other fish usually are first in line. Fortunately the Dolly Varden char *(Salvelinus malma)* has access to only a few of the streams in which Kamloops trout spawn, but where it is present it is an eager and efficient consumer of trout eggs and fry. Kingfishers and herons attack fry migrating downstream from spawning tributaries and follow them into the shallow areas of lakes. There they are joined by mergansers and loons, while ospreys and eagles zero in on trout of yearling size or better.

Corbett Lake near Merritt, a typical eutrophic lake.

Northern squawfish *(Ptychocheilus oregonensis)* are present in some of the larger Kamloops trout lakes, and these fish—which may grow to large size—also tend to feed in the shallows where fry congregate, taking a heavy toll. Large Kamloops trout also sometimes eat smaller ones, although this is not very common and usually occurs only where competition for food is especially intense.

The lake trout *(Salvelinus namaycush)*, mountain whitefish *(Prosopium williamsoni)* and fresh water ling *(Lota lota)* are other predators found in some of the larger Kamloops trout lakes. These fish also compete for some of the same food sources utilized by Kamloops trout, which has an indirect but significant effect on trout survival and growth.

A number of other fish species are native or have been introduced within the natural range of the Kamloops trout. Some provide valuable forage for the Kamloops, some compete for the same food resources, and some do both. The predator-prey-competitor relationship often varies from one lake to the next, for reasons not clearly understood; a species that provides valuable forage in one lake may be a more efficient competitor in another, and there is no certain way to forecast the impact of forage species introduction. It is clear, however, that Kamloops trout cannot coexist with another species in the same lake without one affecting the other. If the presence of another species is not beneficial to the trout, then almost certainly it will prove harmful in some direct or indirect way.

Species that provide prey for the Kamloops—at least some of the time—include the kokanee and its anadromous counterpart, the sockeye salmon *(Oncorhynchus nerka)*, the redside shiner *(Richardsonius balteatus)*, various species of sculpin *(Cottus)*, the fine-scaled sucker *(Catostomus catostomus)*, and the coarse-scaled sucker *(Catostomus macrocheilus)*. Some of the former also compete with Kamloops trout for food stocks in various waters, as do the Eastern brook trout *(Salvelinus fontinalis)*, the carp *(Cyprinus carpio)* and the chub *(Mylocheilus caurinus)*.

Altogether the other fish that share the Kamloops trout's environment contribute little to its well-being; more often, the opposite is true. The single exception is that of the kokanee, which has established its usefulness as a forage fish in a few instances. Fortunately, most Interior lakes—which were free of any fish to begin with—remain free of any species other than the Kamloops.

Animal predators do most of their work along the spawning tributaries in the spring, taking both ripe unspawned Kamloops adults and spawned-out kelts. Bear, lynx, mink, marten and raccoons all get into the act and the bloody evidence of their visits is often visible along the streambanks. Otters also take a heavy toll of trout, hunting efficiently in the lakes throughout the season.

But the greatest predators are humans, usually the only ones who take more than they need. They disguise their predation by calling it sport, and as individuals they are not very efficient—but their cumulative impacts are great. Of all predators, humans alone are capable of reducing trout populations to the point of extinction. They also are the only creatures capable of making large-scale changes to trout habitat.

The mission of fisheries management is to take all these things into account—lake size, depth and productivity; climatic effects; the impacts of predators, competitors and forage fish; angling effort and efficiency; the consequences of human alteration of the environment—and somehow assure continued healthy production of trout from as many lakes as possible. To fulfill this mission, the Fisheries Branch carries on stocking programs, regulation-setting and enforcement activities, habitat restoration and research projects and a host of other diverse activities.

Stocking Programs

The first management efforts consisted of simple regulations to prevent overharvest and limited attempts to stock Kamloops trout in previously barren lakes. As we have seen, many of these early stocking efforts were carried out haphazardly, either with or without government sanction. The outcome often was strictly a matter of luck, but sometimes results were spectacular; the newly planted trout took advantage of untouched food resources and grew to very large size.

Where this happened the best fishing generally occurred in the third, fourth and fifth years after stocking. In most cases the spectacular growth rate leveled off by the sixth or seventh year, then began declining slowly as surplus food stocks were consumed. In lakes with limited spawning habitat, trout populations sometimes reached equilibrium with the food resource, resulting in a relatively stable population of trout of predictable average size. In lakes with abundant spawning habitat, populations increased rapidly and consumed food supplies at the same rate, leading to large numbers of small trout. Other lakes did not fit either pattern because spawning success or fry recruitment fluctuated from year to year depending on water levels, and in these the average size of trout varied widely from season to season. Finally there were many lakes where no spawning took place at all, and these were dependent upon continued periodic stocking.

The reasons for this seem obvious now, but in the early days they were not always clearly understood. That began to change with Mottley's study of the trout populations in Paul, Knouff and Hyas Lakes.

Paul Lake received its first trout in 1909; Knouff in 1917, and Hyas, which lies in the same watershed as Paul Lake, was planted in 1923 with eggs taken from the spawning run that had developed in Paul Lake. Mottley examined records of the average size of the trout in the 1926 spawning runs at all three lakes and found that the fish in Paul Lake, 17 years after the initial plant, averaged 2 1/2 pounds; those in Knouff Lake, eight years after stocking, averaged 8 pounds, and those in Hyas, three years after introduction, averaged 12 pounds. From this he concluded that changes in the size of the trout populations and subsequent depletion of food stocks were responsible for the declining average size of the trout.

Mottley also found that in some lakes natural factors inhibited spawning or reduced survival so that a natural balance was struck between fish populations and food stocks, and in these waters trout remained at good average size. He saw that it would be necessary to establish and maintain such a balance in all waters to assure good fishing in the future, and he understood the way to do it was to treat each lake individually in terms of its productivity.

However, a lot of work had to be done before a management program could be established along these lines. The life history and habits of the Kamloops trout first had to be documented along with the characteristics of each lake targeted for management.

A pondmill (center distance) on Black Lake. Pondmills were used for lake aeration but proved unreliable; now electric aerators are used.

support for a large-scale management program; it was not until after World War II that such an effort materialized. Then a provincial agency called the Fisheries Research Group was established to begin a survey of lakes and gather information about their productivity and the species of fish that inhabited them. The survey yielded data on water temperature, climate, drainage, chemical content and all factors known to influence productivity.

Using this information, a more sophisticated formula for stocking Kamloops trout lakes was developed. The new formula was based on the dissolved mineral content (TDS) of each lake and its shoal area (littoral development, or percentage of bottom at a depth of less than 10 meters). The shoal area multiplied by the TDS value yielded a figure for the productivity of the littoral zone. This information, combined with a determination of the average size and numbers of trout desired and a calculation of expected fry survival, produced a figure for the number of trout to be stocked per unit of shoal area. The remainder of the lake—that portion with a bottom more than 10 meters below the surface—was stocked at one-tenth the rate of the shoal area.

This was the job Mottley set out to do at Paul Lake.

The Paul Lake fishery already was declining when he arrived, so Mottley began studying the lake and its trout to see what could be done to restore it. From his surveys he concluded Paul Lake was capable of producing a yield of 8 to 10 pounds of fish per surface acre. Paul Lake has a surface area of 390 hectares (963.7 acres); rounding that off to 1,000 acres and assuming a fry survival rate of about 5 percent, Mottley calculated that a plant of 200,000 fry should result in a surviving adult population of 10,000 fish weighing 1 pound each.

The plant was made and Mottley's calculations proved almost exactly correct. Paul Lake gave up catches that were very similar numerically and in weight to what Mottley had predicted; the fishery stabilized, and for the first time a program based on sound scientific management had been applied to one of the Kamloops trout lakes.

Mottley's work at Paul Lake was only the beginning. Little or nothing was known of the productivity of other lakes in the area, and they continued to be managed mostly by guesswork. Funds were scarce and at first there was little public interest or

There have been many refinements to the formula since then—shoal area is now considered less than 6 meters deep—and several different formulas are now in use, though all are founded on the same principles. The stocking and management of Kamloops trout lakes nevertheless is still far from an exact science. Biologists often trust their own experience more than any formula, and the majority of Kamloops trout lakes are stocked with fewer trout than the formulas call for—sometimes by as much as 40 to 60 percent. The guiding philosophy is that it's better to remain conservative and understock a lake than overstock it and have to "work backwards" to restore the fishery.

In the early days, trout stocked in the Kamloops lakes came from existing runs of wild fish. This was a satisfactory source as long as the stocking program was limited in scope. Later, when it became evident the province would have to support a widespread stocking program to augment or maintain populations in waters without natural reproduction, the need for eggs and fry became much greater.

To satisfy this need, traps were built in the tributary streams of several lakes so spawning trout could be captured and stripped of their eggs and milt. The eggs were hatched and the resulting fry raised in hatchery ponds until ready for stocking. Unfortunately, this method had several shortcomings. For one thing, there never was money enough to build as many traps as were needed, or pay the personnel to operate them. For another, weather sometimes interfered with operation of the traps; in dry years, spawning runs often lasted such a short time it was impossible to service all the traps and recover the eggs, and in high-water years floods or freshets sometimes swept away traps or left them filled with debris.

In an effort to get around these problems biologists decided to try importing rainbow trout eggs from hatchery stocks in Washington, Oregon and California. The eggs were hatched in British Columbia hatcheries and the fry were planted in some Interior lakes, with results that were nearly disastrous. The eggs were from domesticated stocks bred selectively for early maturation. This is a desirable trait for trout used in "put-and-take" management schemes where longevity and growth are not important and the goal is to raise new "crops" of trout for harvest in the shortest possible time. The eventual result is a trout that becomes sexually mature at an age of 1 1/2 to 2 years, before it has had an opportunity to grow large enough to provide any real sport. The Kamloops trout fishery, on the other hand, is based largely on the harvest of maiden 2- or 3-year-old fish weighing 1 to 2 pounds or more. The imported trout simply could not live long enough to grow to that size, and anglers complained they did not provide sport comparable to the native Kamloops.

These unsatisfactory results made it clear that only native Kamloops trout could provide a satisfactory source of eggs for the stocking program, despite the difficulties inherent in gathering them. But there still remained questions about how fry hatched from these eggs were affected by hatchery rearing before release. The practice for many years had been to hold fry in hatchery ponds before stocking, but nothing was known about their survival and growth after release. Were they able to compete successfully with wild fish? Did they survive and grow as well? More research was needed to find the answers.

Stuart B. Smith, former head of the province's trout hatcheries and later head of the research secretariat for Alberta Environment, selected Corbett Lake near Merritt for an experiment designed to answer these questions. He took trout from the same stock and divided them into two lots, raising one in hatchery ponds and the other in natural ponds under wild conditions. Then both lots were stocked in Corbett Lake. Records were kept of their size at harvest and comparisons made to see which group had fared better. Not surprisingly, the fish raised under natural conditions were found to have done better than those raised in the hatchery, but the difference in growth was not exceptional. There also was no evidence of significant mortality among the hatchery fish. The cost of raising fish in a natural environment also proved higher than the cost of raising fish in a hatchery. From this, Smith concluded that in lakes where anglers made heavy demands upon naturally reproducing trout populations, supplemental stocking with fish reared in a hatchery would be practical, economical and acceptable so long as a wild, native run of Kamloops trout was the source of the hatchery stock.

Present management mostly follows this policy. In lakes where no spawning takes place, stocks are maintained by periodic introduction of hatchery-reared fry taken from the eggs of wild fish. Hatchery-reared fry also are used to augment populations that are at least partly self-sustaining but subject to unusual angling pressure. There is no lack of wild fish to provide eggs for these fry, but it seems there never will be enough money or personnel to build and operate as many egg-taking stations as could be used. Currently there are four, at Pennask, Dragon, Tunkwa and Badger Lakes.

Existing practice is to hold the fry in hatcheries until the fall of their year of birth, then plant them. This costs less than holding them until they are yearlings; there also is evidence suggesting that male fish planted as fry have a lower rate of precociousness (early sexual maturity) than those planted as yearlings.

Kamloops trout from the wild Pennask Lake strain are most often used for stocking purposes, and from a management standpoint these have proven to be good, hardy, all-purpose fish. Other strains have been stocked in certain specialized situations. For example, trout from the long-lived Gerrard or Lardeau strain have been planted in Paul Lake, Lac des Roches and Niskonlith Lake in hopes they would develop a predatory relationship with coarse fish present in those waters (Paul Lake is infested with shiners, Lac des Roches with chub and Niskonlith with suckers and kokanee). In each case the Gerrard strain fish were fin-clipped for identification purposes.

The Gerrard fish planted in Paul Lake appeared in the angling harvest until the third year after they were stocked, then seemed to disappear; none ever turned up in spawning runs. Biologists now theorize the Gerrard fish may have been temperature-sensitive and remained below the summer thermocline while shiners stayed above it where they were not available for the trout to feed on. As a result, the Gerrard strain fish may simply have starved to death. Gerrard strain fish are still present in Lac des Roches and Niskonlith Lake, but their general lack of success to date has caused the Fisheries Branch to reassess their use for stocking purposes.

Stocking the right strain of fish in the right numbers at the right time is only one element of a succesful management program. Setting appropriate regulations is another.

Regulations

The purpose of regulations is to protect fish from people. This is ironic, since the main purpose of management is to

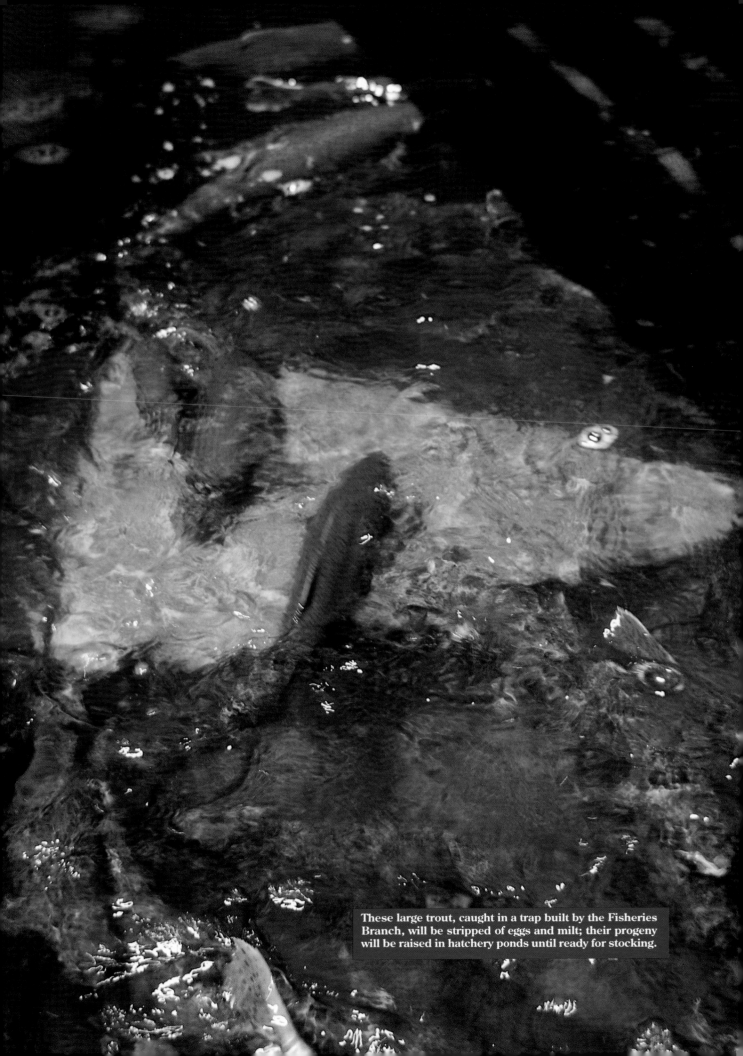

These large trout, caught in a trap built by the Fisheries Branch, will be stripped of eggs and milt; their progeny will be raised in hatchery ponds until ready for stocking.

provide fish for people. Yet because people are so wasteful and so often ignorant of the consequences of their acts, regulations are necessary to prevent individuals from taking a disproportionate share of fish or committing other acts that might damage the use and enjoyment of the fishery by others. No one much cares for regulations, but we have only our own bad habits to blame for them.

The history of fishing regulations in British Columbia is a familiar story to those who study such matters. Starting with simple catch and possession limits applied uniformly to all waters, regulations have gradually become more elaborate, complex and specific. For many years they also were exclusively reactive in nature—that is, they were established in response to problems that already had gotten out of hand—and only recently has British Columbia, like other political jurisdictions, begun to adopt preventive regulations aimed at heading off anticipated problems.

To manage fisheries as efficiently as possible and provide the wide range of recreational experiences sought by the angling public, the Fisheries Branch has divided the province into eight management regions. The natural range of the Kamloops trout spans the heart of two of these, the Thompson-Nicola and Okanagan regions, and spills over into two others, the Kootenay and Cariboo regions. Within each region are many smaller management units of varying size—the Thompson-Nicola region alone has 30. The advantage of such a system is that it allows regulations and management activities to be targeted to relatively small areas with roughly similar habitat characteristics.

In order to set appropriate regulations, biologists must have some knowledge of lake productivity and a good estimate of angling harvest. The latter depends on the intensity of angling effort, which usually is directly proportional to a lake's accessibility.

Many of the population centers of the Southern Interior Plateau are on the shores of major lakes, and many major highways follow natural watercourses, providing access to some of the large, low-lying valley lakes. These lakes, because of their size, easy accessibility, physical characteristics and intermingled species of fish, almost defy any effective management or regulation. For example, it once was estimated that intensive trout management of Okanagan Lake would require stocking 3.5 million fry annually, which could only be done at the expense of hundreds of smaller lakes requiring annual stocking.

So it is in the smaller, higher-elevation lakes that fisheries managers exercise most control, and accessibility is an essential element to be considered in establishing management plans and setting regulations. Easily accessible lakes close to major population centers usually receive the heaviest angling pressure and have the highest harvest rates. They require the most intensive management, including frequent measurements of angling effort and success. Waters somewhat farther from cities or towns, or those reached only by difficult roads, receive less attention and therefore require less intensive management. Nearly inaccessible lakes—those reached only by hiking, horseback or float plane—receive the least fishing pressure. The harvest in these lakes is minimal, and unless there is some specific problem that requires management attention, they may be left largely on their own. There are only a few lakes that still fit this description, however.

Somewhere between 350 and 400 lakes in the Thompson-Nicola region are now under "active management," meaning either that specific regulations have been adopted for them or they are stocked periodically, or both. Of these, 52 are under what the Fisheries Branch calls "quality" management, which means they have regulations restricting use of bait, requiring artificial lures and/or single barbless hooks, reduced limits and so on.

Peterhope, Pennask and Salmon Lakes were among the first to come under such regulations. Beginning in 1970, anglers fishing these lakes were restricted to using artificial flies (British Columbia's "artificial flies" regulation allows the use of any type of angling gear so long as there is an artificial fly at the end of the leader and no flasher or spinner is attached; a slightly more restrictive "fly-fishing-only" regulation exists but is seldom applied). These regulations were adopted partly to satisfy the wishes of fly-fishing activists, but they also represented one of the province's first attempts at preventive regulations. By limiting anglers to artificial flies, managers hoped to reduce trout harvests, extend recreational opportunities and perhaps improve fishing quality by assuring more fish would survive to reach large size. Reducing the harvest also reduced the need for restocking, freeing up more fry for planting elsewhere.

Not surprisingly, the new regulations generated some controversy, but this soon passed and now such measures are commonplace. The artificial-fly regulation has since been removed from Peterhope and a two-fish daily limit adopted in its place, but Pennask and Salmon Lakes remain under artificial-fly regulations and anglers are now required to use single barbless hooks on all three waters. These changes illustrate the continuing trend toward ever more elaborate and specific regulations.

The 1992-94 fishing regulations for the Thompson-Nicola region illustrate that trend even more vividly. They include 20 lakes with a daily limit of two fish, a barbless-hook-only requirement and a bait ban; six lakes with a six-fish daily limit and bait ban; four lakes (Blue, Corbett, Ernest and Warren) restricted to artificial flies only with a two-fish daily limit and barbless hooks; three lakes with a two-fish daily limit and no other restrictions; two lakes (Hatheume and Island) limited to catch-and-release with barbless hooks and a bait ban; two lakes (Jimmy and Pass) with a daily limit of one fish over 20 inches, barbless hooks and a bait ban; two lakes (Pennask and Salmon) restricted to artificial flies only with a daily limit of six fish and a bait ban; one lake with a daily limit of two fish and barbless hooks only, and two lakes with a daily limit of six fish and barbless hooks only. Such a list would have been inconceivable not many years ago.

The list makes it clear that managers are tailoring regulations not only to the circumstances of individual waters but also to the desires of a wide variety of anglers. Obviously a regulation calling for the release of all trout caters to the desires of those who consider fishing strictly a form of recreation rather than a means of obtaining food. Similarly, a regulation that allows anglers to keep only a single trout over 20 inches is intended to provide angling for "trophy"-sized fish, just as regulations permitting use of artificial flies only are aimed at satisfying those who prefer to fish that way.

British Columbia has a long record of success using catch-and-release regulations to preserve declining native steelhead runs on many of its rivers, so it seems surprising that more Kamloops trout waters are not under this type of management. This may reflect the fact that the catch-and-release ethic has been slower to take hold among Kamloops trout anglers than it has in most other locales ("fishing derbies"—the very antithesis of good sportsmanship and conservation—unfortunately are still common on some Kamloops trout lakes). This is true despite educational efforts by the Fisheries Branch, one of the first management agencies to publish instructions on how to release trout without harming them.

As growing numbers of anglers compete for what is essentially a finite resource, the benefits of catch and release are likely to be more widely understood, and it seems probable that more Kamloops trout lakes will come under such management. Catch-and-release, fly-only and "trophy" regulations provide the best promise for the future, assuring there will always be at least some angling of the type that made the Kamloops trout fishery famous in the beginning.

Even with a good management program based on sound biological data and thoughtful regulations, things can and often do go wrong. Some problems—like summer or winter kill—are due to natural causes and may be difficult or impossible to prevent. More often things go wrong because people make them go wrong. For example, a new road built to a previously inaccessible lake almost always leads to a sudden increase in angling effort and harvest which may not have been anticipated by managers. Ice fishing during the winter may take a fearful toll on trout populations. Impacts from logging, land clearing or the introduction of scrap fish may take longer to show up but can be just as devastating.

Some of these problems have eased in recent years. The B.C. Forest Service's belated policy of public participation in the planning process gives the Fisheries Branch early warning of new roads or logging plans, and often steps can be taken to minimize the impacts of these ventures on fisheries. Lakeshore management plans now being written should head off other problems. The Fisheries Branch itself has authority to block development (such as subdivisions) on lakes fronted by Crown (public) land, although this authority does not extend to deeded (private) property.

Indian fisheries are an occasional problem on Kamloops trout lakes. The provincial government has declared settlement of Indian claims a top priority and is committed to a policy

of joint fisheries management with the Indian bands, so the outcome of this issue may be important to the future of the Kamloops trout fishery. For the present, however, biologists rank poaching by non-Indians as perhaps a greater problem than the occasional Indian food or subsistence fishery.

The rapid growth of angling pressure undoubtedly remains the biggest problem faced by managers. This is somewhat paradoxical, since much of that growth is due to the success of the fisheries management program. In a sense, biologists are victims of their own success.

One result is that management "really has become a form of crowd control" in the view of Brian Chan, the biologist who has managed small lakes in the Thompson-Nicola region for the past 12 years. New highway construction has exacerbated the problem. The Coquihalla Highway and the Okanagan Connector have had a severe impact on the Kamloops trout fishery because of the reduced traveling time from both the Lower Mainland and Okanagan Valley, Chan says.

A 1988 survey showed 871,000 angler-days of fishing effort on lakes in the Thompson-Nicola region, and at one point during the 1993 Victoria Day weekend Chan counted 129 boats on Roche Lake alone. Few waters can withstand such pressure very long without suffering a great loss of angling quality.

Chan and other biologists believe some way must be found to distribute angling pressure more evenly to preserve esthetic fishing experiences on "quality" waters. One method, which has been discussed internally within the Fisheries Branch, could be some form of limited-entry system, perhaps requiring daily fee tickets like those used in the British Isles, or permits issued through a lottery. Money raised from the sale of these tickets would be used for management of the lake for which they were issued.

The very thought of limited entry would have been incredible a few years ago, but a similar program already is in effect on some of British Columbia's most popular steelhead rivers, so there is no reason to suppose it could not be applied to Kamloops trout lakes. In a sense, the fish-for-fee waters on the Douglas Lake Ranch already represent a form of limited entry under private management.

The inherent danger of limited entry is that it inevitably alienates part of the constituency that traditionally supports fisheries management and conservation efforts. That in turn could mean less money from license fees, more enforcement problems and less public help in the critical battles that must be fought to preserve fisheries resources. Managers face the unenviable task of somehow finding a delicate middle ground.

Research and Habitat Improvement

Research and habitat improvement are elements of fisheries management that usually don't get much public attention, perhaps because it often takes a long time for results to show, but they are key factors in the overall success of any management effort. In British Columbia these programs are financed by the Habitat Conservation Fund with money raised from the

conservation surcharge on fishing and hunting license sales. Funds are allocated by a board that reviews detailed technical proposals submitted by regional managers and biologists throughout the province. Once accepted, proposals are ranked by priority and funded as money becomes available.

The most common form of habitat improvement is the chemical treatment of lakes to remove coarse fish, an operation that has been carried out many times in the waters of the Southern Interior Plateau—usually to eradicate redside shiners introduced by anglers using them illegally as bait. Such treatment is controversial and expensive and its success is never a sure thing, and growing public opposition to chemical treatment eventually may force biologists to discard it as a management method. This would be extremely unfortunate since it would almost certainly lead to a net loss of habitat for Kamloops trout.

Lake aeration is another common form of habitat-improvement work, involving installation of a variety of aeration devices on lakes with marginal oxygen levels. Early models were called "pondmills," small windmills driving a piston or compressor to force air through a perforated pipe below a lake's surface, enhancing circulation and raising oxygen levels during periods of poor circulation or ice cover to prevent winter kill.

The first pondmill was installed on Black Lake, a small (18-hectare, 44.5-acre) lake near Roche Lake southeast of Kamloops, which now holds brook trout. Further experience demonstrated pondmills were too unreliable, so solar-powered systems were tried next but subsequently rejected for the same reason. Then devices powered by Diesel engines were installed; these worked well but were expensive to operate and became frequent targets of vandalism or theft. Now electric-powered aerators with surface-mounted or suspended diffusers are being used with satisfactory results, although their distribution is limited by lack of power availability in the back country.

Lakes with aeration devices currently installed include Rose, Tulip, Corbett, Bleeker, Lodgepole, Walloper, Stake, Logan and Horsehoe. Aerators usually are turned on in the fall and are left on until winter in some waters. In all, the Fisheries Branch has spent nearly $1 million in Habitat Conservation Fund money on the aeration program throughout the province.

Other typical habitat-improvement projects included work on the inlet to Heffley Lake and the outlet from Chataway Lake. At Heffley Lake, trout ascended the inlet to spawn during spring runoff but the lower reaches of the stream usually dried up before fry could migrate downstream to the lake; as a result, there was no natural fry recruitment to the trout population in the lake. The Fisheries Branch solved this problem by installing an 8-inch pipe in the streambed with a catchment box at the upper end, providing a safe passage through the normally dry section of the stream so fry could reach the lake.

The problem at Chataway Lake was just the opposite: Young-of-the-year fry hatched in the outlet were too small and weak to ascend to the lake. Forced to remain in the outlet, many died and a whole year passed before the survivors were strong enough to gain the lake. The loss of a year's growth in the lake coupled with the onset of early sexual maturation kept many of these fish from reaching a size desirable to anglers. To correct this situation, the Fisheries Branch installed a gravel "spawning platform" at the head of the outlet so that fry hatched in the gravel would have an easy return to the lake.

The Fisheries Branch and its predecessors have a long and distinguished history of innovative fisheries research, which has paid off in the form of numerous management improvements. Today the research program is spearheaded by the Research and Development Section of the Fisheries Branch, based at the University of British Columbia in Vancouver. Kanji Tsumura heads the small-lakes research effort.

Recent projects have included development of a strategy for establishing productive seasonal fisheries in lakes subject to frequent winter kill and experiments suggesting that a method of grading fry by size before planting might reduce the rate of male precociousness in Kamloops trout populations. Ongoing work involves tracking the growth and survival of sterilized female trout planted in Island Lake in the Highland Valley in an effort to eliminate the problems of precociousness and early maturation and produce fish of true trophy size.

Other projects, also financed by the Habitat Conservation Fund, are aimed at developing trout stocks compatible with unusual environmental circumstances in some Interior lakes—specifically, the increasing alkalinity of some waters and the presence of coarse fish in others.

The problem of increasing alkalinity is traced to a succession of unusually warm, dry winters in British Columbia since 1985, perhaps an alarming sign of global warming. This prolonged drought has lowered groundwater levels and slowed the rate of water replacement in many Interior lakes, resulting in a rise in alkalinity. In some cases, such as Stump and Valentine Lakes, alkalinity has increased to the point that planted trout fry have suffered severe mortality. To combat this problem, the Research and Development Section in 1991 began a three-year study to try to identify native trout strains that can tolerate high alkalinity.

Stump Lake once supported a famous fishery for very large Kamloops trout, but its alkalinity—or pH—has risen to 9.2 or above (7.0 is neutral), high enough to subject many trout to fatal alkaline shock. Not all the trout in Stump Lake died, however, and biologists trapped some of the survivors and spawned them in a hatchery. Their offspring, along with those of broodstock taken from another high-alkaline lake, were marked for identification and planted in Stump Lake along with a similar number of ordinary Pennask-strain Kamloops trout planted as a control group. Researchers hope to track the relative survival and growth of these fish to determine if progeny of the alkaline-tolerant parents do better than the Pennask control group. Results and conclusions are yet to come.

The natural or artificial presence of coarse fish in many Interior lakes triggered a second project, designed to identify piscivorous trout strains able to thrive in lakes with coarse-fish populations. Eight small lakes containing one or more species of coarse fish (including redside shiners, peamouth chub, coarse-scaled suckers and squawfish) were selected for the study. These were stocked with offspring from four wild strains of rainbow trout originating in systems with dense coarse fish populations—the Blackwater, Tsuniah, Bootjack and Tzenzaicut strains. Trout from the Pennask strain again were used as controls.

Early results from this work show the Tzenzaicut fish had better survival and growth rates than the Pennask fish in five lakes where they were stocked. The Bootjack strain had a better survival rate but no difference in growth. Tsuniah fish had a lower survival rate but a larger average size in two of three lakes stocked. Blackwater fish had a lower survival rate but a consistently better growth rate than Pennask fish. These results are strictly preliminary, however, and much work remains before any final conclusions can be drawn.

In addition to feeding on coarse fish, the Blackwater strain (from the Blackwater River) also displays an avid disposition for insects, meaning it is able to take advantage of the full spectrum of food available in lakes. It has shown so much promise that the Fisheries Branch is developing a brood stock in Dragon Lake, near Quesnel, where four-year-old fish have reached weights of 11 pounds. So far the only apparent drawback to the Blackwater fish is that they tend to be more gullible, or easier to catch, than others. But that's no drawback as far as most anglers are concerned.

All the activities described in this chapter—and others not described here—make up the complex, costly business of fisheries management. At its best, management never can make all anglers happy all the time; because it must balance a variety of competing interests and conflicting uses and somehow deal with the vagaries of natural systems, it must be content to settle for making some anglers happy some of the time.

Considering the resources it has had available, the Fisheries Branch has done that about as well as any agency could. Whatever it has not done, or has done imperfectly, is likely the result of inadequate funding or the frequently conflicting priorities of the provincial government. Certainly it is not due to any lack of dedication on the part of those men and women who have made the protection and care of the Kamloops trout their livelihood and their profession. To them, anglers owe a debt of enormous gratitude.

4: The Food of Kamloops Trout

Gammarus limnaeus, the common scud of Kamloops trout lakes. *Facing Page:* Sedge adult.

T he diet of the Kamloops trout is as rich and varied as the country it lives in. Its rapid growth and surprising strength are due to the wide assortment of aquatic insects, crustacea, snails, terrestrial insects, leeches and other creatures it has available for food.

The study of these creatures is a fascinating hobby and well worth the investment of an angler's time. It is hardly necessary to memorize a long list of Latin names, although some anglers seem to regard such knowledge as a badge of status and the names are provided here for those who wish them. It is essential to learn to recognize the basic types of insects, to know something of their habits, their seasons of peak abundance and where they are most likely to be found. Armed with such basic knowledge and enough skill to present a fly properly, even an angler new to the Kamloops trout lakes is assured of some success.

Conventional fly-fishing entomology has emphasized the mayfly, and while mayflies are important in some Kamloops trout waters, they are usually much less significant than the sedge, or caddisfly—not to mention scuds, midges, damselflies and dragonflies. This is the reverse of what many anglers have been taught, and the entomology of the Kamloops trout lakes therefore is likely to be at least somewhat new to them. Anglers from other parts of the world also are often surprised by the size of the insects they find in the Kamloops lakes, some

of which are very much larger than anything they have seen elsewhere. The feeding habits of Kamloops trout also may differ from those of other locales—and that seems a good place to begin.

Feeding Habits

Kamloops trout alevins begin feeding as soon as they emerge from the gravel of their natal stream. At first they wait for the current to bring them food, taking myriad small items into their tiny mouths and deciding quickly whether to accept or reject them. In this way they soon learn to recognize what is edible and what is not, and having learned this they no longer wait for the stream to bring them food but begin to seek it actively. They forage for small nymphs or larvae beneath the surface and rise to tiny flies trapped in the surface film.

These feeding habits are continued as the alevins grow to fry and migrate downstream to the lake where they will spend most of their lives. Once in the lake, their schools patrol the shallows and the little fish begin feeding on the more abundant food stocks they find there: Water fleas and copepods, small midges or little terrestrial insects that have fallen to the surface. The fry feed eagerly and well and the mark of their passage is a succession of tiny dimples in the surface near the shore.

Once they reach yearling size, Kamloops trout begin seeking larger prey, feeding on small scuds found in shallow weedbeds or larger nymphs and pupae of aquatic insects. Mostly they continue foraging near shore, but as they grow larger their feeding ventures take them more and more often into deeper water.

As adults, Kamloops trout turn to scuds as the great staple of their diet in most lakes. Nymphs and larvae of aquatic insects also are important, and because of their subsurface abundance, adult trout are content to forage in the depths for much of the year; only a hatch of considerable size and duration will induce them to rise freely and feed on the surface.

Early-season midge hatches may stimulate a fair rise of trout, and there are always at least a few scattered rises to hatching midges throughout the year. Some lakes also have mayfly hatches that produce a fair rise in late May or early June, and the damselfly nymph migration—which often takes place about the same time—usually provokes a violent rise. The appearance of flying ants in late spring or early fall sometimes sets off an eager rise, but the best and most consistent rises occur during the spectacular sedge hatches of late spring and early summer.

Whether it is on or beneath the surface, food is most abundant over weedbeds or shoals—but adult Kamloops trout, having learned the value of caution, will enter such areas only with care. On calm, bright days they may not enter the shallows at all until the light is off the water. On dark or windy days they enter more willingly but always remain wary and alert, and a disturbance—such as that caused by an outboard motor—may cause them to leave for hours at a time.

When feeding, larger trout tend to follow the edges of shoals and weedbeds. If a shoal offers abundant cover, such as dark gravel or a thick carpet of weed, trout may remain for long periods and browse for food within a relatively small area; but if good cover is lacking, they usually will not stray far from the safety of deep water. Shoal contours and the presence or absence of cover often cause trout to follow similar paths as they cruise around looking for food. By studying rise patterns carefully or observing fish movements if the water is clear enough, an angler sometimes can deduce these routes and take station along them to intercept cruising trout. Once such a spot is discovered an angler may return to it with confidence that it will reward him again and again, but keen and patient observation is necessary to find such places.

The feeding patterns of Kamloops trout follow a fairly well established order through the year. When the ice goes off the lakes in spring, the first hatches usually are of small midges; trout take the rising pupae and sometimes feed on the freshly hatched adults. Hatches of larger midges quickly follow, and some lakes have enormous emergences in the last few days of May. When these are in progress midge pupae are so abundant it's a simple matter for a trout to cruise under the surface with open mouth and intercept dozens of pupae at a time. Fishing frequently is poor at such times because naturals are so abundant that imitations hardly stand a chance.

As the midge hatches taper off, mayflies begin to come on. There are mayfly hatches in virtually all Kamloops trout lakes but only a few—Lac des Roches is a notable example—have emergences large enough to stimulate a consistent rise of trout. The best rises usually are to newly hatched duns, often on days when a breeze concentrates the flies in one area. Some mayfly hatches continue sporadically through the summer and it is not unusual to see mayfly spinner flights as late as early September.

A few hot, still days in late May or early June can bring on the flying ants, and great numbers of these may become stranded in the surface film of a lake. Their futile struggles attract the attention of trout and often trigger a vigorous rise.

Warm weather also sets the damselfly nymphs in motion, and under normal conditions their hatching migrations peak during the first two weeks of June. Trout take them avidly just beneath the surface, sometimes with splashy rises that mislead anglers into thinking some surface fare is being taken. Dragonfly nymphs also are active at this time, but their movements are more secretive and they are most often taken by trout in submerged weed thickets or along the bottom.

Mid-June usually brings the first great sedge hatches and trout feed wildly on the emerging pupae and adults. The awkward, fluttering motions of the big traveling sedge adults set off spectacular rises, and this is the most exciting time of year for dry-fly fishers.

The sedge hatches taper off quickly after the first week in July. Then the summer sun warms the lakes, water circulation ebbs and temperature layers begin forming in the depths. The sudden lack of surface fare, coupled with increasing heat and light, drives the trout into deeper water. Scuds now become their most important food, along with snails and leeches. It is a difficult time for the fly fisher on most waters, a time for a slow, deep-fished fly during the day, or hopes for a few rising fish in the twilight of early morning or late evening. The problem is not as severe in cooler, high-elevation lakes, but even in those waters there is often a summer lull to the fishing.

Early in September the flying ants may come again. Their appearance is not certain and if they do come their fall flights are not as prolific as those of spring, but they are much more eagerly received; having gone two months without substantial surface fare, trout rise willingly to the struggling ants and continue taking floating imitations days after the last natural has disappeared.

Warm Indian-summer days often bring on a hatch of backswimmers, but trout usually are slow to respond and do not begin taking the adults consistently until the hatch has been under way for several days.

From early September until ice-up, the scud is the principal source of food for Kamloops trout. On balance, over a year's time, it is the most important food of all. Sedges usually are next, at least in those lakes with good hatches, followed by midges, which continue hatching throughout the season following their peak emergence in the spring. The nymphs of damselflies and dragonflies are next most important in the season-long diet, followed by leeches, water boatmen and backswimmers, mayflies and other organisms. The timing of insect emergences may be accelerated or delayed by the vagaries of weather, but the sequence rarely changes.

Scuds

Among the larger forms of crustacea two members of the order *Amphipoda* are common in Kamloops trout waters. One of these, *Gammarus limnaeus*, is present in nearly all the Kamloops trout lakes and usually constitutes the bulk of the trout diet during summer and fall months. It ranges in length to an inch or a little more and in color from a dull

A hatching damselfly heaves itself out of the nymphal shuck.

The adult is free of the shuck but still looks like a nymph; its wings have yet to unfold.

Now the wings have unfolded and begun to dry.

An adult damselfly rests on a lily pad.

khaki to a brilliant turquoise, with light olive the most common hue. Scuds and the fly patterns tied to imitate them invariably are called "shrimps" by anglers because of their shrimp-like posture when they are at rest. This has prompted many fly tiers to construct imitations on curved-shank hooks, and while these patterns look deadly, they really are not very good imitations; the reason is that the scud's body becomes elongate when it is in motion, and trout rarely take scuds that are not in motion.

Scuds are extremely mobile, using their seven pairs of legs for swimming or to grasp and climb submerged plant stocks. Their normal swimming motion is forward, but they are also capable of swimming upside down and/or backwards, which they do frequently under stress.

The scud's segmented exoskeleton (literally a skeleton outside the body) is formed of relatively hard material manufactured from calcium absorbed from the water. As it grows, the scud periodically sheds its exoskeleton and replaces it with a new and larger one. The abandoned exoskeletons often may be found floating on the surface of lakes.

Gammarus is an omnivorous scavenger that feeds on decaying plant and animal matter. It ranges to depths of 50 feet but is most comfortable at depths of less than three meters, or about 10 feet. It is sensitive to light and in shallow water tends to hide in weedbeds or under rocks during the day, but an angler usually can verify its presence by turning over a few rocks near the shore.

Under favorable circumstances *Gammarus* breeds several times a year, and it is common for anglers to see mating pairs locked in embrace. Females carry their young in brood pouches and these so-called "pregnant" scuds are easily recognizable from the bright orange brood pouch, which actually is the color of the tiny scuds inside it.

Hyalella is the other genus common to the Kamloops trout waters, and at least two species—*Hyalella azteca* and *Hyalella knickerbockeri*—are present. In appearance and habits they closely resemble *Gammarus,* but there are several important differences. Most significant is the difference in size; *Hyalella* seldom exceeds a third of an inch in length. It also appears in a wider range of colors, from blue to bright red, although light brown, yellow and green predominate. *Hyalella* prefers even shallower water than *Gammarus* and is found mostly in aquatic vegetation very close to shore. This preference makes it an especially important food source for juvenile Kamloops trout, and that—plus its diminutive size and enormous numbers—usually discourages anglers from trying to imitate it.

Snails

Snails *(Gastropoda)* are virtually impossible for anglers to imitate, but their importance as trout food in some lakes makes them worth at least brief mention. At home in beds of *Chara* weed or other vegation at depths of 4.5 to 9 meters (15 to 30 feet), they are taken most often during July and August when trout tend to feed in deeper water. In some lakes they are the primary summer food source for trout.

Lymnaea and *Physa* probably are the two most common genera found in the Kamloops trout waters. Both have distinctive spiral shells and the primary means of identification is the direction of the spiral—*Lymnaea* spirals to the right and *Physa* to the left.

Annelida

The annelids include the leeches *(Hirudinea)*, aquatic earthworms *(Oligochaeta)*, flatworms *(Turbellaria)* and roundworms *(Nematoda)*. Of these, the leeches are most important to fish and anglers.

Leeches are flat, ribbon-like creatures found in a wide variety of lengths, although specimens from one to two inches long are most often found in trout stomachs. They swim with a distinctive motion like that of a sidewinder rattlesnake. Common colors are black, muddy brown, dark gray and gray with mottled dark green spots. Their mouths are in a small sucker at the anterior end; another, larger sucker is at the posterior end. They feed on small worms, snails and insect larvae, but they also have a well-known predilection for blood, and anyone who makes a regular practice of swimming in the Kamloops trout lakes should be prepared for the ugly sight of a leech clinging to his or her body.

Leeches are hermaphroditic, each having both male and female reproductive organs. However, they do mate, exchanging packets of sperm cells, and are incapable of self-fertilization. Eggs are laid in cocoons and development and growth are direct without a larval stage. Adults are nocturnal and usually remain hidden under rocks or vegetation in daylight. Like many other fauna in the Kamloops trout lakes, they may be found easily by turning over rocks in shallow water.

Leeches are most abundant at depths of 3 to 15 meters (10 to 50 feet), but also are commonly found in shallow water. Despite their nocturnal preferences, solitary individuals fre-quently emerge from hiding during the day and swim within a meter of the surface, and these are taken readily by trout. They are most important during summer months when they may constitute a substantial portion of the trout's diet, along with scuds and snails.

The other annelids—aquatic earthworms, flatworms and roundworms—are of lesser significance. The first two are fairly abundant but are seldom taken by trout (except for the earthworms used as bait by trollers).

Insecta

Aquatic and terrestrial insects provide much of the food for Kamloops trout and offer a wealth of subjects for imitation by the angler. The insects of greatest importance to the Kamloops trout fly fisher include the damselflies and dragonflies *(Odonata)*, sedges *(Trichoptera)*, midges *(Diptera)*, mayflies *(Ephemeroptera)*, water bugs *(Hemiptera)*, beetles *(Coleoptera)*, and the terrestrial ants, bees and wasps *(Hymenoptera)*.

Dragonflies and Damselflies

The order *Odonata* is divided into two suborders, *Zygoptera*, the damselflies, and *Anisoptera*, the dragonflies. Damselfly nymphs are characterized by long, slim, segmented abdomens culminating in two or three distinctive leaf-like gills that are positioned vertically in relation to the body. They have three pairs of legs attached to the thorax and large eyes set widely apart at the front of the head. They are predators equipped with an extensible labium which they use to capture prey. Nymphs range in color from dark olive to light reddish-brown, always lighter on the ventral surface. Color is not a determinant of species because it may vary among individuals of a single species. The most reliable method of identification is to examine the vein structure of the gills.

Adult damselflies usually deposit their eggs in weeds or rushes near the shoreline just under the surface, or on the surface itself. Once the eggs hatch, the nymphs go through a series of instars, or molts, before reaching maturity. Mature nymphs may be as long as 1 1/2 inches.

Nymphs usually are found clambering over submerged vegetation in shallow water or waiting in concealment, hoping some form of prey will pass within striking distance. In most years, the annual damselfly migration—or emergence—occurs during the first two weeks of June in Kamloops trout lakes at about 1,070 meters elevation (3,500 feet), although it may begin earlier or later if the weather is warmer or cooler than usual. At this time mature nymphs swim to the surface and strike out in a horizontal direction until they encounter rushes, weeds, logs or other structures upon which they can climb out of the water to hatch.

The nymph swims with a sculling motion created by rapid flexing of its abdomen, with the posterior gills acting as a sort of oar. During their migration the nymphs are silhouetted by light from above and become easy targets for feeding trout. During a heavy emergence trout may become extremely selective and anglers must have an imitation that not only closely resembles the natural but somehow imitates its sculling motion. An entirely satisfactory solution to this problem in fly design has yet to be found. However, during the early or late stages of a hatch, trout seem less particular and an imitation close to the natural in color, shape and size usually is adequate.

If a damselfly nymph succeeds in reaching a plant stock, log or other object that protrudes above the surface, it climbs out of the water and rests until the nymphal shuck begins to open and the adult fly crawls out. The adult waits until its wings unfold and dry before it is able to take flight. As an adult it continues its predatory habits, feeding on terrestrial insects or the adults of other aquatic types.

Adult damselflies are a common sight around any lake or pond during summer months. Members of the genus *Enallagma* are practically ubiquitous on North American waters; they are the bright blue and black damselflies familiar to nearly every fisherman. Like all damselflies, they are strong fliers with two pairs of clear, heavily-veined wings that are held vertically over the abdomen while the insect is at rest. Males are more vividly colored than females. Members of the genus *Ischnura* also are common in Kamloops trout lakes; their adults are black with greenish markings on the thorax and blue markings on the tips of the abdomens in males and some females, while other females are brownish or dull orange.

Mating may take place in flight or while the insects are at rest, depending upon the species. The adults usually are not available to trout, but spent flies sometimes are taken on the surface and occasionally trout will rise to adults blown to the surface on windy days.

The nymphs of some dragonfly species are short, stocky and powerfully built; others are long, thick and bulbous in the abdomen. In all species, the gills are inside the abdomen and water is drawn in through an anal opening for respiration. This water may be expelled quickly by muscular action, resulting in a crude form of jet propulsion that drives the nymph forward in quick spurts. But the nymphs also have three strong pairs of legs attached to the thorax which allow them to crawl over bottom debris.

The dragonfly nymph is a fierce predator with a very powerful extensible labium that reaches out with incredible speed to capture prey. Nymphs range in color from olive gray to muddy brown, which provides appropriate camouflage in their preferred habitat of mud or decaying vegetation. Nymphs of smaller species may scarcely exceed an inch in length at maturity; those of some larger species range up to 2 1/2 inches long.

Adults of different species use different means to deposit their eggs; some are laid in weed or plant stems, some are left in silt or mud on the lake floor, and some are merely dropped into the water. After hatching the nymphs go through 10 to 14 molts during a period ranging from several months to a year or more, depending upon the species and the water temperature. When mature nymphs are ready to hatch, they crawl toward shore until they find an object on which they can crawl out of the water, after which their hatching is similar to that of the damselfly. During their shoreward movement they become more vulnerable to trout than at other times, but are still far less susceptible to capture than damselfly nymphs swimming near the surface. Their emergence period in the Kamloops trout lakes is not as clearly defined as that of the damselfly; it may begin as early as late May and continue through June or even later.

Some adult damselflies have wingspans measuring up to five inches. They are strong fliers with clear, heavily-veined wings that are held horizontally at a 90-degree angle to the body when the insect is at rest. Like the damselfly adult, they have two pairs of wings, and also like the damselfly they continue their predatory habits as adults.

Aeschna, Gomphus and *Sympetrum* are common genera in the Kamloops trout lakes. *Aeschna* adults are large with blue markings; *Gomphus* adults also are large with black and yellow markings, while *Sympetrum* adults are smaller with shorter abdomens and a distinctive wine-red color.

Sedges

The *Trichoptera*, caddisfly, or sedge, as it is customarily called in British Columbia, is as important to the Kamloops trout fly fisher as the mayfly is to anglers who fish the British chalk streams or North American spring creeks. Usually it is the only aquatic insect whose hatches are sufficient to set off a really good, consistent rise of Kamloops trout, and these rises occur periodically throughout the duration of the hatch, which may last several weeks. The annual sedge hatch unquestionably provides the best dry-fly fishing opportunities of the season.

Many sedge species are native to Kamloops trout waters. The adults of some are quite small and rise quickly from the surface after emerging; others are extremely large and slow to take flight. The latter frequently rest on the surface for a time, stretching and drying their wings, then spin or flutter for long distances, leaving little V-shaped wakes behind them, before finally taking flight. This behavior provokes even the largest trout to rise, and it is this phenomenon—the "traveling sedge"—that gives the Kamloops trout lakes an extraordinarily exciting type of dry-fly fishing unknown elsewhere in the world.

The sedges of the Interior lakes are case-builders. The larvae begin construction of a case soon after hatching, using whatever materials are at hand. These may include sand or tiny bits of gravel, small empty snail shells, bark, twigs, bits of stem or leaves, even needles from coniferous trees.

Characteristics of case construction vary between species and sometimes among individuals of the same species, so the cases are not a reliable guide to speciation. Regardless of species, sedge larvae are remarkable architects; some build intricate spiral cases from bits of plant fiber, others create cylindrical tubes of sand and gravel, and some make miniature "log cabins" of bark and plant stems. Glands within the larva secrete a sticky silk that binds together the materials of the case.

Since they are made from materials found in the natural habitat, the cases blend well with their surroundings and offer valuable camouflage for their occupants. They do not provide physical protection, however; trout willingly eat the larva, case and all.

The larva is a soft, segmented creature, usually light-colored over the portion of its body that remains inside the larval case. The head and thorax are black or dark brown with a hard, chitinous surface. Legs attached to the thorax allow the larva to crawl slowly and awkwardly over bottom debris, dragging the case behind it. The larva has small hooks on its posterior end to clutch the inside of the case and prevent the larva from being forcibly withdrawn. The larva also may draw its head inside the case when danger threatens, much as a turtle retreats into its shell. Water is drawn into the case by a gentle writhing motion of the larva and respiration is through gills on the abdomen.

The larvae go through several instars, adding to their cases or abandoning them to construct new ones. They are omnivorous feeders. Most species in the Interior lakes go through one generation a year, entering the pupal stage in early spring. The larva seals itself inside its case by constructing a porous membrane across the open end, which allows water to pass so respiration can continue, then begins the transformation to the pupal stage.

This transformation is as remarkable as the metamorphosis of a butterfly. The caddis larva is a humble, awkward, worm-like creature when it seals its case; when the pupa emerges two or three weeks later, it is a strikingly different creature. Its color is darker and its abdomen thicker; two pair of large, hairy wings have grown from its thorax, and two long antennae have sprouted from its head. Its legs are much longer, especially the middle pair, which have hairs along the trailing edge to help in swimming. The pupa struggles out of the case, still enclosed in a membrane, but its legs are free to allow it to swim to the surface. During its slow ascent it is extremely vulnerable to feeding trout and the beginning of a large emergence may start trout on an orgy of subsurface feeding.

Once at the surface the pupa may swim around for a considerable period, using its powerful middle legs like a pair of oars, until finally it heaves itself up through the surface film. Then the membrane splits slowly lengthwise down the back and the adult insect pushes itself out. All through this process—which may take five minutes or longer if the air and water temperature are cool—the hatching sedge is a sitting duck for feeding trout. At least this is true for the larger species; the smaller ones hatch much more rapidly.

After hatching the large sedges stretch and dry their wings, then begin the "traveling" routine, fluttering across the surface as if propelled by a tiny outboard motor. Finally they take tentative, awkward flight, lifting off for short distances and perhaps returning to the surface to repeat the performance a second or even a third time before they finally take wing and fly to shore. While fluttering across the surface they are plainly visible to trout, which pursue them with splashy, explosive rises; an angler can almost feel the mounting excitement of the trout as they chase the large, fat-bodied insects.

At least that is how it is at the very beginning of the hatch. After the hatch has been going on for several days and the trout have fed well, the excitement ebbs and the fish return to their normally cautious and selective ways. Then, even when the hatch is very heavy, an angler may have to work hard to fool a few trout.

Sedge adults that survive the assaults of hungry trout find resting places in shoreside brush or trees, where they may remain for several weeks before mating. Most species mate in flight, but some return to the lake's surface. The adults are easily recognized by their long, tent-like wings, which they fold parallel to their bodies while at rest, and by their long, graceful antennae. The wings exceed the length of the body; usually they are mottled brown and black and covered with tiny hairs. While the flies are on the water, the colors of their abdomens are visible to trout, and this is a key to proper imitation of the naturals. The colors range from black to orange, but shades of green ranging from dark olive to bright emerald are most common among larger sedges; brown and gray occur with less frequency. Anglers are well advised to capture a natural and try to match the color of its body as closely as possible.

Adult sedges do not undergo additional molts, as do mayfly adults, and after mating they deposit their eggs in various ways. In most cases the female goes under water and deposits her eggs in gelatinous strings on the bottom, but some species deposit eggs on the surface and others drop them from flight. Female adults returning to the water to lay eggs sometimes set off another rise of trout.

A full-blown traveling sedge emergence is an awesome sight, especially when seen for the first time. Anglers accustomed to fishing in other parts of the world usually are astounded by both the size of the flies and the size of the fish feeding on them. The sedge adults may exceed 1 1/2 inches in length, requiring a size 8 hook with a 2X long shank for imitation. Fly patterns also must be constructed to float well during repeated long retrieves across the surface to match the behavior of the naturals, a difficult problem in fly design when dealing with such a large imitation.

"Traveling" behavior is typically exhibited by species of the genera *Limnephilus* and *Phryganea,* both common in the Interior lakes. Unfortunately, hatches of these sedges are not as widespread as they used to be. The overstocking of Knouff Lake, which resulted in virtual elimination of its traveling sedge hatches, already has been described, and other lakes have fallen victim to similar circumstances. Once reduced, traveling sedge hatches never have been able to recover under natural conditions, and while there has been occasional talk of trying to transplant sedges from one lake to another, it has never happened and probably never will.

Despite these losses, traveling sedges still hatch in good numbers on many lakes. In a normal season, the first meaningful hatches may be expected around June 15 in a lake about

1,070 meters (3,500 feet) elevation. The hatch will remain heavy for about two weeks, then begin tapering off around the first of July. Fairly good hatches may continue sporadically through the first week of July, but usually by July 10 they start tailing off rapidly and by mid-July the hatch is completely over. The best daytime hatches occur between 11 a.m. and mid-afternoon on most lakes, convenient hours for the angler, but the heaviest emergences often take place at night, stimulating trout to feed even more aggressively than by day.

Egg-laying flights may continue even later than mid-July, sometimes prompting a rise of trout. These flights mostly take place in the evening, just before dark.

At least 10 genera of *Trichoptera,* and probably more, are present in the Kamloops trout lakes. Little work has been done to identify individual species, and the task of identification is formidable—the genus *Limnephilus* alone has about 250 separate species, *Phryganea* about 30.

Midges

The *Diptera,* or true flies, include a very large number of insects. The most important of these in the Interior lakes are the midges of the family *Chironomidae* and the so-called "phantom midge," *Chaoborus.*

Identification of chironomids is difficult; it has been estimated there are more than 2,500 North American species, and the work of classifying all of them is far from complete. The problem is further complicated by small differences between some species.

Chironomid larvae are found over a very wide range of depths, but are most common in shallow water, particularly in areas where the bottom consists of soft mud or silt. Larvae of many species construct tubes, which may either be attached to the bottom or carried around by

Chironomid pupa (bottom) and adult.

Backswimmer (dorsal view).

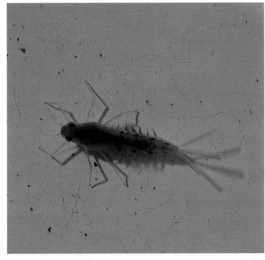
Callibaetis mayfly nymph.

their occupants. The larvae are long, segmented, cylindrical and worm-like, and respire by undulating movements inside their tubes. They feed on algae or planktonic animals.

The larval stage includes four instars and may last from two weeks to as long as four years, depending on the species. In warm, eutrophic lakes, some species go through several generations in a single summer. Some larvae are nearly transparent while others range in color from deep red to shades of green and bronze. The red larvae, known as "bloodworms" because they contain hemoglobin, are especially common in shallow, eutrophic lakes, where they are important trout food. Bloodworm larvae are most active in late summer and early fall, before entering the pupal stage.

The pupal stage is brief and the pupa usually hides in bottom debris until pupation is complete. Mature pupae are easily identified by white, tuft-like gills at the head, a thin segmented body and a developing wing case over the thorax. They swim with a rapid flexing motion of their bodies, but all this hard work propels them at a very slow rate. During their slow, halting ascent to the surface, they are taken in very large numbers by trout, and they are most important to anglers at this point.

When a pupa reaches the surface it assumes a vertical attitude and waits for the pupal shuck to split open; then the adult fly crawls out onto the surface film. On warm days hatching flies may take flight immediately, but on cool or damp days they may rest for a time or buzz rapidly across the surface for some distance before lifting off. Either way, they are vulnerable to rising trout.

Adult chironomids resemble mosquitoes in shape, although many are much larger than any mosquito; pupae and adults of some species range up to an inch in length. The adults have thin, tapered bodies and clear, transparent wings, which may appear white in reflected light. The wings are held flat over the back while the fly is at rest, and in larger species the length of the body exceeds the length of the folded wings. Adult males have prominent feather-like setae protruding from their heads, and all adult chironomids rest on the surface with their forelegs held forward and off the water.

Black is the most common body color in adults, especially in smaller species (the "black gnats"). Kelly green or emerald-colored adults also are common among smaller species while tan, gold, bronze and red colors are found in larger species, usually with black rings where body segments join. The adults join in mating flights over the water or around shore-side brush, and females deposit eggs from flight, on the lake surface or on emergent vegetation, depending upon the species.

Chironomids are available to trout throughout the season, from ice-out to ice-up. They may begin hatching as soon as a patch of open water appears on an otherwise still-frozen lake. Normally these first hatches are of very small insects, many too small for any practical imitation. Hatches grow steadily in volume until the last week or so in May when they peak on many lakes, and by then many larger species are hatching. In some lakes—Tunkwa already has been mentioned, and Minnie is another—insect swarms are phenomenal and constitute a real annoyance. Thankfully, they do not bite.

Hatches taper off in late May or early June, but continue throughout the season, usually heaviest in early evening. By late summer the first large adults begin hatching from the bloodworm larvae. This hatch may continue sporadically for several weeks, from late August to early October. Chironomid adults live from a few days to two weeks, depending on the species, dying after mating and egg-laying.

A heavy chironomid hatch leaves the surface of a lake littered with vacated pupal shucks. The long, tapering, segmented cases, which appear black-and-white in the water, are familiar sights on the Interior lakes—and a possible clue that trout will respond enthusiastically to a pupal imitation.

Chaoborus is a member of the family *Culicidae,* which includes the mosquitoes, but fortunately for anglers *Chaoborus* does not share the biting habits of its kin. Eight species are known, but it has not been determined how many of these are present in the Kamloops trout lakes. The common name "phantom midge" for this insect apparently is derived from its sensitivity to light; the free-swimming larvae stay in deep water during the day, rising to the surface only at night. Consequently they are rarely seen by anglers, except when found in the stomachs of trout.

During its evening ascent or morning descent, the *Chaoborus* larva becomes a likely target for feeding trout, and Kamloops trout often feed on them with a high degree of selectivity. A study by members of the Washington Fly Fishing Club of stomach contents of Kamloops trout in Hihium Lake showed *Chaoborus* larvae were an important item of the trout's summer diet.

Chaoborus is small, seldom exceeding a third of an inch in length. The larvae are very difficult to imitate, not only because of their size but also because they are virtually transparent. If they have any color at all, it is likely to be a pale yellowish orange. Adults bear a superficial resemblance to adult chironomids, but may be identified by their distinctive, blunt proboscis.

Water Bugs

The order *Hemiptera* includes the backswimmers, *Notonectidae,* and water boatmen, *Corixidae,* both of which are of some importance in the diet of Kamloops trout. The *Corixidae* include 121 known species, the *Notonectidae* 30; it is not known how many of each are present in the Kamloops trout lakes.

Water boatmen feed on the tiny plants and animals of the plankton and play an important role in converting this material into a form more readily available to trout. They are short, stocky insects, the adults usually measuring little more than a half inch long, and prefer shallow, weedy water. Water boatmen overwinter as adults and lay eggs in the spring; the eggs hatch after a week or two and the nymphs go through five instars, each lasting about a week. The only noticeable difference is a gradual development of the wings.

Water boatmen have three pairs of legs. The hind pair is most strongly developed, with a fringe of long hair on the trailing edges. These legs are used like oars to propel the insect at high speed through the water, and this distinctive swimming motion is the basis for the insect's common name. They are air breathers, swimming to the surface to gather a "bubble" of air which is held against the ventral surface as they return to the bottom. With this small supply of air they are able to remain submerged for considerable periods.

The wings of water boatmen are finely-mottled black and brown, their abdomens creamy-yellow and segmented. However, the colors of the abdomen usually are obscured by the silvery bubble of air the insects carry with them under water. Adults are capable of flight, but only the nymphs are important to trout—and anglers. Although they are readily available to trout throughout the season, water boatmen are seldom taken in quantity, and then only when other food is lacking.

Backswimmers, by contrast, are extremely fierce predators that unhesitatingly attack creatures larger than themselves, including trout fry. They are somewhat longer, thinner insects than water boatmen and adults may exceed three quarters of an inch in length. Their name is derived from their unusual habit of swimming on their backs, using the rear set of their three pairs of legs which are powerfully developed and equipped with a fringe of swimming hairs like those of the water boatman. Using these paddle-like appendages, backswimmers can swim at astonishing speed.

The swimming habits of the backswimmer have led to color adaptations opposite those of most aquatic creatures. Its

Callibaetis dun.

A dragonfly nymph from the family *Aeschidae*.

INCIDENCE TABLE FOR SCUDS AND LEECHES IN KAMLOOPS TROUT WATERS

	May 15-30	June 1-15	June 15-30	July 1-15	July 15-31	August 1-15	August 15-31	September 1-15	September 15-30
SCUDS	• •	•	•	•	• • •	• • •	• • •	• •	• • •
LEECHES	•	•	•	•	• •	• •	• •	• •	•

Frequency of occurrence in trout stomachs:
- **- - -** - *Abundant; main item in trout diet.*
- **- -** - *Frequent; secondary item in diet.*
- **-** - *Occasional.*

INSECT EMERGENCE TABLE FOR KAMLOOPS TROUT WATERS

	May 15-30	June 1-15	June 15-30	July 1-15	July 15-31	August 1-15	August 15-31	September 1-15	September 15-30
CHIRONOMIDS	• • •	• •	•	•	•	•	•	•	•
DRAGONFLY NYMPHS	•	• •	• •						
DAMSELFLY NYMPHS	•	• •	• •						
MAYFLIES	• •	• •	• •	•					
FLYING ANTS	•	• • •							• • •
SEDGES			• • •	•					

Frequency of occurrence in trout stomachs:
- **- - -** - *Prolific hatches, daily occurrences.*
- **- -** - *Fair hatches, usually every day.*
- **-** - *Sporadic hatches, inconsistent.*

(Calculated for a lake at 1,070 meters (3,500 feet) elevation; local conditions may change emergence dates.)

wings, held over the back beetle-fashion, are mostly light yellow with mottled patches of black or dark brown; its abdomen, which faces upward when the insect is swimming, is flat black and segmented. The backswimmer also is an air breather, but unlike the water boatman it pierces the surface film with the tip of its abdomen and hangs there, suspended, with swimming legs outstretched, taking a much longer time to gather its air supply. Its sudden departure from the surface normally leaves a tiny dimple during flat-calm conditions and these may be noticed by anglers from time to time. The backswimmer stores its air supply in abdominal grooves so that it, too, appears to be sheltered by a silver bubble while under water. Its life cycle is very similar to that of the water boatman, except the backswimmer may go through more than one generation a summer, with adults emerging both in late spring and early fall.

Trout occasionally feed on backswimmers in the nymphal stage, but their greatest interest appears to be during large-scale emergences. Even then a hatch usually must be in progress two or three days before Kamloops trout begin to respond. It would seem the backswimmer is not one of the favorite foods of Kamloops trout, but they will take it when it is available in such numbers it cannot be ignored.

The order *Hemiptera* also includes the giant water bugs of the family *Belostomatidae*, and although these apparently are not widely distributed in the Kamloops trout lakes, they are sometimes important in individual waters. Trout from a small lake in the Thuya chain, for example, were found to be feeding heavily and selectively on these bugs, which may exceed 1 1/2 inches in length. These obloid bugs have a yellowish, segmented abdomen, three pairs of legs, and faintly iridescent black or brown wings which curve over their backs. Respiration is similar to that of the backswimmer.

Beetles

The *Coleoptera*—aquatic beetles—are abundant in only a few Kamloops trout lakes. Those which are present are predaceous members of the family *Dytiscidae*. There are more than 400 species and they vary widely both in appearance and habits, particularly in the larval stage which is when they are most available to trout. Roche Lake has a large population of these beetles—species unidentified—and their larvae are common in the weedy margins of the lake. A survey of Okanagan Lake turned up members of the genus *Hydroporus*. With their free-swimming habits, slim silhouette and pale olive color, the larvae of these beetles are sometimes mistaken for damselfly nymphs.

Kamloops trout apparently feed on the larvae only rarely, when other food sources are not readily available.

Ephemeroptera

The mayfly, *Ephemeroptera,* is much more abundant and important in streams than still waters, but mayflies are present to some degree in nearly all the Kamloops trout lakes and some waters have significant hatches. It is always a treat to watch hatching duns flee before the wind like a fleet of tiny sailboats, and an even greater pleasure to see large Kamloops trout knifing through the waves to take them.

At least five genera have been identified in the Kamloops trout lakes. Of these, the genus *Callibaetis* is undoubtedly most important. It includes 23 species, although the number present in Kamloops trout waters has not been determined.

The nymphs of *Callibaetis* are available to trout from their earliest development. They are at home swimming or crawling through weedbeds in shallow water, where trout like to forage. The nymph has a fairly long, tapering abdomen with 10 segments, typical of all mayfly nymphs. It also has three pairs of legs, each pair attached to a different thoracic segment. Depending upon the species and the water, mature nymphs range from a quarter to a half inch in length and typically are dark gray in color. Possibly because of the abundance of other subsurface food usually available, Kamloops trout do not take the nymphs very often, except during prolific hatches when the ascending nymphs are most vulnerable.

Kamloops trout do feed willingly on the newly hatched adults, however. Called duns or subimagoes, these flies are usually dusky or dark gray in color, with two tails. After hatching, they may rest for a time on the surface before taking flight, especially on cool or wet days (the best emergences often occur between rain squalls), and they are taken eagerly by trout under such circumstances. Those able to escape the rising trout fly to shore and find resting places in timber or brush where they undergo a final molt. The resulting fly is called a spinner, or imago, and has a glossy appearance with shiny, nearly transparent wings. Typical *Callibaetis* spinners have mottled reddish-brown markings along the leading edges of their otherwise transparent, graceful wings. They are dark blue or black along the upper surface of the abdomen and reddish-brown beneath, and their two long tails are smoky blue.

The spinners are so named because of their behavior in the mating flight, which takes place over the water; the flies bob up and down in a vertical posture which makes them look like tiny spinners, their shiny wings flashing like sparks in the sunlight. Female *Callibaetis* spinners may live several weeks, mating and laying eggs before finally falling spent to the surface where again they become vulnerable to rising trout. In many Western waters, the spinner fall interests trout even more than hatching duns, but this does not appear to be the case on the Kamloops trout waters.

Depending upon the elevation of the lake and the progress of the season, mayflies may begin to appear on the Kamloops trout lakes in the last week of May or the first few days of June. Prolific hatches may continue through June and even later on some waters, and *Callibaetis* spinners are sometimes seen even in late July.

Hexagenia, Siphlonurus and *Tricorythodes* are other mayfly genera present in the Kamloops lakes and their hatches may extend from late May or early June through August, but usually they do not appear in sufficient numbers to set off a good rise of trout.

Callibaetis **spinner.**

Terrestrials

Terrestrials are insects whose origins are of the earth rather than the water, but they include many forms whose mating flights or foraging may carry them over water where they become available to feeding trout. They include the ants, bees and wasps of the order *Hymenoptera.*

Of these, ants are by far the most important to the Kamloops trout fly fisher. There are more than 700 North American species, so the task of identification is difficult. For the angler's purposes it probably isn't worth worrying about; it's enough to know that ants are on the water, and to be able to present an imitation of the appropriate size and color.

It is the winged, sexual stage of the male ant that appears on the water after mating flights. The surfaces of Kamloops trout lakes are often littered with the wreckage of these flights to a density of more than a dozen insects per square foot. An ant fall of this magnitude presents a tremendous opportunity for trout and may set off an enormous rise. Several different ant species may be present simultaneously, ranging from tiny black or cinnamon ants less than a quarter inch long to medium-sized brown or golden ants up to an inch in length, or carpenter ants that may be even larger. Sometimes trout will feed avidly on all of them, and sometimes they will feed selectively on only one—confronting the angler with the prob-

Carpenter ant.

lem of figuring out which one is being taken. Occasionally, on very bright, still days, the trout may feed sparingly, if at all, even though the surface is covered with struggling, dying ants. This frustrating circumstance may be due partly to the weather and partly to the fact that the trout have already become sated from the abundance of food.

A string of warm days in late May or early June will start the ants flying. The spring flights usually consist of large black carpenter ants or smaller black ants. The response of trout to these flights is not always consistent because they may occur simultaneously with prolific midge and mayfly hatches or damselfly emergences, and the trout may focus on one of the latter targets. But the fall flights, which usually occur on warm days during the first two weeks of September, seldom fail to stir an enthusiastic response. These flights are often dominated by medium-sized brown or golden ants and typically involve fewer insects than the spring flights, but their appearance almost always triggers a rise that may continue for days.

Bees, yellow jackets and wasps, familiar enough they should need no description, seldom occur on the water in large numbers. Yellow jackets probably are the most common on the Kamloops trout lakes, but even these usually aren't present in sufficient numbers to tempt more than the occasional trout.

5: Fly Patterns

Dave Hughes lands a handsome trout from a canoe.

he first Kamloops trout fly fishers brought with them the angling traditions and fly patterns of the British Isles and those influences remained evident when British Columbia's first indigenous fly tiers began devising their own patterns. From early to mid-20th Century the emphasis was on wet-fly "attractor" patterns for the Interior lakes, usually brightly colored flies with long, sweeping hackles.

It was not until the 1950s that fly tiers began seriously trying to imitate the larvae, nymphs, pupae and scuds common in Kamloops trout waters. By then the bonds of tradition had weakened, new materials and methods were rapidly expanding the horizons of fly tiers, and advances in fly-line technology were making it possible to fish imitations in a more realistic manner.

Since then the trend toward "exact" imitation has become an article of faith, and in at least one area—tying and fishing chironomid imitations—Kamloops trout anglers have advanced the sport to an unparalleled level of sophistication. Local fly patterns, chironomids and otherwise, have become numerous and other patterns from outside the province have been adopted as standards. The work of imitation has been greatly aided by development of new materials and innovative uses for old ones, by new tying techniques, and not least by more selective trout. With fishing pressure increasing steadily and more anglers practicing catch-and-release, trout in many lakes have become highly discriminating and more difficult to fool.

Only realistic imitations fished in a realistic way have a chance of taking such trout consistently, and that has been a powerful stimulus to development of more realistic fly patterns.

Since contemporary patterns are likely to be of most interest to contemporary anglers, we will begin with them.

Contemporary Patterns

• *Scuds:* As the single most important item in the year-round diet of Kamloops trout, the scuds—or gammarids—are obvious targets for imitation. As such they have received great attention from fly tiers, but capturing the exact color, shape and movement of the natural has not been easy and only a few

consistently effective patterns have been developed. The following three may be safely said to fall within that category:

Werner Shrimp
Hook: No. 10.
Tail and Overlay: Deer hair.
Body: Olive-dyed seal's fur or chenille.
Hackle: Brown palmered.
Tying instructions: The deer hair is tied in at the bend of the hook with tips pointing to the rear. The hackle and body material are added, the body is wound forward and the hackle palmered over it. The remaining deer hair is brought forward

This Kamloops trout was fooled by a deerhair sedge pattern.

over the top of the body to form a "shellback," then tied off behind the eye and trimmed.

Mary Stewart, a Vancouver tier, is credited with this pattern, named for Werner Schmid whose use of the fly on Interior lakes led to its widespread popularity. While it is relatively effective, its acceptance undoubtedly is due at least partly to the fact that it is an easy pattern to tie.

Some tiers have experimented with variations on the original pattern. One successful variation, probably more effective than the original, involves substituting olive-dyed mallard breast for the deer hair. This results in a more durable and uniformly colored fly than the original.

'Baggie' Shrimp

Hook: No. 10 or 12.

Body: Olive wool (other colors may be substituted).

Rib: Olive tying silk.

Overlay: Thin strip cut from clear polyethylene sandwich bag.

Tying instructions: Cut a narrow polyethylene strip tapered to a point at each end. Tie in one end at bend of hook. Then tie in wool. Leave enough tying silk at the bend of the hook to use for ribbing. Wrap the wool forward, building up a thick body. Lay the polyethylene strip over the top of the body and tie off behind eye, forming overlay. Then wind ribbing over body and overlay, binding the latter in place. Use a dubbing needle to draw out wool fibers from the lower body; these are meant to resemble the legs of the natural.

The rather inelegant name of this fly stems from the use of a sandwich bag as part of the dressing. It is easy to tie and makes a good imitation.

Golden Shrimp

Hook: No. 10 or 12.
Tying Silk: Olive or tan monocord.
Body: Golden olive rayon floss.
Tail, Legs and Antennae: Ginger hackle.
Rib: Fine gold wire.

Tying instructions: Select a small ginger hackle feather and strip the fibers from one side of the quill, being careful to leave the tip of the feather intact and some long fibers at the butt. The hackle tip is tied in at the bend of the hook so the tip extends rearward and down, forming the tail of the fly. Then tie in the fine gold wire, followed by four to six strands of floss. Wind the floss forward to form a thick, cigar-shaped body. Then lay the hackle feather along the underside of the body with fibers pointing down and tie it off behind the eye of the hook; do not trim the remaining fibers at the butt of the quill. Wind on the gold wire as a rib, binding the hackle feather to the body of the fly and giving the body a segmented appearance. A dubbing needle is used to separate the hackle fibers so they are not bound under the wire; they should remain free to hang down and form the legs of the fly. When the ribbing is complete, the excess hackle is doubled back over the eye of the hook so the long fibers of the butt extend forward over the eye to form the antennae. A whip finish then is applied to the head of the fly.

As the instructions indicate, this is a complex fly to tie. Using a dubbing needle to divide individual hackle fibers to make way for the ribbing is a painstaking and time-consuming process. But the finished fly, if tied correctly, makes a deadly imitation; the floss darkens slightly in the water and provides a very close match for the natural.

Although it may seem immodest for an author to offer his own fly pattern, that is what I have done here. The pattern was developed after nearly five years of experimentation with many different materials and designs. Anglers with the patience to tie this fly correctly have used it with great success in the Kamloops trout lakes for more than 25 years, but the complexity of the pattern probably has kept it from being more widely accepted.

A variation called the Suntan Shrimp calls for light tan or beige floss in place of the olive. It is used in lakes where most scuds are lighter colored. Except for the different-colored floss, the tying instructions are the same.

• *Leeches*: Although leeches make up only a small portion of the diet of Kamloops trout, leech imitations are extremely effective in the Interior lakes—perhaps because they are such big mouthfuls trout can't resist them. Many local patterns have been developed and others from as far away as New Zealand have been adopted for use in fishing the Kamloops lakes. Here is a representative sample:

Black Flashabou Leech

Hook: No. 4 or 6, 4X long.
Tail: A dozen or more strips of black flashabou, extending about an inch past the bend of the hook.
Body: Black chenille, full and thick.
Wing: Long strips of black flashabou, tied in at head like a conventional hair wing.
Optional hackle: Black saddle hackle, tied long and full.

This is a *big* fly, so large and heavy it is difficult to cast for long distances. However, it is very effective for Kamloops trout, especially in the fall months. The pearlescent gleam of flashabou, one of many new artificial fly-tying materials, gives it an attractive quality lacking in most traditional leech patterns.

The pattern is based on an earlier dressing tied with marabou, and many anglers still prefer the latter. Smaller hooks—6 to 10, 2X or 3X long—are most often used for the marabou pattern, and mohair or wool sometimes is substituted for the body material. Black is the most popular color, but brown or gray are sometimes substituted.

Black Matuka Leech

Hook: No. 4 or 6, 2X long.
Body: Black chenille.
Wing: Two long black saddle hackles, tied Matuka style.
Rib: Black tying silk.
Hackle: Black saddle hackle, tied wet and full.

Tying instructions: Tie in chenille at the bend of the hook, leaving a length of tying silk to serve as ribbing. Wind chenille forward to create body, then tie off. Place two long black saddle hackles back-to-back, with tips curving outward, and tie in the butts behind the eye of the hook. Then use the tying silk remaining at the bend of the hook as ribbing, spiraling it forward to bind the hackles in place on top of the body. A dubbing needle should be used to separate the hackle fibers so they are not bound flat by the ribbing. The free ends of the hackles should extend well beyond the hook. Add several turns of full black hackle behind the eye of the fly and whip finish.

The Matuka style of tying originated in New Zealand. Its name is derived from a New Zealand bittern called the Matuka or Matuku whose feathers were used to tie an extremely popular fly used on Lake Taupo. The fly became so popular that the bittern was hunted almost to extinction for its feathers and authorities finally banned the fly to save the bird. The name now identifies the style of tying, which involves binding the wing feathers to the body. Wings tied Matuka-style are much less apt to wrap around the hook when the fly is cast.

Rabbit Leech

Hook: No. 6 to No. 10, 2X or 3X long.
Tying silk: Black.
Body: Black chenille, full.

Wing: Narrow strip of black rabbit pelt.

Tying instructions: Tie in chenille at bend of hook, leaving an extra length of tying silk which will later be used to bind the rabbit pelt in place. Wind chenille forward and tie off behind eye. Cut strip from pelt of black rabbit, tapered to a point at each end, and lay on top of body. Then wind the excess tying silk forward as a rib to hold the rabbit strip in place, using a dubbing needle to separate strands of fur so they are not bound by the rib.

This pattern also is based on a popular New Zealand tying method. The thin, soft rabbit fur takes on a lifelike appearance in the water.

• *Damselfly and Dragonfly Patterns:* Damselfly and dragonfly nymphs and adults are only seasonally important in the diet of Kamloops trout—but when in season they are very important indeed, especially the damselfly nymph. The peculiar sculling motion of the swimming damselfly nymph has presented fly tiers with a problem that so far has resisted a fully effective solution. Imitations, including those given here, may work well at the beginning or end of a hatch, but a pattern that remains consistently effective when the hatch is at its peak and trout are feeding selectively on the seductively wiggling nymphs has yet to be found.

'52 Buick

Hook: No. 8 to No. 12.
Tail: Tuft of dyed yellow mallard breast feathers or light ginger hackle, extending at least a quarter inch past the bend of the hook.
Body: Dubbed olive-dyed seal's fur.
Ribbing: Silver or gold tinsel.
Beard: Same as tail, extending as far as hook point.
Head: Several wraps of peacock herl.

This pattern, attributed to Gary Carlton of Edmonton, Alberta, is most beloved for its colorful name. In its original form it has become something of a generic pattern, sometimes fished as a dragonfly nymph imitation, or—trimmed down and in smaller sizes—as a scud. Substituting olive-dyed mallard for yellow makes it a more effective damselfly imitation.

Damselfly Nymph

Hook: No. 8
Tying silk: Monocord or silk matching color of body material.
Tail: Marabou dyed to match body material, extending at least one-half inch beyond bend of hook.
Body: Olive or light brown chenille, wool, Swannundaze, dubbed seal or dyed hare's mask, thin.
Thorax: Same as body material, built up and covered with wingcase of turkey, duck or pheasant.

This pattern, a composite of many local designs, is a good generic damselfly nymph imitation. The "Self-Bodied" Carey Special and the "Six Pack," both described in the section on traditional patterns, are also used as damselfly nymph imitations.

Damselfly Adult

Hook: No. 8 or No. 10, 2X or 3X fine wire.
Underbody: Thin clump of deer body hair set parallel to hook and bound in place so that tips extend shortly beyond the bend of the hook to form a tail.
Overbody: Electric blue floss, thin.
Rib: Single strand of black floss.
Wing: Deer hair divided and tied flat in a V-shape so each wing extends back from the head at about a 45-degree angle. Wings should not exceed body length.

This pattern is a good generic imitation of an adult blue damselfy and may come in handy on windy days when trout rise to naturals blown on the water. The hollow deer hair underbody and wings help keep the fly afloat, although a liberal application of dressing is also usually necessary. The fly is tied without hackle.

Nation's Blue, described in the section on traditional patterns, is another imitation of the adult damselfly.

The dragonfly nymph emergence is less visible and certainly less spectacular than that of the damselfly. As a consequence, dragonfly nymphs have occupied less attention from fly tiers. A few detailed patterns have been devised, but most anglers seem content with generic patterns like the following:

Dragonfly Nymph

Hook: No. 6, regular or long shank.
Body: Chenille, wool or dubbed seal, very thick and full.
Hackle: Two or three turns of Chinese pheasant rump.

Most often tied in shades of olive or brown, this pattern resembles the Carey Special except for the thickness of its body. It is fished most often during the spring dragonfly emergence, but can also be effective in smaller sizes in late fall when immature dragonfly nymphs are active in some lakes.

The Black O'Lindsay, Nation's Gray Nymph and Nation's Green Nymph, all described in the section on traditional patterns, also make useful dragonfly nymph imitations. Nation's Red is a somewhat fanciful imitation of the red dragonfly adult.

• *Sedges:* Fly tiers and anglers have spent a great deal of time trying to create imitations of the sedge adult, somewhat less on the pupal stage and almost none on the larval stage. The following list of patterns reflects that trend:

Sedge Pupa

Hook: No. 6 to No. 10, 2X long.
Body: Olive wool or dubbed seal's fur.
Wings: Gray duck primaries cut to shape and tied closely against either side of the body, pointing slightly down.
Optional hackle: Gray-green pheasant rump, one or two turns (sparse).

Some variations call for a wingcase and beard hackle in place of the stubby wings, and some tiers use olive wool or seal's fur only for the rear half of the body and brown for the forward half.

Among traditional Kamloops trout patterns, the Knouff

Werner Shrimp

'Baggie' Shrimp

Golden Shrimp

Black
Flashabou
Leech

Black Matuka Leech

Rabbit Leech

'52 Buick

Damselfly Nym

Damselfly Adult

Dragonfly Nymph

Sedge Pupa

Goddard Sedge

Mitch's Sedge

Sedge Adult

Tom Thumb

Vincent Sedg

Halfback

PKCK

TDC

Tunkwanamid

YDC

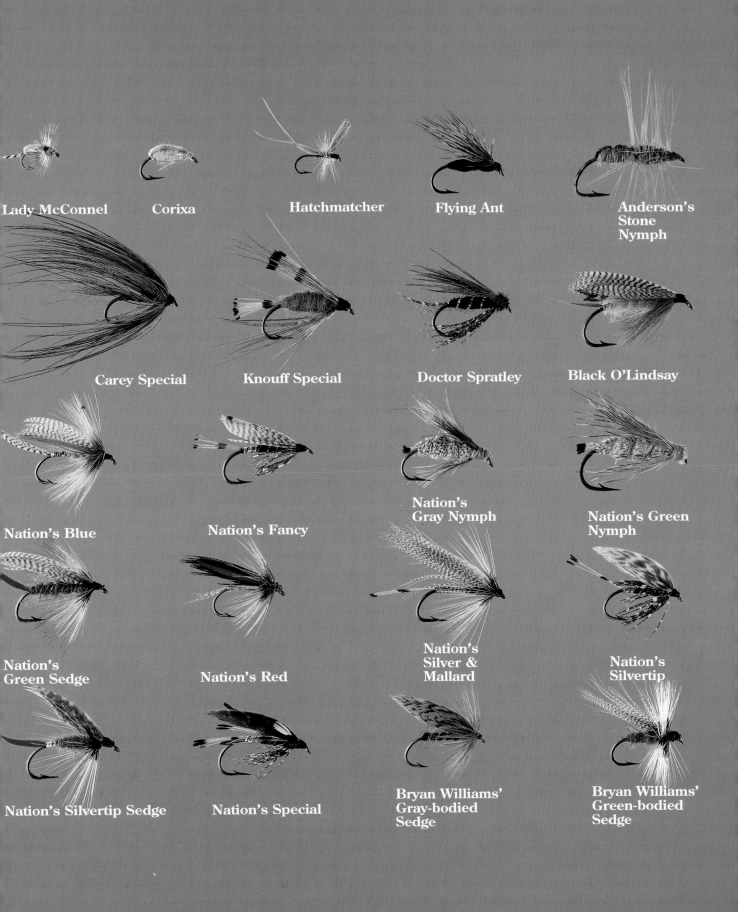

Lady McConnel

Corixa

Hatchmatcher

Flying Ant

Anderson's Stone Nymph

Carey Special

Knouff Special

Doctor Spratley

Black O'Lindsay

Nation's Blue

Nation's Fancy

Nation's Gray Nymph

Nation's Green Nymph

Nation's Green Sedge

Nation's Red

Nation's Silver & Mallard

Nation's Silvertip

Nation's Silvertip Sedge

Nation's Special

Bryan Williams' Gray-bodied Sedge

Bryan Williams' Green-bodied Sedge

Special and Carey Special are sometimes fished as sedge pupae imitations.

There are many excellent sedge adult imitations, some local and some imported from as far away as the British Isles. Following is a representative sample:

Goddard Sedge
Hook: No. 10.
Tying silk: Green.
Underbody: Green silk or floss (see tying instructions).
Overbody and wing: Deer hair, trimmed to shape (see tying instructions).
Hackle: Two red-brown hackles tied full and trimmed on top.
Tying instructions: The green silk or floss for the underbody is tied in at the bend of the hook and left hanging free. Then bunches of deer hair are tied along the hook shank and packed together as densely as possible. Next the deer hair is cut flat along the bottom while the top is trimmed carefully to match the shape of a winged adult sedge. When trimming is finished, the hanging strands of silk or floss are stretched forward under the belly of the fly and tied off behind the eye. Then the hackle is added.

This pattern, developed in England by John Goddard, is not easy to tie, but when tied correctly it is an excellent imitation and almost impossible to sink. This makes it especially useful for imitating the behavior of the traveling sedge, which requires skating a fly across the surface for long distances.

Mitch's Sedge
Hook: No. 8 to No. 12.
Tail and wing: Elk hair.
Body: Blended olive-brown fur and polypropylene dubbing.
Hackle: Brown, tied sparsely.
Head: Elk hair (trimmed butts from wing).
Tying instructions: The hollow elk hair, which provides excellent flotation, is tied along the hook shank in three bunches separated by dubbing. The first bunch forms the tail, which is blended with the rest of the wing to form an overall silhouette of the winged adult. The head, consisting of the butt ends from the last bunch of elk hair, helps keep the fly afloat when it is skated to imitate the traveling sedge.

This pattern is the work of "Mitch" Mikulak of Calgary, Alberta.

Sedge Adult
Hook: No. 8 or No. 10, 3X fine wire.
Body: Braided olive wool doubled over to form a tight loop with the ends tied in behind the eye.
Wing: Dark brown deer body hair.
Hackle: Chocolate brown, three-four turns, optionally trimmed in a V-shape from the bottom.
This generic pattern is quick and easy to tie. The light-wire hook and detached wool body make the fly very light in weight; the deer hair wing provides added flotation. However, the fly should still be dressed frequently to keep it afloat for skating.

It's also a good idea to check now and then to make sure the detached body hasn't become wrapped around the hook.

Tom Thumb
Hook: No. 8 or 10, 3X fine.
Tail, Body & Hackle: Deer hair.
Tying instructions: A thick bunch of long, gray-brown deer hair is held to the hook shank with tips pointing toward the rear and bound tightly with tying silk so the free ends of the hair flare outward in a circle. The tying silk then is carried forward and tied off behind the eye. The flared tips of the deer hair are gathered up, pulled forward and tied off behind the eye, and if this is done properly a neat, barrel-shaped body will be formed, completely enclosing the hook. A few hairs may be left at the rear of the fly to form a tail, but this is optional. The tips of hair left pointing forward after the body is formed may be forced upward to form a wing and secured with tying silk, or they may be cinched tight so they flare outward in a circle to form a hackle. The winged style is more popular than the hackle style and makes a better sedge imitation.

It takes considerable practice to tie this fly properly, but the result is a pattern that is almost impossible to sink and one that may be fished very effectively as a traveling sedge imitation. However, in addition to the difficulty involved in tying it, the fly has another disadvantage: Deer hair is extremely brittle, and a single fish may rip the body apart and make the fly useless.

A common variation of the Tom Thumb calls for a body of olive or green wool with the deer hair laid over the top to form a shellback rather than a full, barrel-shaped body. Sometimes a conventional feather hackle also is added. These variations essentially convert the Tom Thumb into a Humpy or Goofus Bug, popular Montana patterns.

Vincent Sedge
Hook: No. 10 or 12.
Tail: Brown-tipped deer body hair, "not too long, but fairly heavy."
Rib: Narrow light green floss.
Body: Light olive green seal's fur or wool.
Underwing: Same as tail.
Outerwing: Mottled gray-brown turkey primary, sprayed with lacquer.
Hackle: One or two brown hackle feathers, tied dry.
Tying instructions: Tie in the ribbing material first. Then tie in a short but fairly substantial clump of deer hair after evening it in a "stacker." The butts of the hair should extend two-thirds of the way up the hook shank toward the eye. In binding down the hair, ease pressure on the tying silk near the rear of the hook to keep the hair from flaring. Then add the body material and wind it two-thirds of the way up the hook shank and add the ribbing. A second clump of deer hair then is evened in a "stacker" and tied in on top of the front of the body material (do not tie it directly to the hook shank or it will flare badly). Next take the lacquered turkey feather and cut out a strip about half an inch wide, depending on the size of the fly. Double it over

and cut a "V" in the rear end. Place the strip over the deer hair underwing, gathering in any stray hairs. Try to keep the lower edge of the wing close to, and even with, the side of the body. The wing should be tied in when it has been positioned correctly. Then add the hackle and the fly is complete. Green or olive tying silk usually is used.

This fly, created by Jack Vincent on Roche Lake in 1975, is tricky to tie but ranks as one of the most deadly sedge patterns ever devised for the Interior lakes.

• *Chironomid Patterns*: The importance of chironomid pupae in the diet of Kamloops trout has only been recognized by fly fishers in the past 30 years. Some remarkable things have happened during that period, however, not only in fly-pattern development but also in chironomid fishing tactics. Now there are scores of chironomid imitations and it seems each tier has several favorites. Those presented here include some of the most widely used.

Halfback
Hook: No. 8 to No. 12.
Optional tail: Brown pheasant rump hackle, short and sparse.
Body: Bronze peacock herl, tapered thicker toward head.
Wingcase and hackle: Brown pheasant rump tied over forward half of body with tips tied down and back to form beard hackle.

This pattern made its appearance in British Columbia about 30 years ago. Its origin is in doubt, although various accounts say it was first developed in Alberta or Montana. While not an especially good imitation, it is often fished as a chironomid pattern (sometimes with the beard trimmed off); it also makes a good exploratory pattern not suggestive of any particular insect.

A variation called the Fullback usually is tied on a No. 8 4X long-shank hook. The pattern is the same except the wingcase extends over the full length of the body, bound by a single turn of tying silk in the center.

PKCK
Hook: No. 10 to No. 14. Sometimes long-shank or low-water Atlantic salmon hooks are used.
Tag: Silver tinsel.
Body: Single strand of dark green or olive wool.
Rib: Single strand of stripped eyed peacock herl.
Wingcase: Brown turkey primary section.
Gills: Two short (about 3/16-inch) strands of white emu or ostrich, one on either side of head.
Tying instructions: Wind on tag near bend of hook, then tie in stripped peacock herl and wool. The wool is wound forward about two-thirds of the length of the hook shank and tied off. Then the stripped herl is added as a rib. Next one end of the brown turkey section is tied in and the remaining wool is wound forward and built up to form a thorax, without ribbing. The turkey section is brought forward over the top of the thorax and tied off behind the eye to form a wingcase. Emu or

ostrich strands are added and the fly is finished.

This pattern was developed by Jim Kilburn and Dave Powell to imitate chironomid pupae during the heavy spring emergence at Minnie Lake.

TDC
Hook: No. 8 or 10, 1X long.
Body: Black wool or chenille, tapered larger toward the head.
Rib: Silver tinsel.
Hackle (gills): White ostrich herl, several turns.

This fly, the grandfather of chironomid pupal imitations, was first tied in the 1950s by Dr. Richard B. Thompson, now retired from the (U.S.) National Marine Fisheries Service. Nearly every chironomid pattern developed since has followed its simple but highly effective design.

Tunkwanamid
Hook: No. 8 to No. 16.
Tag: Silver tinsel.
Body: Peacock herl.
Rib: Silver tinsel.
Gills: White emu or ostrich.

Another chironomid pupa pattern, very close to the original TDC. The name stems from Tunkwa Lake, noted for its very heavy early season chironomid hatches.

YDC
Hook: No. 8 to No. 16, 2XL.
Body: Black polypropylene yarn, thin.
Rib: White thread.
Thorax: White ostrich herl.
Wingcase: Pheasant rump or oak turkey overlay.

Another pattern in the tradition of the TDC, this one developed by Wayne Yoshida of Kamloops.

Other popular body materials for chironomid pupa imitations include moose mane, Chinese pheasant tail or rump feathers, Swannundaze, Body Glass or blended fur dubbing in various colors, and more new synthetic materials are joining the list all the time. Ribbing runs the gamut from dental floss to gold, silver and copper tinsel, with the latter assuming more importance recently. Foam and antron are becoming popular substitutes for ostrich and emu to imitate the feathery white gills of the natural, and some tiers favor curved rather than straight-shank hooks for chironomid imitations.

Adult chironomids are much less important than pupae as food for Kamloops trout and fly tiers have not devoted nearly as much effort to devising imitations. Occasionally, however, Kamloops trout will rise well to chironomid adults, which are especially vulnerable as they emerge from the pupal shuck. Some good fishing may be had at such times if the angler is equipped with a good imitation, such as the following pattern:

Lady McConnel
Hook: No. 10 to No. 18, fine wire.

Tail: Light grizzly (barred rock) hackle tip, short
Body: Gray polypropylene yarn.
Shellback: Light brown or gray deer body hair.
Hackle: Grizzly (barred rock).

This pattern is credited to Brian Chan, biologist for the Fisheries Branch in Kamloops. The grizzly hackle tail simulates the empty portion of the pupal shuck just vacated by the adult crawling out onto the surface, as represented by the rest of the fly.

Variations on this pattern include the use of teal feathers for the tail (which I personally find more effective), substituting other colors (particularly yellow) for the body, and palmering the hackle over the forward part of the body instead of tying it

behind the eye. Some tiers also use polypropylene yarn instead of deer hair for the overlay or shellback, although the result doesn't float as well as a fly dressed with deer hair.

• *Backswimmers and Water Boatmen:* As befits their rather insignificant role in the diet of Kamloops trout, there are few good imitations of backswimmers or water boatmen. The following pattern by Jack Shaw may be used interchangeably for both:

Corixa
Hook: No. 10 or No. 12

Bare Lake, B.C.

Body: Light yellow wool yarn, picked out, with single strand of tinsel tied lengthwise along the bottom.

Wingcase: Mottled turkey wing feather tied in at both ends with a few strands pulled out on either side to simulate legs.

• *Mayflies: Callibaetis* is by far the most important mayfly in the Kamloops trout lakes. Since it is a widespread genus, anglers in other parts of North America long ago developed imitative patterns that were appropriated for use by Kamloops trout fly fishers. These have worked well enough to forestall the need for local development of new patterns.

The Pheasant-Tail Nymph and the Gold-Ribbed Hare's Ear Nymph work well as nymphal imitations, and both are such old and well-known patterns it is unnecessary to repeat their dressings here. As for adults, the Adams makes a good imitation of either the *Callibaetis* dun or spinner. Its dressing also has been published so many times it hardly seems necessary to give it here. However, there is another dressing, not so familiar, that I do feel compelled to list because I have found it more effective than any of the old standbys. It is known variously as the Hatchmaster or Hatchmatcher.

Hatchmatcher

Hook: No. 12 to No. 16, 3X fine.

Tail, Body, Wing: Dark gray goose flank feather or substitute.

Hackle: Very dark blue dun or natural black.

Tying instructions: A small gray goose flank feather is selected and the center quill is cut about two-thirds of the way up from the butt. The tip is then cut off, leaving a V-shaped section about half an inch long. A dubbing needle is used to pick out the last two fibers on the upper end of the V, one on either side of the quill; these will be left undisturbed to form the twin tails of the fly. All the remaining fibers are grasped between thumb and forefinger and pulled forward until they bend toward the base of the quill rather than the tip (the fibers may require repeated stroking until they behave); these will form the body of the fly. A bed of tying silk is built up on the hook shank about a third of its length behind the eye. The body of the fly is positioned on top of this bed of tying silk and tied down tightly with the twin tails pointing to the rear. The fibers left extending forward over the eye of the hook are coaxed upward and secured in an upright position by a figure-8 weave of tying silk, then trimmed to shape to form the wing. The hackle is added, with at least two turns behind the wing and the remainder in front. The darker the feathers used for both body and hackle, the more effective the imitation.

The tying instructions make the pattern sound complicated, but after a little practice it becomes easy to tie and makes an amazingly lifelike imitation. Its soft, flexible materials also make it incredibly durable; many times I have caught more than 20 fish on the same fly without any sign of wear. These virtues make the Hatchmatcher the best adult mayfly imitation I know.

The pattern given here is for the dun or newly hatched mayfly adult which has yet to undergo its final molt and become a spinner. It is easily varied to imitate the spinner, usually by going to a hook one size smaller and substituting a different feather for the body and wing. Popular substitutes include dyed dark-blue mallard breast or the iridescent green feather from the neck of a Chinese pheasant rooster. Other materials may be substituted to imitate mayflies of other genera or colors.

• *Terrestrials:* The flying ants that appear in spring and again in early fall are the most important terrestrials on the Kamloops trout's menu. Next to the traveling sedge, ants may provide the best dry-fly fishing of the year. Trout often abandon all caution when fallen ants are littering the surface and it doesn't take a terribly detailed or sophisticated imitation to fool them. The following pattern has worked well for me:

Flying Ant
Hook: No. 8 to No. 16, fine wire
Tying silk: Black.
Body: Black polypropylene yarn or foam, tied ant-style in two bulbous segments.
Wing: Sparse dark deer body hair, tied flat and divided.
Optional hackle: Single turn of natural black saddle

hackle, either behind the eye of the hook or in the center between the two segments.

Large flying ants are more common in the spring, although it's not unusual to see ants of several different sizes on the water at the same time. Even when that happens, trout appear to be more interested in the larger specimens. For that reason I carry more of these flies in hook sizes 8 to 12 than any others.

The fall flights are less predictable than those of spring. When they do occur, the ants usually are smaller and sometimes of a different color. One common variety is dark brown on the back and a sort of washed-out yellow underneath. Trout respond well to an imitation tied according to the pattern listed above, except that a No. 12 hook is used and beige or brownish-yellow polypropylene yarn is substituted for black.

• *Other patterns:* Where forage fish are present they may be an important source of food for Kamloops trout, but their very presence usually puts a damper on fly fishing. That may be a reason no local patterns have been developed to imitate forage fish. Anglers who wish to experiment with such imitations would be well advised to start by trying some of the traditional streamer-fly patterns developed to imitate forage fish in the brook trout and landlocked Atlantic salmon waters of the Northeast.

Since stoneflies are found in running water and not in lakes they are absent from the diet of Kamloops trout, but that hasn't stopped Anderson's Stone Nymph from becoming a popular lake fly. As its name indicates, the pattern was developed as a stonefly nymph imitation, but it also has worked well in still waters, where it may be taken as a dragonfly nymph. It is especially popular on Dragon Lake, near Quesnel, famous for its large rainbows, but also has been used with good results in the Kamloops trout lakes farther south. The pattern listed here is different in several respects from that given in the last edition of this book, but I believe it is more faithful to the original tie.

Anderson's Stone Nymph
Hook: No. 4 or 6, 2X long.
Body: "Dirty" yellow-green wool.
Overlay: A half-dozen strands of peacock herl.
Rib: Tying silk.
Hackle: Dark olive, palmered and trimmed over front half of body.
Tying instructions: Tie in the strands of peacock herl and yellow-green wool body material at the bend of the hook. Wind the wool forward to the center of the hook to form the rear half of the body, which should be stout. Tie in the hackle at the center of the hook and resume winding the wool to build up the forward half of the body, tying it off a short distance behind the eye of the hook. Lay the strands of peacock herl over the top of the body along its full length and tie off. Then take tying silk and wind a spiral rib back to the bend of the hook; reverse direction at that point and spiral the silk back to the eye, creating a series of cross-hatched ribs that bind the overlay to

the body. Then palmer the hackle forward over the front half of the body and tie it off. Trim the hackle on the top and bottom, leaving fibers on both sides.

Traditional Patterns

• *The Carey Special:* Any discussion of traditional Kamloops trout fly patterns must begin with the Carey Special. It is by far the most widely known Kamloops pattern and its fame and use have spread far beyond the borders of British Columbia. It is tied now in countless versions and has been used effectively for rainbow, cutthroat and brook trout along the Pacific Coast and inland to Montana. Even in this era of exact imitation, it remains a staple fly of Northwest anglers, the single pattern most likely to be found in every fly book. In its many variations it is used to imitate many things its originator probably never intended, and often it is fished by anglers who have no idea it was ever meant to imitate anything at all.

Although it bears the name of Colonel Carey, once an officer in the British Army (some say his first name was Tom, but he was known almost universally as "the Colonel"), there is some evidence the original idea may not have been his. Tommy Brayshaw spoke of a fly called the Pazooka that was being used on Knouff Lake early in the 1930s and called it a "forerunner of Carey's Dredges" (as the Carey Special was called early in its history). So it is possible Carey borrowed at least some features of the pattern from one that was in use even earlier.

Some accounts, including the first edition of this book, say the Carey Special was devised by Colonel Carey and Dr. Lloyd Day in the Beaver Lake chain near Kelowna to imitate emerging sedge pupae. However, Brayshaw, a contemporary of Colonel Carey, disputes this and offers a rather precise account of the origin of the fly:

"He (Colonel Carey) started the fly when he was camped at Arthur Lake and I think dressed it for a dragonfly nymph," Brayshaw wrote. "At any rate, we did the same thing at Knouff with the 'Pazooka' and fished it the same way: Throw it out, lay the rod down, fill a pipe, light same, half smoke it and then, wallop! You had him!

"The old boy used to use ground-hog hair (or do you call it fur?) quite a lot and I am not sure that his tail and body may be that . . . The body is made by winding the hair around the hook and ribbed for protection with waxed black linen thread in the reverse direction . . ."

Another striking feature of the pattern was its hackle, several turns of at least two Chinese pheasant rooster rump feathers. This produced a very full hackle of long, sweeping flexible fibers that gathered around the body of the fly as it was being retrieved, giving a fine illusion of movement. The hackle is about the only feature of the original that survives in the many modern versions of the pattern, although now it usually is tied sparsely.

The original pattern also incorporated a short tail of ground-hog hair fibers. Here is the original pattern, as nearly as it can be traced:

. Carey Special
Hook: No. 6.
Tail: Thick bunch of ground hog hair fibers, short.

Body: Ground-hog hair wrapped around the hook shank, with heavy black tying silk (or "linen," as Brayshaw called it) wrapped in the opposite direction to bind the hair in place.
Hackle: Two brownish-gray Chinese pheasant rooster rump feathers, tied very full with several turns each.

Depending on how it was fished, the original pattern worked equally well as an imitation of a dragonfly nymph or an emerging sedge pupa. Many anglers also were quick to see that a more sparsely tied version made an excellent damselfly nymph imitation, and many modern Carey Special designs were constructed with that intent.

One of the most popular and effective modern versions is the so-called "Self-bodied" Carey, which employs the pheasant rump feather for both body and hackle. The body feather is tied in at the bend of the hook with the tip fibers extending rearward to form a tail. The remainder of the feather is twisted forward around the hook shank to form the body and tied off behind the eye. Any fibers left sticking out from the body are trimmed off. The hackle is tied sparsely with one or two turns of a separate rump feather.

Another variation, called the "Six Pack," is tied the same way except the rump feathers are dyed olive. Both the Self-bodied Carey and Six Pack make good damselfly nymph imitations.

Other variations involve substitution of the body material. Common substitutes include floss, chenille, moose mane, peacock herl, wool, dubbing, tinsel and mylar. Some tiers add a short tail of golden pheasant tippet feathers. Patterns with stout bodies of olive or brown chenille and sparse hackle make effective dragonfly nymph or sedge pupa imitations.

Regardless of how it is tied, the Carey Special evidently has a look about it that fish find appealing, and that undoubtedly accounts for its long and widespread use.

• *Knouff Special:* As its name indicates, this fly was developed on Knouff Lake where it was fished as an imitation—albeit a highly impressionistic one—of an emerging sedge pupa. The date of its origin is unknown, but the pattern goes back many years. The use of Chinese pheasant rooster rump feather for the hackle prompts speculation this fly may once have been known as the Pazooka, the pattern Tommy Brayshaw described as the forerunner of the Carey Special, but there is no direct evidence to support this.

Knouff Special
Hook: No. 6.
Tail: Thick clump of long golden pheasant tippet fibers.
Body: Green wool, thick.
Rib: Orange wool, wound so that segments of green and orange are of equal width.
Wing: Golden pheasant tippet feather.
Hackle: Brown-gray Chinese pheasant rooster rump feather, tied very full.

The Knouff Special is a very colorful and handsome fly that remains in use to this day. Modern tiers sometimes substitute chenille for the wool body and rib.

• *Doctor Spratley:* Next to the Carey Special, the Doctor Spratley probably is the best-known pattern to come from the Kamloops trout waters. Attributed to Dick Prankard of Mount Vernon, Washington, it was named after Dr. Donald A. Spratley, a dentist who popularized the fly in the Interior lakes before his death in 1968. It is now more often called the "Doc Spratley." The original pattern:

Doctor Spratley
Hook: No. 6.
Tail: Guinea hackle fibers.
Body: Black wool, cigar-shaped.
Rib: Silver tinsel.
Hackle: Guinea, tied down as beard.
Wing: Red-brown fibers from Chinese pheasant rooster tail feather.
Head: Peacock herl, several turns.

The pattern now is often tied with barred rock (grizzly) hackle instead of guinea, and the peacock-herl head usually is omitted. Popular variations incorporate green, yellow or red floss or wool for the body in place of the black wool used in the original.

The Doctor Spratley bears little resemblance to any of the insects common in the Kamloops trout lakes, so its effectiveness is difficult to explain. Perhaps, like the Carey Special, it is simply one of those flies with a certain indefinable quality that appeals to fish. However, some anglers trim the pheasant-tail wing to about a third its normal length to produce what they claim is an effective dragonfly nymph imitation. Others sometimes trim both wing and hackle so that virtually only the body of the fly is left, and this makes an acceptable chironomid pupa imitation.

• *Black O'Lindsay:* Virtually unknown outside British Columbia, this fly is one of the oldest and certainly one of the most beautiful Kamloops trout patterns. It dates before World War I when it was originally developed as a grasshopper imitation for trout fishing on the Thompson River. Judge Spencer Black of Lindsay, California, is credited with the pattern, which he fished in the Walhachin reach of the Thompson during late summer months when warm breezes carried hoppers from the hillsides onto the river. The judge's name and home town gave the fly its colorful name.

The fly later was adopted by other anglers for use in the Interior lakes, where it was fished primarily as an attractor pattern. Some anglers also claimed it was a good dragonfly nymph imitation and its silhouette certainly bears a resemblance to the natural even if its colors do not.

Here is the original pattern, as well as can be traced:

Black O'Lindsay
Hook: No. 6.
Tail: Dyed blue saddle hackle fibers.
Body: Yellow wool, thick.
Rib: Embossed gold tinsel.
Throat: Dyed blue saddle hackle fibers.

Hackle: Light brown, tied down as beard over throat.
Wing: Barred mallard breast, parallel to hook, laid over 6 to 8 strands of peacock sword.

As with most popular patterns, the Black O'Lindsay spawned its share of variations. Most common was the use of brown hackle rather than blue for the tail and elimination of the blue throat. Some tiers substituted black hackle for the brown, and occasionally tied the fly with a full hackle rather than a beard. Other variations included a dubbed body of yellow-dyed seal's fur and jungle cock cheeks.

The Black O'Lindsay has largely fallen into disuse over the past two decades, but may still be found occasionally in the fly boxes of veteran Kamloops trout anglers.

• *The Patterns of Bill Nation:* In addition to being the foremost Kamloops trout guide of the 1930s, Bill Nation also was a prolific fly tier. Some of his patterns became standards for Kamloops trout fly fishers, remaining in use for decades.

Modern fly tiers sometimes chuckle over Nation's flies. They are not what one would call classic patterns; many are bulky to the point of being awkward, and few have the precise, trim, carefully proportioned appearance that is the pride of most contemporary tiers. This was partly by design—Nation tied flies that way because he intended them to look that way—but it also probably was due partly to the limited selection of materials he had available. Paul Lake in the 1930s was not the most easily accessible place, and Nation often had to make do with whatever materials he happened to have on hand.

Nation sold flies to some of the anglers he guided (his advertisements said the flies were "guaranteed to kill") and a number of his flies survive in various collections. His patterns are not often used any more, but they form an enduring part of the legacy and lore of Kamloops trout fishing and fly tying. Following is a list of his most popular patterns:

Nation's Blue
Hook: No. 8
Tail: Long, thin strands of barred mallard breast.
Body: Rear two-thirds, flat silver tinsel; front third, blue floss.
Rib: Oval silver tinsel over both body sections.
Wing: Barred mallard breast, tied parallel to hook, with topping of blue chatterer (kingfisher) wing.
Hackle: Badger, tied wet and full.

This pattern was a fanciful attempt to suggest a pair of damselflies locked in mating flight. That it was a wet fly apparently did not bother Nation; he reasoned that if it were fished close to the surface, trout could not tell whether it was in the water or the air—certainly one of the more bizarre theories in the history of fly tying! The fly was effective at times, although it seems likely trout took it as a drowned spent damselfly.

Nation's Fancy
Hook: No. 6.

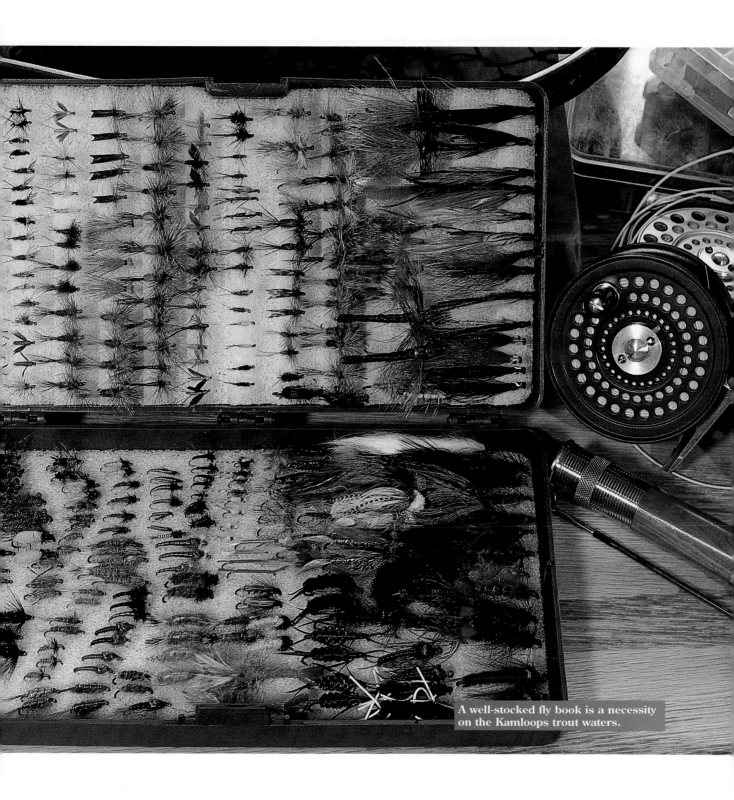

A well-stocked fly book is a necessity on the Kamloops trout waters.

Tail: Thick clump of long golden pheasant tippet fibers.

Body: Rear half, silver tinsel; front half, black floss.

Rib: Oval silver tinsel over both sections of body.

Wing: Barred mallard breast with several strands of golden pheasant tippet enclosed.

Hackle: Guinea.

This fly is well named. It appears to have been a flight of fancy on Nation's part, not meant to imitate or suggest anything in particular.

Nation's Gray Nymph

Hook: No. 6.

Tying silk: Olive green.

Tail: Very short clump of golden pheasant tippet with only the ends showing.

Body: Gray wool, very thick, with barred mallard breast wound over and around it.

Rib: Gold wire.

Wing: Ground hog or other short, stiff hair, thick.

Beard: Ground hog hair or other short, stiff hair, shorter than above.

This was Nation's imitation of a small dragonfly nymph. It is broad and bulky, like the natural, and the use of mallard breast wound over the body gives it a realistic appearance in the water.

Nation's Green Nymph

Hook: No. 2.

Tying Silk: Gold.

Tail: Very short clump of golden pheasant tippet fibers.

Body: Light green wool or chenille, built up very thick, with barred mallard breast wound over it.

Rib: Gold tying silk wound in one direction, gold wire in the other.

Wing: Ground hog hair or other short, stiff hair, thick.

Beard: Ground hog hair or other short, stiff hair, shorter than above.

This was Nation's version of a mature dragonfly nymph, on the verge of hatching. The barred mallard breast wound over the green body gives the fly an effective appearance when both are wet. The fly's size and bulk made it difficult to cast on a light line and Nation sometimes let it trail behind the boat, which was rowed at very slow speed.

Nation's Green Sedge

Hook: No. 6.

Tail: Red-dyed swan or duck.

Body: Spun seal's fur dyed dark green.

Rib: Gold tinsel.

Wing: Barred mallard breast, parallel to hook shank.

Hackle: Badger.

This was Nation's impression of the green-bodied sedge that hatches on Paul Lake and so many other waters. Again, it was a wet pattern even though the adult sedge rides on the surface. The pattern bears a close resemblance to the traditional Grizzly King.

Nation's Red

Hook: No. 2.

Tail: Thin strands of barred mallard breast.

Body: Rear two-thirds, flat silver tinsel; front third, red wool or spun fur.

Wing: Barred brown mallard flank, parallel to hook shank.

Sides: Strips of red-dyed swan or duck.

Hackle: Badger, tied full and wet.

This was the counterpart to Nation's Blue. Sometimes known as Nation's Red Dragon, it was intended to represent adult red dragonflies *(Sympetrum)* in their mating flight. It was a somewhat more popular fly than Nation's Blue and tiers who copied it sometimes tied it on hooks as small as No. 8.

Nation's Silver and Mallard

Hook: No. 6.

Tail: Thin clump of long golden pheasant tippet fibers.

Body: Rear two thirds, thin flat silver tinsel; front third, thin black wool.

Rib: Flat silver tinsel wound over both body sections.

Wing: Barred mallard breast, parallel to hook.

Hackle: Badger, tied full and wet.

This pattern also has been called the Silhouette Sedge. It was sometimes used to imitate a female sedge laying eggs under the surface, with the tinsel intended to represent a silvery air bubble clinging to the body of the sedge. It also was fished as a fry pattern at Adams and Little Rivers.

Nation's Silvertip

Hook: No. 6.

Tail: Small clump of golden pheasant tippet fibers, about half the body length.

Body: Rear one-fourth, flat silver tinsel; front three-fourths, black floss.

Rib: Oval silver tinsel over both body sections.

Wing: Brown mottled turkey feather, tied parallel to hook with a few strands of golden pheasant tippet enclosed.

Hackle: Guinea, tied down as beard.

This may have been Nation's most popular fly. It was widely used during the 1930s and remained popular into the 1960s. In one survey of 80 "record" fish taken from Paul Lake over a 10-year period, the Silvertip accounted for half. Though not suggestive of any insect, it was an excellent attractor pattern or exploratory fly.

Nation's Silvertip Sedge

Hook: No. 6.
Tail: Red dyed swan or duck.
Body: Two or three turns of flat silver tinsel at the end; remainder dyed green spun seal's fur.
Rib: Gold tinsel.
Wing: Brown mottled turkey, tied parallel to hook shank.
Hackle: Badger.

Another wet sedge pattern with the added bit of flash that Nation apparently felt was a necessary part of any good Kamloops trout fly.

Nation's Special

Hook: No. 6.
Tail: Small clump of golden pheasant tippet fibers, about half body length.
Body: Rear one-third, flat silver tinsel; front two-thirds, black floss.
Rib: Oval silver tinsel.
Wing: Brown mottled turkey, parallel to hook shank, with a few strands of golden pheasant tippet enclosed.
Sides: Jungle cock.
Hackle: Guinea.

This was another popular pattern, not suggestive of any particular insect but useful as an exploratory fly. It bears a close resemblance to the Silvertip, but Nation regarded the two flies as separate patterns.

Nation was meticulous in his directions for tying and fishing his flies and experimented with many variations before arriving at the patterns listed here. His flies are not only distinctive in appearance but also represent a curious compromise between traditional influences and Nation's own highly individualistic impressions of the natural insects of the Kamloops trout lakes— a not-always-comfortable blending of the old and the new.

• *Bryan Williams' Sedges:* Bryan Williams' floating sedge patterns were among the first dry flies ever tied specifically for Kamloops trout. These flies, graceful and realistic in design, were imitated widely and their influence may still be seen in the designs of some modern tiers.

There were two patterns, the Gray-bodied Sedge and the Green-bodied Sedge. In a letter to Lee Richardson, quoted in *Lee Richardson's B. C.*, Williams told about the origin of these flies: ". . . June fishing brings back memories of Knouff, where I first originated the grey sedge fly, and later at Hyas where I found the green-bodied sedge. It was in Hyas Long Lake (as it usually was called then) I killed a fifteen-and-a-quarter pound fish on the dry fly. Certainly they are great fighters, and not only make terrific runs but tremendous jumps. I have never seen any other fish clear such heights."

The pattern for the Gray-bodied Sedge, based on inspection of an original:

Bryan Williams' Gray-bodied Sedge

Hook: No. 8.
Body: Gray goose primary feathers, wound on the hook shank and trimmed to form a slim, even body.
Rib: Black wool, single thin strand.
Hackle: Two light brown hackles tied dry and very full.
Wing: Mottled gray sections from tail of Chinese pheasant rooster, paired and tied parallel to hook shank.

The pattern for the Green-bodied Sedge, based on photographs (to my knowledge, no originals have survived):

Bryan Williams' Green-bodied Sedge

Hook: No. 8.
Body: Seal's fur, dyed light green.
Hackle: Two badger hackles, tied dry and very full.
Wing: Barred mallard breast sections, paired and tied parallel to hook shank.

Both patterns are excellent imitations of the naturals in size, color and silhouette. They probably were fished with a dead float, since their absorbent materials would have made it difficult to skate them across the surface very long without sinking them. Even without movement, they were undoubtedly effective imitations of newly emerged sedges that had yet to begin "traveling" across the surface.

• *Other Traditional Patterns:* A number of wet-fly patterns have enjoyed considerable popularity on the Kamloops trout lakes at various times. These include the Cummings Fancy, a bright attractor fly; the Lioness, once a favorite on Peterhope Lake, and the Rhodes Favorite, another bright pattern often used as an exploratory fly. The Egg 'n' I was an emergent sockeye alevin imitation often used on the Adams and Little Rivers, and the Big Bertha was an elaborate and colorful pattern used on the same waters. The dressings for all these patterns are given in the first edition of this book. They are omitted here because time has caught up with them and they are rarely used any longer. They are now mostly of interest to fly-tying historians.

Many patterns from beyond the borders of British Columbia also have been used in the Kamloops waters at one time or another. A partial list includes the Alder, Alexander, Black Gnat, Butcher, Claret and Mallard, Leadwing Coachman, Gray Hackle, Grizzly King, March Brown, Montreal, Muddler Minnow, Professor, Queen of the Waters, Royal Coachman, Teal and Green, Teal and Red and Teal and Silver. As with many of the early patterns developed within the province itself, most of these have long since fallen into disuse.

The future undoubtedly will witness many more changes to the list of popular fly patterns used for Kamloops trout. Tradition will remain important, as it always has, but the ideas and experiments of modern tiers will certainly bring forth new patterns to take their place alongside the old.

6: Tackle and Technique

his chapter is about fly fishing. That will come as no surprise to anyone who has read thus far. It reflects the author's prejudice and his assumption that the reader also is a fly fisher or is willing to become one. If that assumption is wrong, then it is hoped this discussion—and the book as a whole—will lead the reader to consider fly fishing as a desirable alternative to his or her present method.

Fly fishing is the most effective and enjoyable way to fish for Kamloops trout. It allows the angler to probe the weedy, food-rich shallows that are the most productive parts of any lake and offers the chance to try the greatest possible variety of lures or imitations. Fly fishing also is simply more fun than any other method; the connection between angler and fish is direct, with no intervening weight, so the trout is free to run or jump without restraint. Finally, fly fishing is the method most consistent with conservation; it permits undersized or unwanted fish to be released unharmed.

The angler who caught this trout is handling it carefully so it can be released.

While the following discussion considers a variety of equipment and accessories for use in fly fishing for Kamloops trout, most anglers will accumulate these items a few at a time over many years. To start it is really necessary only to have a basic outfit including a rod, two or three lines, a reel with a couple of extra spools, a few leaders and some appropriate flies—all of which may be obtained without mortgaging the house.

Rods

Choosing a fly rod is a highly personal matter. While there are tests to determine the dynamic characteristics of a rod, most anglers judge rods subjectively by appearance and "feel." All things considered, that may be the best approach. A rod that looks good and feels right in the hand—one that is not too fast or too slow, one that seems well-balanced and never top-heavy or awkward—is a thing to be treasured.

Aside from subjective considerations, however, there are some important factors to consider in choosing a rod for Kamloops trout fly fishing. Even smaller lakes in the B.C. Interior are occasionally swept by high winds that make casting difficult, so a basic rod for Kamloops trout fly fishing must be strong enough to contend with such circumstances. Length also is critical, with float-tube anglers needing longer rods than boat fishermen to obtain more clearance and greater leverage. Weight is most important; a long day spent casting a heavy rod and line can be extremely tiring, and an angler who must rely on a single rod for all fishing is well advised to choose the lightest rod consistent with other requirements. Fortunately there are many rods of bamboo, graphite or other composite materials that fit these demands, although the weight factor may tilt the choice toward a graphite or composite rod.

Whatever material is selected, a basic rod for all-around Kamloops trout fly fishing should be at least 8 1/2 feet long—longer if the angler expects to fish from a float tube—with a strong, fast action matched to a 6- or 7-weight fly line, preferably the latter. Such a rod in the hands of a capable caster should have the strength to throw a long line even when the wind is blowing. Of course it is not necessary to make a long cast every time, but more often than not an angler will be fishing "blind" over water where no fish are rising and then it is a simple matter of logic that the longer the cast, the greater the probability a fish will see the fly when it is being retrieved back to the starting point.

Float tubers usually must do with a single rod, but boat anglers often carry several. They may have one rigged with a weight-forward sinking line for wet-fly or nymph fishing, another with a sink-tip line for fishing shallows or probing holes in weedbeds and a third with a floating line ready for dry-fly or surface-film action. The first is likely to be a long, strong rod capable of throwing a good-sized fly (such as a big leech pattern) at least 60 feet in the wind. The others need not necessarily be as long or stout since they are more likely to be used at close quarters or in more precise fishing situations, but again that is largely a matter of personal preference. Having them all rigged and ready for action saves time when it's necessary to change tactics.

A good rod is a precision instrument and a dependable tool. It may represent many hours of a craftsman's labor and a sizable investment of the owner's money. It is something to be chosen with care and treated with respect, especially when intended for use against a quarry like the Kamloops trout. There is no single rod, or set of rods, that is "right" for the Kamloops lakes; the choice is up to each angler, perhaps to be made after a long but pleasant process of trial and error.

Lines

Modern anglers may choose from a bewildering variety of fly lines designed to cope with nearly every conceivable angling situation. With few exceptions, however, the Kamloops trout angler will need only the three types already mentioned—sinking, sink-tip and floating lines.

Different manufacturers use different nomenclature to describe sinking lines, but generally there are four or five types with different sink rates specified in inches per second. One with a sink rate of 2 to 3.5 inches a second is probably best suited for all-around wet-fly fishing in the Kamloops trout lakes. If kept clean, it will sink a fly fast enough that the angler won't have to wait long before starting the retrieve, but not so fast that it continues to pull the fly toward the bottom between strips of the retrieve. This allows the angler to retrieve the fly at a steady angle, keeping enough tension on the line to detect strikes easily. However, there will be times—especially on bright, warm summer days, or when a thermocline is present—that a faster-sinking line is needed. Weight-forward designs or shooting heads are best; they make long casts easier.

Sink-tip lines are made so that only a short section of the terminal end sinks while the remainder of the line stays afloat, which makes the sink-tip ideal for certain specialized situations. With a sink-tip it is possible to cast to deep pockets in shallow weedbeds or fish a wet fly or nymph over a shallow shoal without much danger of hanging up. The productive weedbeds around the islands at the north end of Leighton Lake or at the extreme south end of Roche Lake are examples of places where sink-tip lines might be employed.

Sink-tip lines are made with 5-foot, 10-foot and 20-foot sinking sections with different sink rates. A 10-foot sink-tip with a sink rate of 2.5 to 4 inches a second probably is the most versatile for use in the Kamloops trout lakes, but personal preference and experience may dictate otherwise.

An inherent characteristic of any sink-tip line is that the tip submerges at an angle to the rest of the line, and the longer the tip is allowed to sink the greater the angle will be. This prevents the energy of a strike from being transmitted directly and the fish may be gone by the time the angler realizes a strike has occurred. The solution to this problem is to watch carefully for any movement of the floating portion of the line, just as one would keep a close eye on a "strike indicator" on a floating line. If the angler reacts to any sign of movement of the line, he or she will not miss many fish.

Again, a weight-forward design is best.

Floating lines are used for fishing dry flies on the surface and nymph or pupae imitations in or just beneath the surface film. Lines with high-visibility colors are best for the low-light conditions when much dry-fly and surface-film nymph fishing is done. Because imitations fished just beneath the surface are often taken very softly by trout, some anglers also like to attach brightly colored "strike indicators" to floating lines. These

Angler in float tube probes the shoalwater of a Kamloops trout lake.

signal the very slight movement that occurs when a feeding trout gently sucks in the fly, allowing the angler to set the hook. Strike indicators are especially important in certain types of chironomid fishing. Polypropylene yarn, pinch-on foam strike indicators or small floats are all used.

A weight-forward design is probably less critical with floating lines than other types, but it's still best for those occasions when a long cast is needed to reach a trout rising far out, or when the wind is blowing.

Whatever type of line is used, it should be attached to a long length of backing on the reel spool. A strong, well-conditioned Kamloops trout can take out a surprising length of line and backing on its initial run, and things will end quickly if there's not enough backing on the reel. I once watched an angler on Lundbom Lake hook a huge trout that ran without pause, taking all 35 yards of line and 100 yards of backing until the last turn came up tight against the spool and the leader snapped. Few fish will run that far, but those that do are the ones you least want to risk losing.

Braided dacron is the most common type of backing material, usually in 18- or 20-pound test. At a minimum, a reel should hold 50 yards of backing plus the fly line; 100 yards or more is better.

Leaders

The leader's purpose is to disguise the fly's connection to the line. Water clarity, size of fish and size of fly all must be considered in deciding what length and strength of leader should be used.

A leader tippet with a breaking strength of 3 to 4 pounds is heavy enough to handle the fly sizes most commonly employed in fishing for Kamloops trout, although it may be necessary to use a 6-pound tippet for large, bulky flies such as dragonfly nymphs or leech patterns. Tippets in this strength range also will hold most of the trout an angler is likely to hook.

Most leaders are made of nylon, but there is little consistency among manufacturers and different brands often have different diameters for equivalent breaking strengths. For instance, one manufacturer's material may have a rated breaking strength of 2.75 kilos (approximately 6 pounds) for a diameter of .011 inches, while another's may have the same rated breaking strength for material with a diameter of .090 inches. To avoid the confusion that results from such differences, it is easier to discuss leader material in terms of breaking strength rather than diameter.

In fishing for Kamloops trout, I have never used a leader of more than 6 pounds breaking strength, nor do I think it ever would be necessary to do so. If handled carefully, even fish larger than 10 pounds can be landed easily on 6-pound tippets. In fact, I rarely use a leader that heavy unless fishing deep in opaque water where I expect to hook only large fish, or unless using a large fly that cannot be delivered properly with a lighter leader. A tippet strength of 3 or 4 pounds is well suited for wet flies in most circumstances and a 3-pound tippet is adequate for most dry-fly fishing, although I have occasionally found it necessary to go down to a tippet of 1 pound breaking strength or even less when fishing for spooky trout in clear water under bright sunlight. Again, if one is very careful, it is possible to land surprisingly large fish on such cobweb tippets, but the range of fly sizes that may be used with them is obviously limited. There is also the constant risk that a violent strike will snap the tippet before the angler even has a chance to react.

Unless the water is clouded with algae—in which case the length and diameter of the leader is not so important—a long, fine leader usually brings best results, especially on bright days. However, there is no established "correct" length for a leader; it really depends upon the skill of the caster and whether the leader is properly designed. My preference is a leader measuring at least 11 feet for a sinking line and 13 feet for a floater. The latter may be lengthened to 15 feet for fishing in clear water under bright conditions.

A number of ready-made tapered leaders are available commercially in various tippet strengths and sizes, usually lengths of 7 1/2 or 9 feet; the longer length is recommended. Manufactured leaders have the advantage of lacking knots that might pick up bits of algae or weed in the water, but in spite of that many anglers still prefer to tie their own leaders. By joining sections of different strengths and diameters it is possible to form tapered leaders of almost any length, and there are many different formulas for doing so. It is also easy to replace sections weakened by wind knots, which is not true for manufactured leaders. However, self-tied leaders do suffer the disadvantage of having many knots that may pick up weed.

The knot joining the leader to the fly line is critical. Nail knots and needle knots are strong and have slim profiles that allow them to slide easily through the rod guides. Both knots are described in many different publications and there is no need to repeat them here.

The clinch knot and the single or double turle knot are most often used to attach a fly to the leader tippet. My preference is the double turle; it is easy to tie, permits realistic movement of the fly and provides a strong connection; only rarely have I lost a fish to knot failure.

Reels

A fly reel should provide adequate storage for line and backing and a steady drag offering consistent resistance no matter how fast a fish is running or how much line and backing remain on the reel. It must be durable enough to put up with heavy use yet light enough not to be an encumbrance to the angler. Most modern fly reels offer these qualities, but they come with a hefty price tag.

Many anglers attach great importance to the sound a reel makes. A few fly fishers prefer silent reels, but most enjoy the thrilling sound of a noisy reel under the stress of a heavy running fish. More than one reel has been purchased just for the quality of its sound. Obviously this is another matter of personal choice.

A single reel with two extra spools—one spool each for a

sinking, sink-tip and floating line—is enough to equip an angler for most Kamloops trout fishing.

Floating Devices

Although it is possible to cast from shore or wade the shallows of many Interior lakes, some sort of floating device usually is necessary to reach the best fishing.

Float tubes have become extremely popular in recent years, but like any other floating craft they involve compromises. Their advantages include comparatively low cost, portability and ease of maneuverability, but they also have limitations, including a close-to-the-water vantage point that keeps users from seeing as much as they could from a higher platform. This low vantage point also distorts distance perception, creating the illusion that objects are farther away than they actually are, and this sometimes causes float-tube anglers to blunder into water being fished by someone else—a breach of etiquette that can lead to angry words or worse. Exacerbating the problem is the fact that float-tube anglers must travel backwards and often don't turn around to see where they're going. Anglers who try to use float tubes in shallow or weedy water also frequently stir up so much mud or silt they spoil the fishing for themselves and others. These problems have given float tubers something of a bad name in the eyes of many who fish by other means, but most can be overcome by the exercise of a little common sense and courtesy. Properly used, float tubes are well suited for fishing the smaller Kamloops trout lakes under most conditions.

Small, inflatable rubber rafts have some of the same advantages of float tubes: They are light in weight and easily portable. Deflated, they can be stuffed into a pack and carried on an angler's back. A sheet of plywood placed in the bottom of a rubber raft makes it a more stable craft and may allow an angler to stand up and cast. This also gives a higher vantage point and greater range of vision than is possible when fishing from a float tube. As with float tubes, however, rafts are best suited for small waters and do not handle well in wind.

Some fly fishers prefer canoes, although their relative lack of stability makes it difficult to stand up and cast, particularly on windy days.

On waters accessible by road, boats unquestionably provide the safest, most efficient means of covering the water. For anglers who fish alone, a light, durable, 8- to 12-foot cartop boat works well. Desirable features for fly fishing include a flat or nearly flat bottom and wide beam for stability, ample freeboard, and absence of obstructions inside the hull. This automatically eliminates boats with round hulls or narrow beams as well as double-hulled or catamaran designs, which have interior obstructions. Wooden boats with removable floorboards also are an abomination unless a rubber mat or piece of indoor-outdoor carpeting is placed over the boards.

Fiberglass boats are durable and require little maintenance, but they are also heavy and may be difficult for one person to handle, especially if they must be loaded on or off a vehicle. Fiberglass hulls also transmit noise rather well, although this can be minimized by placing a mat on the floor of the boat. However, most fiberglass designs lack all the features desirable in a good fly-fishing boat.

Wooden boats are costly because of the labor required to build them, and they are less common than they once were. Now most wooden boats are built by home craftsmen, and those knowledgeable in such matters can easily design a craft with all the features needed by a fly fisher. Wooden boats tend to be heavy, though, and they require lots of maintenance.

Aluminum boats and prams are light in weight, durable and require little maintenance. Many designs are available and a good number of them are well suited for fly fishers. Their disadvantages are that they are expensive and noisy; even a small object dropped inside an aluminum boat can make enough noise to scare fish away. Again, this problem can be minimized by placing a mat or carpet on the floor of the boat and keeping the oarlocks well lubricated.

After spending much of my life in small boats, I now own one I consider the best I have ever used for fly fishing. It is a 9 1/4-foot aluminum pram that weighs only 68 pounds and can be handled easily by one person. It has a flat bottom, wide beam and high freeboard but is still highly maneuverable and remains stable even in strong winds. The noise problem has been licked by placing a rubber mat on the floor with a layer of indoor-outdoor carpeting on top of that. I have used this boat more than 20 years with no maintenance other than a single coat of paint and periodic cleaning. Unfortunately, the manufacturer long ago stopped making the model I have, but I have seen others similar in size and design that probably would be just as good.

Anchors are essential in fly fishing from a small boat. Two should be carried, one to be let down from the stern and the other from the bow to prevent the boat from swinging in a wind so that a belly forms in the line, making it difficult or impossible to hook a fish.

Almost any heavy object will serve as an anchor—even a heavy stone in a pinch—and it should be attached to a rope about twice as long as the maximum depth the angler expects to be fishing. The extra length is necessary to provide enough "scope" for the anchor to hold when a stiff breeze is pressing on the boat. Various pulley arrangements for anchor ropes are sold commercially and these are a great convenience.

There is no justification for using an outboard motor of more than 4 or 5 horsepower on any but the largest Interior lakes. A motor of that size is enough to get an angler to or from the fishing grounds in short order, which is its only legitimate purpose. Larger motors do more harm than good.

Motors are not necessary at all on smaller lakes. Those who insist on using them merely make life miserable for other anglers and the trout. When trout are feeding in the shallows an outboard motor may frighten them into deeper water for the rest of the day, spoiling things for everybody. Big wakes left by too-powerful motors operated at full throttle also may pose a real danger to the safety of unsuspecting fly fishers standing up in boats or fishing from float tubes. Common sense alone should keep people from using an outboard in shallow water, or running a large one at full throttle on a small lake crowded with anglers, but common sense is all too often lacking among weekend boaters. Outboards should be used only on larger lakes, only when necessary and only with discretion. At all other times, oars are perfectly adequate—and they always start.

Accessories

A rod, reel, line, leader, flies and a floating device are all that is necessary to fish the Kamloops trout lakes. But fly fishers are fascinated by gadgetry and countless accessories have been developed to cater to their whims. Some are a bit frivolous, but others have real value in convenience, comfort and efficiency.

Flies, of course, are an essential part of an angler's kit and so is something to carry them in. Many types of plastic, leather or metal fly boxes or wallets are available for the purpose. Size, ease of access and storage capacity are points to consider in choosing one of these devices, and the final choice may boil down to a matter of whether the box or wallet will fit in a jacket or vest pocket. Metal fly boxes should be made of aluminum alloy to inhibit rust and plastic boxes should be sturdy enough to withstand the inevitable knocking about they will receive.

Extra spools of leader material may be carried in boxes or kept on lengths of dowel inserted through holes in the center of the spools. Anglers who tie their own leaders also may wish to carry a small micrometer to measure the diameter of leader material.

A clipper or small pair of sharp scissors is indispensable for trimming knots or removing flies from leaders. A small pair of pliers also is necessary for pushing down hook barbs to comply with the barbless-hook regulations now in effect on many lakes—or just to make it easier releasing fish. Surgical forceps also are very handy for removing flies from fish.

I am never without a pair of Polaroid sunglasses while fishing. They cut surface glare, keep my eyes from tiring and offer protection from errant casts. They also make it easier to spot submerged weedbeds or shoals surrounded by deep water. In clear water over a marl bottom, a good pair of Polaroids may make it possible for an angler to see individual cruising fish and lead them with a cast, then watch the result as the fish comes to the fly. For me, nothing is more exciting.

Having lost several pairs of polaroid glasses overboard, I now attach them to a cord—actually a length of old fly line—around my neck. It makes me look a bit like an old-fashioned schoolteacher, but I haven't lost a single pair of glasses since I began wearing the cord.

Other handy accessories include a hook-sharpening file or stone, a thermometer to take the water temperature, a notebook for keeping a journal, a scale, and a measuring tape. A good pocket knife with screwdriver, bottle opener and other attachments also is extremely useful.

Some anglers prefer to carry a landing net, but I find nets unnecessary—especially if one does not plan to keep very many fish.

Anglers who smoke should carry an ash tray and use it. Trout are prone to swallow discarded cigaret butts or matches but can't digest them, and such items have doubtless brought many trout to uncomfortable, untimely ends. The same is true for pull-tabs from beverage cans; I have seen trout stuck in the plastic web that once held a six-pack of cans together and it's not a pretty sight.

Any angler who respects the fish or the water he or she fishes will never throw garbage or refuse in a lake. They should treat each lake as if it were their own living room, remembering that it is, in fact, the trout's living room, and litter may be lethal to fish or other organisms that live there. Boat anglers in particular should always carry an ash tray and litter bag.

It's difficult to enjoy fishing if one is wet or too warm or cold, and proper clothing is a critical part of any angler's equipment. The frequently changing weather of the British Columbia Interior calls for a wide variety of clothing. Hats are especially important; they shade the eyes and face from the sun, offer protection from flying hooks and provide at least some insulation from rain and hail. Anglers planning a trip to the Interior also should pack long underwear, heavy sweaters and warm jackets. These items can always be taken off if the weather turns warm, but if they aren't available when it's cold an angler will surely regret it. Full or partial gloves also should be worn by anglers whose hands are sensitive to cold. Good rain gear, capable of keeping a person dry in a torrential thundershower, is absolutely essential.

Insect repellent and a good sun-block lotion are extremely important for an angler's personal comfort. Mosquitoes can be thick and fierce around some Interior lakes, especially early in the season, and a good repellent is necessary to keep them at bay. The sun also can do lots of damage to a fisherman, especially at the high elevations of most Kamloops waters. A painful dose of sunburn can ruin a fishing trip and may lead to more serious complications, such as skin cancer. With many effective sun-block lotions now available, it's a simple matter to take precautions against such unpleasantries.

Technique

There is something slightly intimidating about one's first view of an unfamiliar lake. Usually there is nothing to indicate what secrets it may hold, nothing but an opaque expanse of water, perhaps marked only by a random rise. The rocks and wrinkles that are telltale signs of trout hiding spots in streams are missing, and there is no easy guide to where the fish may be. Reading a lake is much more difficult than reading a stream.

The problem becomes less complicated if an angler remembers that trout in lakes have exactly the same requirements as trout in streams—food, cover and comfort—but meet them in different ways. In streams, food is carried by the current, cover is available beneath undercut banks or overhanging limbs, and comfort is found in rocky pockets sheltered from the flow. In lakes, trout must actively move around and search for food

Rubber rafts, like other floating devices, involve compromises—but these are quickly forgotten when a fish is hooked.

since there is no current to bring it to them. They seek cover in weedbeds, over dark gravel bottoms or in the sheltering depths, and they find comfort in the layer of water offering the most favorable oxygen and temperature regime.

The shallow areas of any lake are most productive of the scuds and insects that trout feed on, and if other circumstances are favorable some trout will nearly always be found feeding in or near these areas. Obviously that means the shallows immediately offshore are the first places to look, but other good spots sometimes can be found by inspecting the lay of the land around the lake. For example, a long, gently sloping point extending well out into the lake may continue its descent under the surface, providing a shallow place where trout may congregate to feed. Similarly, a bay lying in a concave hollow might offer a broad expanse of shallow water. Not all shallow areas are so easy to locate, however; offshore shoals or "sunken islands," as anglers like to call them, can usually be found only by searching.

Once the shallow areas of a lake are found and noted, it is time to try some exploratory fishing. If there is no obvious feeding activity, the angler should anchor near the edge of a shallow area and cast into deeper water in hopes of intercepting trout that may be cruising the edge of the shallows. Almost any shallow area is likely to have trout feeding over or around it at some time of day, although early morning and late evening are the most reliable times; the absence of light gives trout a sense of security then. Gravel reefs or marl-covered shoals often are especially productive areas.

The mouths of inlet streams are other good places to try. Trout sometimes gather off inlets to feed on insects swept down by the current or to enjoy cooler, more highly oxygenated water. The mouths of tributary streams also may have aprons of gravel or silt that are good food producers themselves.

The main point to remember is that trout in lakes must aggressively seek their food, and because the shallows—areas less than 5 meters deep—produce most of it, trout are most apt to be found feeding there.

The wind also can determine where trout will be feeding in a lake. A breeze blowing from the same direction all day will concentrate hatching or spent insects on the windward side of the lake, and hungry trout will quickly take advantage of the fact; observant anglers will do likewise. If the wind is strong enough to stir up a chop, there will usually be "slicks"—narrow stretches of flat water extending for long distances through the waves—and veteran anglers know it pays to "fish the slicks." The reason is simple: Fish can see insects in the calm water of a slick more easily than in the broken water around it. "Fishing the slicks" can be especially rewarding during a good sedge hatch or ant flight.

When the wind dies, it also may leave drift lines of spent insects and other flotsam, and trout sometimes will cruise these drift lines rising to spent flies.

Deep water is an excellent source of cover for trout in lakes and they are quick to take advantage of it if they sense danger.

Conversely, they are invariably nervous and wary when they leave the security of deep water to feed in the shallows, so they must be approached carefully. When a trout is hooked in shallow water its first response is likely to be a long run in a frantic bid to return to the safety of the depths.

Cover is most important in shallow, clear-water lakes with marl bottoms, where trout may be highly visible. In this type of environment they tend to congregate over patches of submerged weed or rock, where they sense they are less visible from above.

When trout are not actively feeding, cover becomes a paramount concern and they will spend most of their time in areas where they feel safe. In the absence of any visible feeding activity, it's a good idea for anglers to fish areas of obvious cover.

In early spring and late fall, when oxygen levels and temperatures are most amenable, trout feel comfortable almost anywhere in the water column and their movements will be dictated mostly by their need for food or cover. During the hot summer months, when many lakes develop thermoclines, trout are forced to seek the most comfortable thermal zone; once they find it, their subsequent movements will be confined largely within that zone. Anglers usually can find out where this is by fishing a sinking line and keeping track of how long it takes to reach a depth where consistent action results, or by using a depth thermometer to determine the level of the thermocline.

The very best anglers I know all have one thing in common and that is the ability to concentrate fully on what they are doing. By honing every faculty to a keen edge and using it to focus on everything happening around them, they can pick up subtle clues—the nearly invisible surface bulge that may indicate a feeding fish below, a slight shift in wind or light that may suggest a different angling strategy, a change in behavior of birds or insects that sometimes is a tip-off to the behavior of the fish. They are able to maintain this fierce level of concentration for hours at a time, which takes great energy and endurance. From this description, you might think these are single-minded individuals whose only interest is fishing, but that is not the case at all; they are simply people who find maximum enjoyment through maximum involvement, a quality they frequently bring to other endeavors. The ability to develop and maintain such concentration can be acquired through practice, and anyone who takes up fly fishing would do well to practice it.

Dry-fly Fishing

If a hatch is in progress, the first thing to do is determine what insect is hatching and then choose a fly of the same general shape, size and color of the natural. Good imitations are perhaps even more important in lakes than streams because the still-water environment gives trout more opportunity to inspect a fly before deciding whether to take it.

If trout are feeding on the hatch, good results often can be obtained by casting to individual rising fish. When a trout rises, the angler should cast to it as quickly as possible in hopes the fish will still be there to see the fly. Failing that, the next best strategy is to try to determine from the rise characteristics what direction the fish has taken and attempt to place the fly in its path.

The dry-fly angler also must decide whether to move the fly or let it sit still. This is extremely important; movement of the fly, or lack of it, is probably the most significant factor in dry-fly fishing on lakes, and one must carefully observe what the naturals are doing and try to imitate them. If traveling sedges are on the water the angler should try to move his or her fly at the same speed as the naturals. A retrieve that is too fast or too slow may spell the difference between success and failure. This is especially true on a calm surface; if the wind is blowing up a chop, the speed of the retrieve is somewhat less important.

Angler trolls a fly from a wooden boat on Corbett Lake.

Since a traveling sedge hatch involves large insects in motion, it is the most complex hatch to fish correctly—but also usually the most rewarding. Other hatches are less complicated. Mayfly dun imitations should always be fished without motion, or at most with only an occasional twitch, to conform with the behavior of the naturals. Flying ants should be fished half-drowned in the surface film, again with only an occasional tiny twitch to imitate the motions of a struggling natural. Emerging chironomid imitations also should be fished without movement, but imitations of fully emerged adults often should be skated across the surface to match the behavior of the naturals. The best advice is to keep a close eye on what the real insects are doing and try to imitate them.

I have often enjoyed excellent dry-fly fishing late in the season even though no hatch was in progress and no flies were on the water. The technique is to find a good feeding or sheltering area and cast over it with a well-dressed, high-floating fly, usually a small sedge pattern, then retrieve it as quickly as possible. The rapid movement of the fly across the surface often brings up fish from considerable depths, perhaps triggering some sort of psychological response. Because the fly is moving so rapidly it is not always easy to hook fish, but their spectacular response to the skated fly is always exciting—especially under conditions that would seem to rule out dry-fly fishing.

In fishing a dry fly under any circumstances, it is important to keep a straight line from the rod tip to the fly. If the wind is coming at an angle it will quickly cause a belly to form in a floating line, making it very difficult to set the hook in a rising fish. If wind is a problem, the angler should take position with the wind at his or her back and cast parallel to the wind direction. The fly always should be moved by retrieving line rather than lifting the rod; the rod tip should be as close to the

surface as possible so there is no sag in the line between the rod and the surface that might prevent setting the hook in a rising fish (the same applies in fishing nymphs or wet flies).

A dry fly obviously must remain afloat to serve its intended purpose. Large patterns, such as traveling sedge imitations, or any fly the angler intends to skate across the surface should be treated with a floatant before use. Commercial preparations such as Mucilin paste or Gehrke's Gink are good for this. During use the fly can be dried by false casts, but it's a good idea to apply another coat of dressing after a fish is taken—and when the score reaches several fish it's probably time to change the fly.

The Kamloops trout is a swift riser and the angler's response to a rising fish must be equally swift; the rod must be raised quickly and firmly, tightening the line to set the hook in the trout's jaw. The timing requires some practice; if the response is too swift, the angler may pull the fly out of the fish's mouth; if it is too violent, the leader is almost sure to break, and if it is too slow the fish will be gone before the hook can be set. Only experience can teach the correct timing and pressure—but what a pleasant way to learn!

Nymph Fishing

There is no clear line between nymph fishing and wet-fly fishing. The usual definition of a nymph is that it imitates the immature stage of an aquatic insect while a wet fly does not necessarily imitate anything in particular.

Nymphs may be fished on any type of line. When a floating line is used the angler may encounter many of the same problems of dry-fly fishing, such as wind interference, but there similarity ends. In nymph fishing, both the fly and the strike often are invisible.

A floating-line presentation is necessary when fish are feeding on nymphs just beneath the surface. Such activity usually is apparent from the characteristic surface bulges left by trout taking nymphs or pupae, although sometimes nymphing fish will leave only small, delicate rings to mark their passage. If the angler has a good idea what nymphs or pupae are likely to be present or is able to capture a sample from the water, he or she should put up an appropriate imitation and begin casting to feeding fish.

The choice of whether to retrieve the fly or fish it without motion again depends upon the behavior of the natural. Imitations of emerging sedge pupae or damselfly nymphs should be retrieved accordingly, although some experimentation probably will be necessary to establish the correct rate of retrieval. The take may be surprisingly gentle, so the angler should be prepared to set the hook at even the slightest feeling of resistance. The surface bulge will not become visible until after the fish has made its pass at the fly, and by then it is far too late to set the hook.

Fishing chironomid pupal imitations requires different techniques, and over the past couple of decades some Kamloops trout anglers have refined these to astonishing degrees of sophistication. The most common method requires a stable casting platform—usually a boat firmly anchored fore and aft—a floating line, a strike indicator, and a leader trimmed to match the depth of water the angler is fishing. Sometimes this means using a leader as long as 25 feet and a weighted fly; at the opposite extreme, there are times when it's appropriate to use a short leader and grease all but the last few inches so the fly hangs just beneath the surface film. Veteran chironomid anglers often spend as much time measuring depths, tying knots and adjusting leader lengths as they do fishing—but the results they get are worth the effort.

The pupal imitation, which should match the natural both in color and size, usually is fished without motion, although a *very* slow retrieve is sometimes used. The secret of this technique is to keep a close eye on the strike indicator and react to even the slightest hint of movement. It takes lots of practice and even greater amounts of patience to become truly proficient at this method, but it may be the single most consistent and effective way to catch Kamloops trout. In other words, it can be absolutely deadly.

Chironomid pupal imitations also can be fished on sinking lines. Again a stable casting platform is necessary, and the technique is to make a measured cast equal in length to the depth being fished, then allow the line to sink until the fly is hanging nearly straight down. At that point a very slow retrieve is started, matching the fitful, halting progress of a natural struggling toward the surface. The angler should be prepared to strike at the least feeling of resistance. Obviously a fast-sinking line is best, but this method requires much patience even with a fast-sinking line and usually is not quite as effective as the floating-line technique. However, it can be very effective at times.

Damselfly nymph and/or sedge pupae imitations also may be fished on any type of line, although floaters or sink-tips are best. The technique is simply to cast, allow the fly to sink to the desired depth, then retrieve at an appropriate rate. Strikes usually will be felt as a slow, sullen resistance, but it also pays to keep a close eye on the floating portion of the line for any telltale movement that may signal a more subtle take.

Dragonfly nymph imitations are best fished on sink-tip or sinking lines with a slow retrieve. Scud patterns are effective at almost any depth, and the line choice should be made accordingly. Regardless of what type of line is used, a slow retrieve is best.

Leech patterns are usually fished on sinking lines with an erratic retrieve from deep to shallow water. Perhaps because they feel more secure in deep water, Kamloops trout seem to respond to deeply-sunk patterns with less caution and the takes are often violent. In most cases the fish hooks itself

before the angler can react.

It's worth repeating that the angler always should strive to keep a straight line between the rod and fly, free of any slack.

Wet-fly Fishing

Wet-fly fishing has been called the "chuck-and-chance-it" method, a disparaging term probably coined by dry-fly purists to show their contempt. While unnecessarily harsh, the term is essentially an accurate description of the method: Wet-fly fishing involves using non-imitative fly patterns which are cast more or less at random. In the Kamloops trout lakes, wet-fly fishing usually involves "attractor" patterns, often brightly colored flies or "lures" designed for maximum visibility and movement. These patterns may be fished with sink-tip or fast-sinking lines, depending upon the depth and character of the water.

Many veteran Kamloops anglers consider attractor patterns a last resort when imitative flies and methods have been tried and failed. The attractors are fished at varying depths with varying retrieves until a fish finally takes hold. The fish may then yield a stomach sample that will prompt the angler to change back to an imitative pattern; if not, he or she will continue using the attractor, fishing it the same way that brought results the first time. Casts will be made randomly only to the extent that the angler cannot see the fish, for surely he or she will have chosen a spot where fish are likely to be present, or one that has produced results on earlier occasions.

Wet-fly fishing with attractor patterns can be surprisingly productive when trout are not actively feeding on a hatch; sometimes a bright, colorful fly stimulates a response when nothing else will. These patterns also can be effective during thick algae blooms because they are more visible in the water. Wet-fly fishing may lack the skill and refinement demanded by dry flies or nymphs, but it gets results—and it should be a part of any angler's repertoire.

Anyone who fishes the Kamloops trout waters, by any method, should not expect uniform success. The Kamloops trout lakes, like trout waters everywhere, can be very fickle, and sometimes they withhold their rewards stubbornly—but only to those who give up easily. Anglers who practice their skills diligently, fish patiently and remain observant will soon find results.

Playing and Landing Fish

In the split second between the fish's take and the angler's first inkling of contact, the trout already has begun its response. Its usual reaction is to run with all its strength or throw itself recklessly into the air. How quickly and how well the angler reacts in these first few moments often determines the outcome of the battle.

If a trout runs there is little point in trying to stop it unless it is headed for some obstruction. If the fish is a large one, any attempt to slow it down is likely to result in a broken leader anyway. So the best thing to do is sit back and enjoy it, and let the fish run as far as it wants—so long as it does not strip all the backing from the reel. There may be potential danger if a large fish runs in a curving direction, however; that will cause a belly to form in the fly line as it slices through the water behind the fish, and water resistance on the line may increase enough to cause the leader to part. The danger can be minimized to some extent by keeping the rod pointed at the fish and trying to recover as much trailing line as possible.

Once a running fish has taken up all the slack and is "on the reel," it is best to continue to play it from the reel and avoid retrieving line by hand; the latter method should be reserved for smaller fish that pose less hazard to the leader.

If a hooked fish jumps—either at the moment of the strike or any time later—the correct response is to instantly lower the rod tip and ease the sudden strain on the leader. A violent leap against the pressure of a taut leader may tear out the hook or increase the chance that the leader will break if the fish should fall on it. Dipping the rod usually creates enough instant slack to cushion the shock of a strong leap.

A favorite tactic of the Kamloops trout—particularly when it has just made a long run—is to reverse course and run straight toward the angler. This move creates instant slack so there is no longer any feeling of resistance, and it may fool even an experienced angler into thinking he has lost the fish; the sudden slack also may allow the fish to escape before the angler realizes what has happened. One way to guard against this is to watch the line carefully; even when there is no longer any feeling of resistance, if the line keeps moving there is certainly still a fish at the end of it. The challenge then is to recover slack line quickly enough to restore a tight connection. Sometimes a reel simply can't be wound fast enough to take up slack when a fish is running directly toward the angler, and then it becomes necessary to start stripping line rapidly by hand. This is the only exception to the rule that a large fish always should be played from the reel.

A hooked Kamloops trout spends its strength freely trying to escape with long runs or jumps, but if these don't work the fish eventually settles down and tries to win through brute strength. A large Kamloops trout often will shake itself like a wet Spaniel, trying to dislodge the hook—a tactic that frequently succeeds. Sometimes a trout will roll itself up in the leader or manage to tangle the tippet around its ventral fin, gill, or mandible. This impedes its freedom of movement so that it may come meekly to the angler, but the strain placed on the leader is dangerous and the trout may suddenly free itself at the last moment and catch the angler unprepared for a sudden run or jump.

The key to success during this phase is to keep steady pressure on the fish so it has no chance to rest or regain its strength. The rod should be kept at an angle and direction calculated to keep up consistent pressure, and if the trout changes direction the angler should respond accordingly. Line should be recovered at every opportunity. These tactics will soon tire the trout enough for the angler to gain control.

The "end game" is as crucial in landing a trout as it is in chess. Probably more fish are lost next to the boat than at any other stage of the contest. Any number of things can go wrong: The fish may tangle the leader around the anchor rope, bolt at the sight of a landing net or cut the leader on a sharp corner of the hull. These things are more apt to happen if one tries to land a trout too soon, before it is tired out. The fish should be played until the angler is confident he or she has control of it (but not too long, or it will jeopardize the trout's chances for recovery if released). Then, if the fish is to be netted, the net should be placed in the water and the fish led gently over it.

The growth of the "catch-and-release" ethic has prompted many anglers to stop using nets. Instead, on those rare occasions they decide to keep a fish, they play it close enough to take a firm grip on its lower jaw with their thumb and forefinger. This momentarily paralyzes the trout, making it possible to lift even a very large fish out of the water. But it takes some practice and must always be done with care.

Trout destined for release must be handled carefully. The B.C. fishing regulations include an excellent summary of release techniques that seems worth repeating here:

"A fish that appears unharmed may not survive if carelessly handled, so please abide by the following:

"1. Play and release (the) fish as rapidly as possible. A fish played too long may not recover.

"2. Keep the fish in the water as much as possible. A fish may injure itself out of water, and scale loss is more likely out of water.

"3. Handle the fish gently with your bare, wet hands. Keep your fingers out of the gills, and don't squeeze the fish or cause scales to be lost or damaged.

"4. Remove the hook as rapidly as possible using longnose pliers. Be quick, but gentle. Barbless hooks are recommended. If the fish is deeply hooked, cut the leader and leave the hook in.

"5. Take the time to hold the fish in the water, moving it back and forth to pump water over its gills . . . When the fish begins to struggle and swim normally, let it go."

And it will be there for you to catch a second time when you return.

Etiquette

With numbers of anglers growing steadily there is bound to be conflict as waters become more and more crowded. This is especially true with the increase of casual "weekend" anglers who remain largely ignorant of the traditions and subtleties of the sport. The rules of angling etiquette are designed to prevent or minimize such conflicts, but etiquette is really just a fancy word for common courtesy, and an angler who follows his or her best instincts is not likely to have any trouble.

In fishing lakes, that means giving a wide berth to anglers who already have anchored and begun casting and keeping well away from the water they have chosen to fish. Float-tube anglers should make it a rule to stay twice as far away from other fishermen as they think necessary to compensate for the distorted distance perception they necessarily experience

from being so close to the surface. Anglers fishing from a boat with an outboard motor should never operate the motor in shallow areas where trout may be feeding, and should always throttle down to a slow, safe speed when passing other anglers in any type of water.

Good angling etiquette also means offering advice only when asked, or seeking another angler's permission to fish close by or pass through water within his casting range (and the latter should be done only when there is no other route to take). It means not getting in the way of someone who has chosen to drift and cast before the wind, and it means keeping a clean and quiet camp on the lakeshore. In sum, it means

doing nothing to interfere with the sport of any other angler, or his or her enjoyment of the surroundings or the day.

Most experienced fly fishers are aware of all this and rarely come in conflict with one another; when conflict does occur it often involves anglers of different persuasions, frequently trollers. Trollers by definition are not very sophisticated anglers, and in their more-or-less aimless perambulations around a lake it seldom occurs to them that they may be spoiling things for other fishermen by disturbing the water they have chosen to fish. It's not uncommon to see trollers steering their outboards into shallows where fly fishers are at work, prompting all the fish to flee, or coming so close to an

anchored fly fisher that he or she must stop fishing. More than once I have seen unwary trollers accidentally hooked by a fly fisher's backcast—and sometimes it was not an accident.

Such incidents often lead to angry words or sometimes worse, and each party leaves with unhappy feelings. There is little reason such conflicts should occur; a fly fisher uses only a small circle of water while a troller has access to all the rest, and there is no need for trollers to intrude on water being fished by someone else. But it happens, and when it does a fly fisher's patience may be sorely tried.

Not that trollers have a monopoly on bad manners; there are bad apples among the fly-fishing fraternity as well. Usually these are individuals whose eagerness and enthusiasm get in the way of their judgment, to the extent that they make life miserable for other people around them. Fortunately, there are not many such individuals, and usually peer pressure straightens them out sooner or later.

Finally a word about ethics: Any angler who does not faithfully observe fishing rules and regulations has no right to expect anyone else to observe them. Rules also should not be considered targets; numerical and size limits are not meant to be goals, but maximums. Anglers who observe the rules and keep less than their limit do themselves and others a great favor; they assure the future of the sport.

7: Favorite Waters

Hihium Lake in early May, with the ice just melting off. *Facing Page:* The lodge at Corbett Lake Country Inn.

The Kamloops trout lakes are within the economic reach of almost any angler. There are lakes with elaborate resorts that cater to an angler's every whim, lakes with fishing camps that range from comfortable to primitive, lakes with developed campsites and lakes with no development at all. Some lakes lie next to highways, others are reached over dirt roads that range from good to torturous, some are accessible only on foot or by horseback, and a few can be reached only by air. Within this broad range there are bound to be at least a few waters to suit the taste and pocketbook of any angler.

The problem, of course, is to find them. With thousands of waters to choose from, this can be a formidable task for someone not familiar with the country. Fortunately, the British Columbia government does several things to make the task easier, with help from private business.

One very useful thing the government does is publish an annual directory of tourist accommodations listing virtually every hotel, motel or bed-and-breakfast in British Columbia. Fishing camps are included, along with a brief description of their location, services provided, rates, and how to get in touch with them. The directory also includes maps of major highway routes, information on air, bus and rail service, and a lot of other helpful information. Copies may ordered by writing to the Ministry of Tourism, 1117 Wharf St., Victoria B.C. V8W 2Z2. Ask for the *British Columbia Accommodations Guide* for the current year.

Another useful publication is *British Columbia Freshwater Fishing Vacations,* published by the B.C. Fishing Resorts and Outfitters Association. Its chief value is a list of all member fishing camps, guides and outfitters, along with a description of their services and how to reach them. Copies may be obtained from the association, Box 3301, Kamloops B.C. V2C 6B9.

Good maps also are essential. Detailed topographic maps are available in various scales from the Geological Survey of Canada, Map & Pub-

Preparing for a pack trip to a remote lake.

lications Sales Office, 100 W. Pender St., Vancouver B.C., or from MAPS-B.C., Ministry of Lands & Parks, Surveys and Resource Mapping Branch, 1802 Douglas St., Victoria B.C. V8V 1X4, or from commercial map dealers. Catalogs or indexes may be obtained for mail orders.

Good as these maps are, they are updated only at intervals of 10 to 15 years, so they quickly become out of date as new roads are built and old ones fall into disrepair. More recent local maps showing the latest road changes may be purchased at most sporting-goods stores in the Interior. These may not always be accurate to scale, but in combination with the federal or provincial topographic maps they can be very helpful.

Another good source is the commercially published *B.C. Fishing Directory & Atlas* (Art Belhumeur Ent., Ltd., 1640 Western Drive, Port Coquitlam, B.C. V3C 2X3). Updated annually and printed in a magazine format, the atlas includes good area maps and capsule descriptions of many lakes. It is sold at many sporting-goods stores and book shops.

Finding good maps probably is easier than finding a place to buy a fishing license. Most sporting-goods stores sell them, but not all have nonresident licenses. Licenses may be obtained at any regional office of the Fisheries Branch, but these are not always conveniently located—nor are they always open when an angler is passing through on a tight schedule. However, most fishing camps and resorts have them, and stores or other commercial outlets that sell them usually post signs saying so.

Licenses must be carried while fishing. When buying one, it's also a good idea to pick up a copy of the current angling regulations and study it carefully.

Even after an angler has bought a license, read the regulations and studied the most recent maps, it is still advisable to seek local information before heading off to a remote lake. If the lake has suffered a recent winter or summer kill, those who live nearby are bound to know it—and such information could save a visitor lots of time and trouble. Local advice on the most recent road conditions also can be worth its weight in gold, and

it is always wise to assume the roads probably are a bit worse than they are reported to be. Anyone planning to drive the back roads of the B.C. Interior should carry chains, axe, saw, shovel, jacks, power winch or "come-along" (hand winch), extra cable, and a full set of tools, and know how to use them.

This advice should not be taken lightly. Even with all the recent highway construction and other improvements, many back roads leading to the Kamloops trout lakes remain marginal at best, particularly in wet weather, and one who has never traveled them has no concept of what to expect. Anglers unaccustomed to such rugged conditions should not be intimidated, however. Some fishing camps provide their own transportation from the nearest highway or community, and there are many excellent lakes within easy reach of the family car.

There are so many Kamloops trout waters one could not hope to fish all of them in a lifetime. The number of lakes and the difficulties involved in reaching some of them also complicate the task of preparing a list that is comprehensive and accurate. The list that follows therefore is necessarily limited to those waters about which I have personal knowledge or information from sources I consider reliable. It also largely reflects my own angling experience, which has been mostly on the waters of the Merritt-Kamloops-North Thompson axis. So it is by no means a complete catalog of all the Kamloops trout lakes, and no lack of merit is implied for any waters not included.

The figures provided for lake elevations and surface areas are not precise down to the last meter or acre, but they are more than sufficiently accurate for planning a fishing trip. Other descriptions were valid at the time of preparation, but readers should keep in mind that conditions on the Interior lakes can and do change rapidly—and sometimes radically. This is true for access routes as well as fishing opportunities, so it's always best to ask questions locally and try to get the latest information before starting a trip.

Merritt Area

Most visitors now approach the Kamloops trout lakes from the south via the Coquihalla Highway (Highway 5), passing from the wet coastal climate and its fir-dominated forests to the rolling grasslands and pine forests of the Interior. Merritt, the first town they reach, sprawls across the floor of a broad valley where the Coldwater River joins the sluggish Nicola on its westward course to the Thompson.

Merritt is an important road junction. The Coquihalla

Highway skirts its south side, then continues north to Kamloops. The Okanagan Connector comes in from the south, then extends north of Merritt as Highway 97C to the Highland Valley, where it provides the main east-west connection between Logan Lake and Ashcroft. Highway 8 comes into Merritt from Spences Bridge to the west, and Highway 5A, the old Merritt-Kamloops route, heads east along the shore of Nicola Lake, then bends north to Kamloops. All these routes provide access to important lakes.

• *South of Merritt* (MAP, page 132): Of the many lakes in the hills south of Merritt, **Murray Lake** is one of the first accessible to an angler traveling from the south over the Coquihalla Highway. It is reached from the old Coldwater Road (which parallels the Coquihalla Highway) about 56 kilometers (35 miles) southeast of Merritt. The Juliet Creek Exit from the highway provides a connection. The last 6 kilometers (4 miles) to the lake are steep and rocky and a truck may be necessary.

The lake is at an elevation of 1,060 meters (3,478 feet) with a surface area of 35 hectares (86 acres). It is a clear, relatively shallow lake with a marl bottom and not much weed growth. It is not a particularly rich water but does have a good sedge hatch. Dry-fly fishing can be excellent when the hatch is on, although trout seldom exceed 2 1/2 pounds and most are a good deal smaller. There is a small camping area and access at the south end of the lake. The north end has a number of private cabins.

From its junction with the Coquihalla Highway just south of Merritt, the Okanagan Connector climbs steeply into the hills southeast of town. The well-marked, well-lighted intersection at the turnoff to **Lundbom** and **Marquart Lakes** is 13 kilometers (8 miles) from town. A good gravel road, easily traveled by cars, leads first to Marquart, then to Lundbom, a total distance of only about 3 kilometers (1.8 miles) from the highway. Both lakes are at an elevation of about 1,128 meters (3,700 feet). Marquart has a surface area of 22.6 hectares (55.8 acres) while Lundbom covers 45 hectares (111 acres).

The sad fate of these two lakes already has been related in some detail. Once they were among the most productive of all Kamloops trout waters, offering wonderful fly fishing for trout as large as 14 pounds, but overwhelming pressure and abuse have damaged both fisheries to the point they are no longer worth the attention of serious anglers. Marquart, after successive winter kills and shiner infestations, now is managed as a mixed brook trout-Kamloops fishery. Shiners were introduced to Lundbom about five years ago by fishermen using them illegally for bait, but the lake also still holds Kamloops trout and remains capable of producing large fish. It is best visited—if at all—on weekdays early in the season before school lets out, or again in late September after most of the crowds have gone.

About 17.5 kilometers (10.5 miles) south of Merritt a gravel road leaves the west side of the Okanagan Connector and extends about 5.5 kilometers (3.5 miles) to the first of the Kane Valley Lakes, which include **Harmon, Upper and Lower**

Kane and **Englishman**. These scenic little lakes are at elevations ranging from 1,060 to 1,090 meters (3,475 to 3,575 feet). Harmon Lake, the largest, covers 30 hectares (74 acres); Upper Kane is 8 hectares (20 acres) and Lower Kane 7 hectares (17 acres); Englishman is about the same size.

These waters were once quite popular with fly fishers, but repeated shiner infestations have hurt their productivity. Harmon and Englishman have both been reinfested since they were last chemically treated to remove shiners, but the Kane Lakes so far have managed to remain free of shiners. All these waters produce fair fishing for Kamloops trout up to 2 pounds. Limited camping is available and the lakes are easily accessible by car.

On the east side of the Okanagan Connector 18 kilometers (11 miles) southeast of Merritt is **Corbett Lake**, accessible from the highway via a limited public right-of-way or through Corbett Lake Country Inn. Despite being located next to the highway, Corbett has remained a viable fishery by virtue of a reduced bag limit and barbless hook-artificial fly regulations.

Ideally suited for fly fishing, with extensive weedy shallows, the lake is at an elevation of 1,060 meters (3,475 feet) and covers an area of 20 hectares (49 acres). It has a wide assortment of aquatic life, including spring chironomid emergences and a good *Callibaetis* hatch. Recurring problems of winter kill and low water due to irrigation withdrawal appear to have been solved by installation of an electric-powered aerating device and a new dam that raised the lake's water level about 1 meter. Corbett Lake provides consistent fishing for feisty trout up to a pound with occasional larger fish to 3 pounds or more. Current regulations require artificial flies with single barbless hooks. The daily limit is two fish.

Next to those in Paul Lake, trout in Corbett Lake probably have been studied more thoroughly than those in any other Kamloops trout water. There are many good reasons for this: The lake is easily accessible and small enough that its trout population can be controlled without much difficulty and accurate creel censuses can be obtained. But I suspect the most compelling reason biologists have chosen to do much of their work on this lake is the presence of Peter McVey as proprietor and chef-in-residence at Corbett Lake Country Inn.

McVey trained in France and held several prestigious culinary positions in England before moving to British Columbia to indulge his first love, fly fishing. After a short stint as operator of Thuya Lakes fishing camp near Little Fort and an abortive attempt to establish a camp on Minnie Lake, he settled at Corbett Lake where he has held forth in grand style ever since. On any given night his guests may include anglers from several provinces and states, come to sample the culinary artistry which McVey continually performs over the big gas range in the old kitchen at the inn.

Possessed with an endless supply of ideas and limitless energy and enthusiasm to carry them out, McVey has done much to improve the fishing in Corbett Lake and any number of others nearby. His efforts include transplanting gammarids to provide more food for the trout in Corbett Lake and the original development of Minnie and Stoney Lakes as trophy-fishing waters. He is himself an accomplished fisherman, one of the finest casters in the province, and so often did his name appear on the Merritt Fish & Game Club trophy for the season's largest fish that the club finally gave up and awarded him permanent custody of the trophy. When not otherwise occupied, he retreats to a workshop behind the inn and builds custom bamboo fly rods for a growing list of customers. His reputation as a rod builder made Corbett Lake the logical location for the first-ever conclave of bamboo rod builders in 1988, an event which has been repeated at two-year intervals ever since.

In addition to its famous host and dining room, Corbett Lake Country Inn has comfortable cabins, some with handsome stone fireplaces, and maintains a small fleet of rowboats for cabin guests or drop-in customers. There is no camping around the lake.

Just south of Corbett Lake the highway skirts the western edge of **Courtney Lake**, a beautiful lake surrounded by gently rolling hills freckled with groves of pine, fir, aspen and wild rose. At an elevation of 1,045 meters (3,428 feet), Courtney has a surface area of 60 hectares (148 acres) and is made to order for fly fishing, with many broad shoals and weedbeds easily visible through its clear water. Unfortunately, a consistent run of bad luck has kept it from ever reaching its potential. It has been chemically treated twice to remove infestations of scrap fish, and more recently was the subject of a right-of-way dispute between the provincial Department of Highways and the Douglas Lake Ranch, which controlled access to the lake. As a result, access was closed until the Fisheries Branch was able to swap lands with the ranch and gain control of the access. At this writing Courtney was scheduled for yet another chemical rehabilitation to remove yet another infestation of shiners, and a recovery period of two or three years may be expected before the lake is restored to full trout production.

Courtney has produced Kamloops trout up to 6 1/2 pounds at times in the past, and with appropriate regulations and an absence of scrap fish there is no reason to suppose it may not do so again in the future. All the usual aquatic fauna are present, although the lake's sedge hatch is not especially prolific. The lake's shallow character makes it difficult for trollers to fish, and in the past this has been a limiting factor on angling pressure. There is no camping around the lake and its proximity to the highway makes it an undesirable place to camp anyway.

Near Aspen Grove Store, 39 kilometers (24 miles) south of Merritt, the Okanagan Connector turns sharply east and old Highway 5A continues south toward Princeton. About 5.5 kilometers (3.5 miles) south of Aspen Grove on the old highway a good, well-marked road leads east to a provincial park on **Kentucky** and **Alleyne Lakes. Crater** and **Bluey Lakes** also are accessible via this route.

These scenic lakes lie at elevations ranging from 1,005 to 1,035 meters (3,300 to 3,395 feet). Crater, the northernmost, has a surface area of about 20 hectares (49 acres), Alleyne is 55

hectares (136 acres), Kentucky 40 hectares (99 acres), and Bluey 30 hectares (74 acres). All are fairly deep and lacking in shoal water, so they are not especially well suited to fly fishing. However, they are fished heavily by trollers and produce good numbers of trout in the 2-pound class with some larger.

The water in Kentucky Lake is quite clear and it is possible to see trout cruising at considerable depths. A shallow, sheltered bay at the south end sometimes offers exciting fishing because it is one of the few places where it is possible to stalk individual trout, cast to them and watch them come up to a fly.

All these lakes have small camping areas.

The Okanagan Connector east of Aspen Grove offers access to a host of lakes, including the **Paradise Lake** chain, **Pennask Lake** and **Hatheume Lake** and surrounding waters, all lying north of the highway.

Paradise Lake, largest in the chain that bears its name, is at an elevation of 1,515 meters (4,970 feet) and covers an area of 50 hectares (124 acres). A fishing camp that once operated on the lake is now closed and as of mid-1993 a private developer reportedly was planning to build homes on the lake.

Nearby waters include **Boot**, 1,485 meters (4,872 feet), 30 hectares (74 acres); **Boulder**, 1,545 meters (5,070 feet), 20 hectares (49 acres); **Elkhart**, 1,600 meters (5,250 feet), 20 hectares (49 acres); **Island**, 1,485 meters (4,872 feet), 50 hectares (124 acres), **Bobs**, **Johns**, **Skunk**, **Reservoir** and **Walker**. Some are accessible by road, others only by trail.

Situated in rocky, heavily timbered country, most of these high-elevation lakes have dark, amber-tinted water. Most also produce small trout in large numbers and are what the Fisheries Branch calls "good family lakes"—meaning plenty of action for the kids—although Island and Boot have histories of producing some fairly sizable trout in the past. Because of their high elevation the fishing usually holds up well during the summer.

Pennask Lake, which lies to the northeast, is at an elevation of about 1,425 meters (4,675 feet) and covers an area of 955 hectares (2,360 acres) with an irregular shoreline and several islands. It has a maximum depth of slightly less than 21 meters (70 feet) and a mean depth of a little more than 9 meters (30 feet), but there are broad reaches of shallow water made to order for fly fishing. The trout in Pennask tend to be small, however, with 12 to 14 inches about average. Current regulations limit anglers to artificial flies with barbless hooks. There is a provincial park on the lake.

Nearby Hatheume Lake, accessible via gravel road extending about 20 kilometers (12.5 miles) from the Sunset exit on Highway 97C (Okanagan Connector), has been headquarters for one of the Interior's best-known fly-fishing resorts since 1959. Hatheume is due east of Pennask Lake at an elevation of approximately 1,400 meters (4,593 feet). The lake has a surface area of 135 hectares (334 acres) and is currently managed as a catch-and-release lake, one of only two in the region. Anglers must use artificial flies and barbless hooks.

Hatheume's trout were disappointingly small in the spring

Sun breaks through on a day of unsettled weather at Lundbom Lake.

of 1993, perhaps a result of accidental double stocking due to a "failure of communications" within the Fisheries Branch, but some larger fish to 3 1/2 pounds appeared later in the season. Nearby smaller waters include **Rat**, **Jerry**, **Jenny**, **Rock**, **Rouse** and **Ellen Lakes**, which offer a variety of angling experiences.

• *Northwest of Merritt* (**MAP**, **page 133**): From the point where they diverge just north and west of Merritt, Highways 8 and 97C both offer access to several lakes. Highway 97C heads north into the Highland Valley, then west toward Ashcroft—hardly a scenic route, since it passes through the worst strip-mining devastation. But it does connect with the Calling Lake Road, a good gravel road that winds through the ravaged landscape of the Highland Valley copper mine, then climbs south into the timbered hills where it affords access to **Island Lake**, also sometimes known as Big O.K. Lake. The turnoff to the lake is about 6.5 kilometers (4 miles) from Highway 97C and the last kilometer to the lake is very rough; a truck is advised.

Island Lake is at an elevation of 1,485 meters (4,872 feet) and has an area of 24 hectares (60 acres). Like many Kamloops trout waters, it was a natural lake whose level was raised by a dam, but while most such impoundments were created for irrigation purposes Island Lake was enlarged to provide water for a nearby silver mine. The mine has since closed and most traces of it have been obscured by heavy timber, making Island Lake quite an attractive place.

The lake has vast shoal areas, excellent hatches of large chironomids and *Callibaetis*, an abundant population of scuds and a wonderful sedge hatch—all the ingredients necessary for growing large trout. As mentioned previously, it has been planted with sterilized female trout in an experimental effort to eliminate the problems of early sexual maturation. Ordinary, unsterilized Pennask-strain Kamloops trout also have been planted as a control group, but the lake has no natural spawning so these fish will be unable to reproduce. Currently the lake is managed as a catch-and-release fishery, one of only two in the region, with only artificial flies and barbless hooks permitted. Trout in the 3 1/2-pound class are common, 7 1/2-pounders are not unusual and even larger fish are available; however, as usual in such situations, the fishing never is very fast.

Primitive campsites are located along the north shore of the lake.

The Calling Lake Road also offers rough access (4x4) to **Calling** and **O.K. Lakes**. Calling is at an elevation of 1,500 meters (4,921 feet) and covers about 30 hectares (74 acres). It is a shallow lake offering good fly fishing, but is subject to periodic winter kills and Indian fishing. O.K., a much smaller lake of only about 8 hectares (20 acres), is at an elevation of 1,615 meters (5,300 feet). Both lakes have produced trout of 3 pounds or larger.

Highway 97C continues west past the Calling Lake Road to **Willard** and **Barnes Lakes** on the benchlands overlooking the Thompson River canyon and the town of Ashcroft. Willard is visible on the north side of the highway and Barnes Lake lies just out of sight beyond Willard. Both are accessible by a good gravel road.

Barnes covers an area of about 53 hectares (131 acres) while Willard is about half that size. Both lakes are at an elevation of 700 meters (2,230 feet) and both are shallow with silty bottoms and heavy weed growth. The Fisheries Branch stocks Barnes Lake with trout, knowing that some will find their way through its outlet into Willard; some natural spawning also occurs. Both lakes are subject to irrigation drawdown; that, plus their low elevation, limits fishing opportunities to early spring and late fall. They are especially popular in the spring, but are also known as "powerboat heaven" at that time. On occasion these lakes have produced trout of 4 1/2 pounds or better, but their easy year-round accessibility (they are also favorite targets of ice fishermen in winter) exposes them to heavy angling pressure, creating uncertain prospects from year to year.

There are campsites on both lakes. Boat launching is easy in the spring when the lakes are full but can be a problem after irrigation drawdown.

From its junction with Highway 97C outside Merritt, Highway 8 continues a short distance west to the village of Lower Nicola where a well-marked hard-surfaced road leads north and connects with a good gravel road providing access to **Chataway Lakes**. There are many spurs and side roads along the way, but the route to Chataway is well marked. Total distance is about 27 kilometers (16.5 miles) and a car is adequate.

Chataway Lake is at an elevation of 1,380 meters (4,528 feet) and has a surface area of 20 hectares (49 acres). It was named for George Chataway, a prospector who found copper ore in the area early in the century and operated a small mine for several years, hauling the ore out by pack train. The remains of his mine can still be seen near the lake.

A small fishing camp opened on Chataway about 1955, catering to a private clientele of doctors, lawyers and other professionals. In 1967 the camp was bought by Bill Roddy, a former Vancouver police officer, who spent most of the first years of his ownership building new cabins and other amenities. His comfortable lodge has a large room with walls of upright peeled logs (they were built in upright "palisade" style because Roddy did most of the work himself and had no help to raise the walls), a big central fireplace surrounded by easy chairs and sofas, and framed trout-fly plates hanging on the walls. The family-oriented camp also has house-keeping cabins, central hot showers and a sauna, and campsites with fireplaces, picnic tables, piped-in water and a playground for children.

Besides Chataway itself, lakes fished out of this camp include **Abbott**, 1,325 meters (4,347 feet) and 15 hectares (37 acres); **Antler**, 1,335 meters (4,380 feet) and 20 hectares (49 acres); **Billy**, 1,460 meters (4,790 feet) and 25 hectares (62 acres); **Dot**, 1,335 meters (4,380 feet) and 40 hectares (99 acres); **Echo** (also known as Knight Lake), 1,600 meters (5,250 feet) and about 7 hectares (17 acres); **Gump**, about

The late Enos Bradner with a 6-pound Kamloops trout on Lundbom Lake in the "old days."

1,326 meters (4,350 feet) and 8 hectares (20 acres); **Gypsum**, 1,290 meters (4,232 feet) and 10 hectares (25 acres); **Le Roy** (spelled Le Roi on some maps), about 1,402 meters (4,600 feet) and 8 hectares (20 acres) with smaller satellite ponds; **Roscoe**, about 1,585 meters (5,200 feet) and 40 hectares (99 acres); **Tyner**, 1,305 meters (4,281 feet) and 25 hectares (62 acres), and **Tupper**, about 1,330 meters (4,363 feet) and 8 hectares (20 acres). Antler Lake requires a hike of about a quarter of a mile from the nearest road and Echo Lake is a short walk from the northwest shore of Roscoe Lake. The others are accessible by rough roads and a 4x4 is required.

A spring day on Corbett Lake, looking north from the lodge with the boat dock in foreground.

These small lakes offer a wide variety of angling, from very fast fishing for very small trout to challenging dry-fly fishing for larger fish to 5 pounds or more. Natural reproduction keeps some of the lakes perpetually overpopulated, and these provide good angling for children. Others, such as Abbott and Antler, are shallow, weedy lakes that usually provide good fishing for trout up to 3 pounds and sometimes larger, although both lakes experience up-and-down cycles. Dot, Billy and Tupper Lakes all have produced large fish from time to time. Gypsum and Tyner both have excellent sedge hatches, especially the latter, and both are especially well suited to fly fishers. Gypsum has broad shoal areas and a rocky shoal in the middle where trout gather; Tyner is shallow and so full of weeds it can be fished only with a fly. It also has good hatches of damselflies and *Callibaetis* mayflies. Unfortunately, it is susceptible to frequent winter kills, suffering one most recently in the winter of 1992-93.

Echo Lake is little more than a high-elevation, dark-water pond, but it has an interesting legend. The lake supposedly is haunted by a spirit known as "The Presence" that sometimes manifests itself through the sudden touch of a cold hand on the back of one's neck. Mysterious camps also are said to appear and disappear around the lake, with pots and pans and other implements rearranged each morning as if they had just been used—but the camps always are deserted and no one ever sees who made them. Perhaps the strangest part of the tale, however, is that the spirit never appears to anyone who has heard of the legend before visiting the lake—and now that you have, you don't need to worry. As for the fishing, Echo has abundant populations of small scuds and chironomids and

routinely produces trout in the 10- to 14-inch class.

Also in the same vicinity is **Gordon Lake**, accessible via logging roads (with active logging going on in the area, access routes are subject to frequent change). A 4x4 may be necessary. The lake is at an elevation of 1,400 meters (4,593 feet) with a surface area of 28 hectares (69 acres). A shallow lake, it fishes best early and late in the season and has produced large trout at times, although 2 1/2 pounds probably is the maximum to be expected most years. Rough camping is available at the lake.

Although no sign is posted at the turnoff in Lower Nicola, the route to Chataway Lakes also provides the best access to **Pimainus Lakes**. Access also is possible via the Skuhun Creek Road, which departs Highway 8 about 23 kilometers (14 miles) east of Spences Bridge, or by a very bad 4x4 trail south from the Calling Lake Road in the Highland Valley. The Pimainus chain includes three small lakes at an elevation of 1,500 meters (4,921 feet) containing wild populations of small Kamloops trout in large numbers. A fishing camp offers cabins, camping and boats.

• *Northeast of Merritt* (**MAP, page 134**): Highway 5A, the old Merritt-Kamloops route, heads northeast to the little community of Nicola at the western edge of Nicola Lake. There a road branches off along the north shore of Nicola Lake to Monck Provincial Park. Beyond the park the Mab Lake Road climbs steeply into the hills, finally providing difficult 4x4 access to **Bob Lake** at an elevation of about 1,495 meters (4,905 feet). The lake has a surface area of about 25 hectares (62 acres) and has produced trout to 6 pounds or better, although it is subject to occasional winter kill.

Beyond the turnoff to Monck Provincial Park, Highway 5A skirts the southern and eastern shore of Nicola Lake on its way to the historic community of Quilchena. Just past Quilchena a good gravel road, easily traveled by cars, leaves the highway and winds southeast into rolling grasslands about 19 kilometers (12 miles) to **Minnie Lake**. Access to the lake is through a gate controlled by the Douglas Lake Ranch and fishing is available for a daily fee.

Minnie is a shallow, rich, weedy lake at an elevation of about 1,100 meters (3,610 feet) covering an area of about 121 hectares (299 acres). It lies between open, grassy slopes with little protection from strong winds that frequently sweep the area. What makes anglers willing to battle the wind and pay for the privilege is Minnie Lake's ability to grow large trout—up to 13 pounds.

Just a kilometer down the road lies **Stoney Lake**, about half the size of Minnie. Stoney also is mostly shallow, although it has spots where the depth is more than 12 meters (40 feet) and provides some areas of shelter from the prevailing wind. Fishing in Stoney also is managed on a daily fee basis through the Douglas Lake Ranch.

Both lakes are natural bodies of water whose levels

Peter McVey, fly fisher, gourmet chef, bamboo rod builder, energetic entrepreneur and black-belt conversationalist, holds forth behind the bar in the dining room at Corbett Lake Country Inn.

were raised to provide storage for irrigation. Before the mid-1970s Minnie provided good fishing from time to time but winter-killed with disconcerting frequency, while Stoney remained barren because trout could not survive winters there. Then Peter McVey, now proprietor of Corbett Lake Country Inn, tried to establish a fishing camp on both lakes and diverted a stream into Stoney Lake in hopes it would provide sufficient circulation to prevent winter kill. The plan worked; trout survived the first winter after the stream began flowing into the lake and grew rapidly on the abundant natural feed. But when McVey abandoned the fishing camp idea there was no one to look after the stream; beavers soon blocked its flow and the following winter all the fish in Stoney Lake died.

Never one to give up easily, McVey later returned to try again. He stocked both lakes with trout raised at a private hatchery and opened them to daily fee fishing in a cooperative venture with the Douglas Lake Ranch. At first the ranch operators took little notice of the venture, but it wasn't long before Minnie and Stoney began producing trophy-sized trout and more and more anglers started paying for the chance to catch them. Suddenly recognizing a new revenue opportunity, the ranch took over management of the lakes from McVey in 1989.

Minnie and Stoney are noted for spectacular early-season chironomid emergences and both lakes have a full larder of other aquatic life, lacking only a hatch of large sedges (although small sedges are abundant). Both lakes bloom very heavily during the summer months and the best fishing usually is from late May through early July and again from mid-September through mid-October. Careful water management

by the ranch appears to have solved the problem of seasonal kills, at least temporarily.

Since the lakes are under its private management, the ranch sets its own regulations: Fly-fishing only, no internal-combustion motors (although electric motors may be used) and a one-fish daily limit. For those able to afford the daily fee (currently $100 a day, Canadian funds), Minnie and Stoney Lakes offer the chance for some truly spectacular angling. My last visit to Stoney yielded trout as large as 8 1/2 pounds and in three hours on Minnie Lake I landed 10 trout over 5 pounds before being chased off by a wind clocked at 98 kilometers (60 miles) an hour—a fairly typical day on Minnie.

Accommodations for anglers are now available at the Minnie Lake ranch house, not far from the lake, with bookings through the Douglas Lake Ranch.

Returning to Highway 5A, about 5 kilometers (3 miles) north of Quilchena the Douglas Lake Road leaves the highway and heads east; a striking church built of logs marks the intersection. The road is good, easily traversed by cars. About 6.5 kilometers (4 miles) from the highway is a large B.C. Hydro transformer yard and just beyond it a good gravel road, also suitable for cars, leads 12 kilometers (7.3 miles) north to **Glimpse Lake**.

Glimpse, at an elevation of about 1,210 meters (3,970 feet) with an area of 95 hectares (235 acres), offers an interesting variety of water with extensive shoals and weedbeds. A fishing camp that used to operate at the north end of the lake is now closed and a large colony of private homes and cabins has grown up along the southeastern shore. Two public campgrounds and an Indian camp also are located on the lake, so it receives heavy fishing pressure; nevertheless, Glimpse remains popular with fly fishers and offers interesting angling during the spring chironomid emergence and later during the sedge hatch. Trout to 3 1/2 pounds have been reported in recent years, but the average size is much smaller.

North of Glimpse Lake a rough road leads 1.5 kilometers (1 mile) to **Blue Lake**, also accessible via logging road from Peterhope Lake to the northwest. Either way, a truck is necessary and a 4x4 may be needed in wet weather. The lake is surrounded by heavy timber at an elevation of 1,075 meters

(3,527 feet) and covers an area of 12 hectares (30 acres). Nearly circular in shape, it has shoals around the shoreline that slope out of sight into a deep hole in the center of the lake. The water is extremely clear and trout are very cautious and wary when they enter the shallows.

The trout are large—fish of 7 1/2 pounds are not uncommon—and the fishing is not easy, although it is usually best during the sedge hatch. Sometimes, when conditions are right, it is possible to see and stalk individual fish, cast a dry fly in their path and watch them come up and take it—an extraordinarily thrilling sight when the fish is a large one. But a careful approach is necessary and the trout do not allow the angler to make even a single mistake.

Current regulations permit artificial flies with single barbless hooks only and a daily limit of two fish—if you can catch that many. Stocking is limited to assure the average size of fish remains large. Rough camping is available, but space is limited.

The Douglas Lake Road continues beyond the B.C. Hydro transformer yard through the Douglas Lake community, headquarters for the giant 230,000-hectare (568,000-acre) ranch, and eventually reaches **Salmon Lake**, about 48 kilometers (30 miles) east of Highway 5A. The lake also is accessible by road from Westwold, a distance of about 32 kilometers

Corbett Lake in the fall, looking north from the lodge.

(20 miles). Either route is easily traversable by car.

Salmon Lake lies at an elevation of 936 meters (3,070 feet) with a surface area of 123 hectares (304 acres). While it has a maximum depth of 12 meters (39 feet), it is mostly shallow with a silty bottom and extensive weedbeds, especially at its west end where the best fly fishing is found. Trout run to 4 1/2 pounds, although most are smaller. Current regulations limit anglers to artificial flies with single barbless hooks only.

A resort at the east end of the lake offers housekeeping cabins and campsites. Now operated by the Douglas Lake Ranch and managed by Dan and Trish Geary, the resort has new cabins equipped with fireplaces and electric heat, a cen-

tral washroom with showers and a laundry. A liquor license held by the former owners has been relinquished and 10 p.m. "quiet hours" established to make the resort more pleasant for families.

While Salmon Lake itself remains open to the public and may be fished by anyone willing to pay a daily boat-launching charge, the resort also serves as headquarters for the ranch's daily fee fisheries. In addition to Minnie and Stoney Lakes, already described, these include **Sabin Lakes**, **Pikes Lake**, **Little Chapperon Lake** and **Harry's Dam**, all artificial impoundments. Dan Geary is responsible for overall management of these waters, but the ranch also employs a consulting

biologist, Vic Lewinsky.

Big and Little Sabin Lakes are near the airstrip at the ranch headquarters. Big Sabin covers about 34 hectares (85 acres) while Little Sabin and nearby Pikes Lake both are about half that size. All three provide anglers the chance to catch large numbers of trout in the 2- to 4-pound class. Harry's Dam is a 15-acre pond which is kept purposely overstocked to provide fast fishing for children. Daily fees on these lakes currently range from $35 to $75 in Canadian funds (the fees are pegged to the quality of fishing available).

Little Chapperon Lake has a squawfish population that requires periodic netting to keep under control. In 1992 the lake was stocked with 3,000 steelhead fry in hopes they would grow up to prey on smaller squawfish. Steelhead were chosen because the ranch's fisheries managers believed they would be more aggressive predators than Kamloops trout and because they had a lower mortality rate than Gerrard-strain Kamloops displayed in earlier stocking experiments.

Except for the steelhead, brood stock for all these lakes has come from Minnie Lake, descendants of the trout originally planted there by Peter McVey. Ripe fish were trapped in the lake's inlet stream and older, larger fish selected for spawning. These were stripped of eggs and milt and the fertilized eggs taken to a private hatchery for hatching and rearing. However,

Sunset over Willard Lake near Ashcroft.

the ranch also hopes to begin using stock from Campbell Lake near Little Fort and perhaps develop a brood stock from the steelhead planted in Little Chapperon when they mature.

When the Douglas Lake Ranch first took control of Minnie and Stoney Lakes, 85 percent of the visiting anglers were Americans; now it's about a 50-50 split between Americans and Canadians, with a few Asian and European visitors as well. Geary attributes the success of the private fisheries program to the quality of angling available. "If they (visiting anglers) go to a place like Big Sabin and catch 30 2-to-4-pound trout in a day for $50, that's probably the best day of fishing they ever had," he says. "So they come back, rather than go to a public lake where they have a good chance of getting skunked."

The Douglas Lake Ranch expects to open three more fish-for-fee lakes in the next few years and more will be added later, "depending on the financial viability of the enterprise."

Highway 5A continues north beyond Nicola Lake for about 10 kilometers (6 miles) to a gravel road, adequate for cars, that leads east 8 kilometers (5 miles) to **Peterhope Lake**. This famous lake is at an elevation of 1,113 meters (3,650 feet) with a surface area of 116 hectares (287 acres). It is oval-shaped, about a mile and a quarter long, with clear water and a rich marl bottom. Wide shoal areas reach out from the shorelines and a couple of "sunken islands" provide ideal water for fly fishers.

While its maximum depth is a surprising 33 meters (108 feet), more than half the lake is less than 9 meters (30 feet) deep. All the usual orders of aquatic life are present, though the once-abundant sedge hatch has declined over the years.

Peterhope once yielded trout of 8 to 16 pounds, many on dry flies, although the size of the fish varied greatly from year to year due to uncertain spawning survival during periods of low water. In some years this meant little or no increase in the lake's trout population, reducing competition and resulting in rapid growth of trout already in the lake.

During the late 1970s and 1980s, fishing in Peterhope was spotty at best, with most trout running on the small side, and word got around that the lake was "fished out." Then came a succession of low-water years when the inlet dried up altogether and several whole year classes of fry were lost. These culminated in the long, hot summer of 1992, when the water level dropped so low that thoughtless vandals began driving 4x4 rigs on the dried-up shoals. The Fisheries Branch, which had relied on natural spawning to keep the lake stocked, was forced to begin planting fish again.

These problems kept many anglers away from Peterhope, but as before they also sharply reduced competition among trout already in the lake and allowed survivors to grow to huge size. Fishing wasn't fast, and few anglers knew about it, but those who persevered experienced fishing of a quality to match that of the old days, with trout as large as 12 pounds taken in the fall of 1992 and spring of 1993.

Peterhope Lake Fishing Camp on the northwest shore of the lake has housekeeping cabins and boats and there is a large government campground on the northern shore. A number of private cabins also have been built along the eastern edge of the lake.

Beyond the Peterhope turnoff, Highway 5A skirts the western shore of **Stump Lake**, a sprawling lake more than five miles long at an elevation of 750 meters (2,460 feet). For many years, after it was poisoned to remove scrap fish, Stump Lake was famous as a producer of king-sized trout, some over 151/2 pounds. It is a rich, shallow, weedy lake, with clear water and several small islands, some of which become shoals when the water is high. Broad shallow areas at both the north and south ends of the lake are especially attractive to fly fishers.

All the usual aquatic fauna are present in abundance, along with an unusually large snail population. Kokanee also were planted in the lake early in the 1980s and grew to weights of 4 to 6 pounds. However, as related earlier, prolonged drought beginning in the mid-'80s caused lower water levels in Stump

Bill Roddy, who built Chataway Lakes Lodge mostly with his own hands.

Lake and increased its pH to 9.2 or above, resulting in severe mortality to both Kamloops trout and kokanee. There are still some of both species in the lake, including some very large trout, but the fishing—never fast even when the lake was at its best—is very slow and difficult. Chances may be best in early spring, especially during the damselfly emergence, or late in the fall; due to its relatively low elevation, the lake's water becomes quite warm during the summer.

At the north end of Stump Lake a road leads off Highway 5A through the Stump Lake Ranch, offering access to **Plateau Lake**, a distance of about 10 kilometers (6 miles). The road is narrow and rocky and may be difficult in wet weather; a truck is recommended. However, the trip is worth it, because Plateau is a fly fisher's dream. A long, narrow lake at an elevation of 1,210 meters (3,970 feet), it has a surface area of 17 hectares (42 acres). A deep trench runs lengthwise through the middle of the lake with broad, shallow shoals spreading from either side all the way to the shoreline. The bottom is a rich golden marl and the lake is fed by springs which may be seen boiling up through the marl in the shallows at the north end. The lake has a good population of the usual orders of aquatic fauna, including a good sedge hatch. Spring evenings offer exciting dry-fly fishing when large trout prowl the shallows to feed on hatching sedges.

In the past Plateau was subject to occasional winter kill, which made it an uncertain prospect from one season to the next. At its best, after several years without kill, it produced trout up to 10 1/2 pounds, although fish of this size were quite rare. At the time of this writing it had survived several years without winter kills and large fish again were available.

There is a pleasant campsite and boat-launching area on the western shore of the lake where the road comes in. Plateau also is accessible by a rough road from Peterhope Lake.

Kamloops Area

As the principal city of the Interior, Kamloops is the hub of a vast road network. The main north-south route is Highway 5, providing a link with Merritt to the south and via the North Thompson River to Little Fort and Clearwater to the north. The Trans-Canada Highway (Highways 1 and 97) is the primary east-west route, reaching westward to Savona and Cache Creek and east to Monte Creek and Salmon Arm. The old Lac le Jeune Road, which now parallels Highway 5, also runs south from Kamloops, as does old Highway 5A, once the main connection to Merritt. Scores of lakes are accessible from these and numerous secondary roads.

Near the end of the day's fishing on Glimpse Lake.

Unfortunately the fast-growing population of Kamloops and steady improvements to both main and secondary roads have combined to change the character of many lakes close to the city. Visited by ever-growing numbers of anglers and other recreationists, these waters not only have lost their pristine qualities but in some cases have become ringed by subdivisions. Nevertheless, some still provide surprisingly good angling opportunities.

Plateau Lake.

maximum depth of 26 meters (84 feet). Easily explored in a day of fishing, it is fed by a small, seasonal stream, probably without sufficient flow to support a run of spawning fish in most years. Heavy angling pressure makes stocking a necessity in any case.

McConnell has fairly abundant populations of the usual orders of insect life and gammarids, but is not particularly well suited for fly fishing. Except for a shoal area along the eastern shore, the lake floor shelves off rapidly into deep water. The water level fluctuates from one year to the next and low-water years probably offer the best fly-fishing opportunities. There is a small provincial camping area on the lake with a daily fee of $6 that entitles you to firewood and garbage pickup.

About 3.2 kilometers (2 miles) farther south the road skirts the western shore of **Stake Lake**, a shallow lake perfectly suited for fly fishing. The lake is at an elevation of 1,380 meters (4,528 feet) with a surface area of 23 hectares (57 acres) and maximum depth of 9 meters (30 feet). Although its aquatic fauna have been grazed down by repeated stocking of trout, Stake still has a decent sedge hatch and is a good place to fish when the hatch is on. The best fly water is on the west side, near the highway, where the lake bottom slopes gently to a depth of 3 to 5 meters (10 to 15 feet). When the light is good and the wind is down, it is sometimes possible to see and cast to individual cruising fish.

Decades ago, after it was first stocked, the lake produced trout averaging 8 pounds, but as with so many other waters the size of its fish declined rapidly as surplus food stocks were consumed. With no natural spawning, periodic stocking is necessary to maintain its trout population. The Fisheries Branch also has installed an aeration device to prevent winter kill.

Stake Lake now produces trout up to 2 pounds with occasional larger fish. It receives tremendous pressure because of easy access and usually there are plenty of bait fishermen and trollers competing for space on the water. The Highway 5 extension from Merritt to Kamloops runs within view of the lake and noise from the constant flow of traffic is a distraction. What used to be a small camping area at the lake has been changed to a picnic area with day-use only permitted.

Beyond Stake Lake a fork in the road heads east about 1.6 kilometers (1 mile) to **Lac le Jeune**. The lake is at an elevation of 1,275 meters (4,183 feet) and covers an area of 155 hectares

• *Southwest of Kamloops* (south of the Trans-Canada Highway and west of Highway 5A, the old Merritt-Kamloops route)(**MAP, page 135**): The Lac le Jeune Road leaves the Trans-Canada Highway just west of Kamloops and climbs southward into the hills. The first time I traveled it, shortly after World War II, it was merely a pair of ruts with grass growing high in the center and the journey to Lac le Jeune seemed arduous and endless. Now it is a highway and the trip to Lac le Jeune, which once required hours, takes only minutes.

The first lake accessible from this road is **Jacko**, only a few minutes' travel from downtown Kamloops. A dirt road heads east about 1.6 kilometers (1 mile) off the blacktop, climbing over a low ridge to the lake. Late on spring afternoons, when the shops close in Kamloops, there is often a small parade of vehicles over this road as anglers head out to catch the evening rise.

Jacko has a surface area of about 40 hectares (99 acres) and lies at an elevation of about 880 meters (2,887 feet), so it warms quickly in the summer; early spring and late fall are the best times to fish it. Located in open country, the lake is rimmed with tules and has a gently sloping shoreline; the bottom is mostly a soft, black ooze of decaying organic material. There is limited natural spawning but the trout population in the lake is augmented by regular stocking.

Jacko has produced large fish in the past and trout up to 4 1/2 pounds are still caught occasionally. It is a pleasant lake to fish with a fly and trout sometimes cruise the edges of the tule beds in the evenings, where a well-placed nymph will take them. Access is controlled by the Kamloops and District Fish & Game Club, which prohibits overnight camping at the lake.

Farther south, a total distance of about 26 kilometers (16 miles) from Kamloops, **McConnell Lake** lies just off the west side of the Lac le Jeune Road. An attractive lake surrounded by thick timber at an elevation of 1,275 meters (4,183 feet), McConnell has a surface area of 30 hectares (74 acres) and

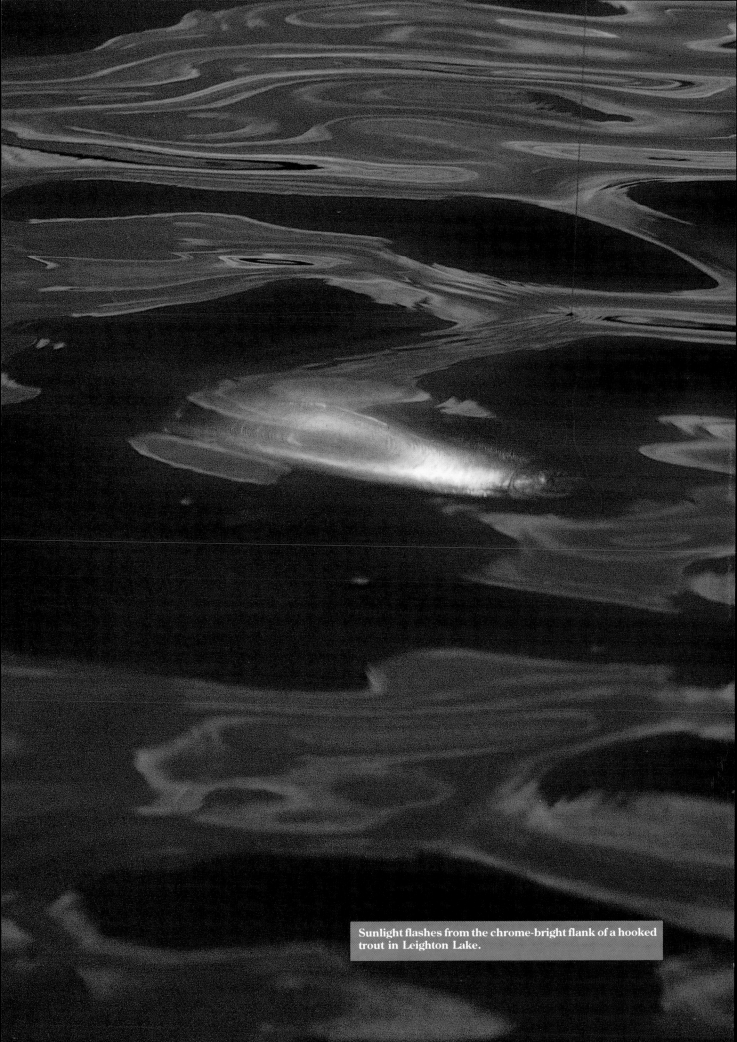

Sunlight flashes from the chrome-bright flank of a hooked trout in Leighton Lake.

(383 acres). Needless to say, it is no longer the pristine lake where Indians fished and Lambert reported daily catches of hundreds of trout at the turn of the century. Now it has two elaborate resorts with conference centers, restaurants, exercise rooms, hot tubs and saunas, plus a huge provincial park and many private homes and cabins on its shores. On summer weekends its population probably outnumbers that of many small towns in the Interior. Yet many of the visitors are non-anglers, so the fishing can still be surprisingly good at times, especially during the sedge hatch in late June and early July. Fish to 3 pounds may be expected.

From the north end of Lac le Jeune a rough dirt road, suitable for 4x4 trucks only, heads east about 5 kilometers (3 miles) to **Ross Moore** Lake, also accessible by a better road from Knutsford on Highway 5A. The lake is at an elevation of 1,240 meters (4,068 feet) with a surface area of 50 hectares (124 acres). It has a silty bottom and brushy shoreline and is not particularly well suited for fly fishing, but does produce trout up to 4 1/2 pounds. A rough spur road, negotiable by 4x4, leads to nearby **Fred Lake**, which lies at the same elevation and covers a surface area of 7 hectares (17 acres). It produces trout of similar size.

The southern (right-hand) fork in the Lac le Jeune Road continues south about 3.2 kilometers (2 miles) to a connection with the Logan Lake exit from Highway 5 just west of **Walloper Lake**. Walloper is at an elevation of 1,255 meters (4,117 feet) with a surface area of 35 hectares (86 acres). It has a silty bottom with a maximum depth of only 7.6 meters (25 feet) and a mean depth of only 2.75 meters (9 feet).

With abundant populations of scuds and leeches, Walloper can provide excellent fly-fishing at times, but is subject to heavy blue-green algae blooms during the summer months. The lake also has suffered frequent winter kills, but the Fisheries Branch has installed an electrically driven aerator to alleviate that problem. In past years, after remaining free of winter kill for several seasons, Walloper has produced trout as heavy as 4 pounds, but now is full of little wild trout from 6 to 12 inches and makes an excellent family-fishing lake. A resort on the lake's east end offers cabins, boats and campsites. What used to be a provincial campground on the western shore has been changed to a picnic area with day-use only permitted.

South of its junction with Highway 5, the Lac le Jeune Road swings west on its extension to the town of Logan Lake. About 6.5 kilometers (4 miles) west of the junction a gravel road heads south off the pavement and offers access to **Surrey, Sussex** and **Frogmoore Lakes**. A map posted on a sign near the road entrance shows the routes.

The distance to Surrey is 10 kilometers (6 miles) and a car is adequate; Sussex lies 2 kilometers (1.2 miles) farther and a 4x4 is needed for the last stretch. Both lakes are at elevations of about 1,395 meters (4,577 feet); Surrey is the larger of the two with a surface area of 55 hectares (136 acres), while Sussex covers 25 hectares (62 acres). A fishing camp on Surrey Lake offers housekeeping cabins and central showers; there is a provincial campsite on Sussex. Both lakes offer consistent fishing for trout in the 12- to 14-inch class.

Frogmoore Lakes, a pair of lakes at an elevation of about 1,448 meters (4,750 feet), are about 3.2 kilometers (2 miles) east of Surrey Lake on a very rough 4x4 road. Together these lakes have a total surface area of about 80 hectares (198 acres) and offer fast fishing for smaller trout. Rough camping is available. An old fishing camp on these lakes has ceased operating but is now owned by Lac le Jeune Resort, which may develop it for future use.

About 1.6 kilometers (1 mile) west of the road to Surrey and Sussex a good gravel road departs the Lac le Jeune Road and heads north. This is the Paska Lake Road, suitable for cars, which leads to **Face** and **Paska Lakes**, a distance of 12 kilometers (7.2 miles). Paska, southernmost of the two, is at an elevation of 1,440 meters (4,724 feet) and has a surface area of 50 hectares (124 acres). It is connected by a stream with Face Lake, which lies about 1 kilometer to the north at about the same elevation. Shaped like a giant slingshot with its prongs pointed north, Face has a surface area of about 60 hectares (148 acres). Both lakes have abundant chironomid and gammarid populations and decent sedge hatches and produce trout to 3 pounds, although most are smaller. The fish in these lakes also have harmless external parasites that resemble the sea lice found on anadromous steelhead and salmon.

Both lakes have B.C. Forest Service campgrounds, Paska has many private homes, and Face Lake has a fishing resort. The latter, originally built in 1940 by "Corny" Cornwall, has changed hands several times. Now it has modern cabins and facilities and a lodge with dining room.

Nearby **Wyse Lake** is a small, shallow lake at an elevation of about 1,495 meters (4,905 feet). On occasion it has produced trout up to 5 pounds but is very prone to winter kill.

Just beyond its intersection with the Lac le Jeune Road west of Kamloops, the Trans-Canada Highway meets Highway 5 in a major interchange. Another 8 kilometers (5 miles) west of the interchange, the Greenstone Mountain Road leaves the south side of the Trans-Canada Highway and climbs steeply for a distance of 3 kilometers (1.8 miles) before it forks. The western (right-hand) fork leads about 13 kilometers (8 miles) to **Duffy Lake**, a clear-water lake at an elevation of 1,150 meters (3,773 feet) with an area of 24 hectares (59 acres). The road is steep but a car should be adequate.

Deep in the middle with extensive shoal areas around the shoreline, Duffy Lake is a rather enigmatic water capable of producing trout up to 3 1/2 pounds when it "turns on." Camping is available at a B.C. Forest Service recreation site at the lake.

The eastern (left-hand) fork of the Greenstone Mountain Road winds steeply uphill to **Dominic Lake**, a distance of about 24 kilometers (15 miles) from the forks, traversable by car. A spur road leads to the **Dairy Lakes**, about the same distance from the forks, but a truck may be necessary for the final 3 kilometers (1.8 miles)

Dominic, a 35-hectare (86-acre) lake at an elevation of 1,515 meters (4,970 feet), also is accessible from the south via the Paska Lake Road. A fishing camp on the lake offers housekeeping cabins with wood stoves and a shower house. Campsites also are available and there are a number of private summer homes and cabins on the lake. Trout are plentiful but not large—16 inches usually is about tops—and the fishing holds up well through the summer due to the high elevation.

Dairy Lake has a surface area of 25 hectares (62 acres) and is at an elevation of about 1,380 meters (4,528 feet). It suffers periodic winterkill and summer irrigation drawdown, but when these conditions are absent for several years running, Dairy can provide excellent fishing for large trout. Camping is available at a B.C. Forest Service recreation site at the lake.

Three other small lakes lie to the east and south. The largest is less than half the size of Dairy Lake. Fishing varies depending on conditions, but can be good at times.

Leaving the Greenstone Mountain Road behind, the Trans-Canada Highway continues west, paralleling the south shore of Kamloops Lake, until it reaches Savona, a sleepy little town at the western end of the lake. Just east of town a good road, easily traveled by cars, heads off the pavement to the south and climbs slowly about 26 kilometers (16 miles) to **Leighton** and **Tunkwa Lakes**, a pair of natural lakes enlarged to provide water for irrigation. They are at an elevation of about 1,130 meters (3,707 feet) in rolling country, surrounded by meadows and thick stands of pine. Tunkwa, the larger of the two, has a surface area of 295 hectares (729 acres); Leighton is 50 hectares (124 acres).

Surely these two are among the richest of the Interior lakes. All common aquatic fauna are present in abundance, and partly because of this abundance the trout in these two lakes—especially Tunkwa—often are very hard to catch; natural insects are so numerous that imitations face stiff competition. Yet this same abundance also produces some very large trout.

Tunkwa Lake has an irregular shoreline with many small peninsulas and bays and broad shallow reaches around its north and south ends. It is fed by several small streams entering from the south, one used by the Fish and Wildlife Branch as an egg-taking station. Tunkwa Lake Fishing Camp, on the east side of the lake, has both cabins and campsites. There is also a very large provincial campground and several private cabins on the lake. The easy access to this lake has led to mob scenes on holiday weekends, but at other times it can be a quiet, pleasant place to fish. However, there is little shelter from the wind, and Tunkwa can become very rough at times.

Tunkwa produces an incredible hatch of chironomids in late May. The insects are so thick they become an irritant, flying into the eyes, ears and sometimes mouths of anglers. Emerging pupae are so numerous it is an easy task for a trout to cruise along beneath the surface with its mouth open, capturing dozens with little effort. At such times the odds against angling success are great, but persistence with a good imitation can pay dividends.

The outlet of Tunkwa Lake at its north end is controlled by an irrigation lock and a short but spectacular waterfall plunges from the lock into Leighton Lake. In the spring it is common to see ripe trout trying vainly to ascend the falls, sometimes stranding themselves on the rocks. Leighton also has several shallow bays and flats and there are two small islands along its eastern shore when the water is high in the spring. There is a campground on its eastern shore and a few private cabins, but no other facilities. Its smaller size makes it easier to cover than Tunkwa and it is somewhat more protected from the wind. Both lakes have silty bottoms and thick growths of aquatic vegetation.

Leighton also has a heavy early hatch of chironomids and an excellent hatch of damselflies in early June. A good damselfly nymph imitation works wonders then. Both Leighton and Tunkwa are drawn down for irrigation during the summer so the water level always is low in the fall. A bloodworm imitation fished over the weedbeds in shallow water produces very well in late September and early October.

The trout in these two lakes average anywhere from 1 to 4 pounds, with occasional fish as large as 7 pounds. Tunkwa fish, on average, are a little larger than those in Leighton. Unfortunately, excessive irrigation withdrawals sometimes cause one or both lakes to suffer summer or winter kills.

• *Southeast of Kamloops* (south of the Trans-Canada Highway and east of Highway 5A, the old Merritt-Kamloops route) **(MAP, page 136)**: About 37 kilometers (23 miles) south of Kamloops on old Highway 5A, a good road, easily negotiated by cars, leaves the highway in an easterly direction and proceeds 11 kilometers (7 miles) to **Roche Lake** at an elevation of 1,120 meters (3,675 feet). Roche, about 2 1/2 miles long and no more than a quarter of a mile wide, has a total surface area of about 130 hectares (321 acres) and lies in rolling, timbered country. Poisoned to remove scrap fish in the late 1960s, it was stocked with Kamloops trout and immediately became popular with Kamloops-area fly fishers.

One of its chief attractions is a fine sedge hatch, usually beginning about mid-June and continuing at least through the first week in July. The lake also produces abundant chironomid and damselfly hatches and has good populations of scuds and leeches. Trout reach an average weight of about 2 pounds, but fish twice that size are not unusual.

Roche has a marl bottom, extensive shoal areas, large underwater weedbeds and four rocky islands. As with so many lakes in the area, it is used as a source of water for irrigation and a lock on the outlet stream controls the water level. Usually this means high water in the spring, while the lock is kept closed to store water for later use. If the water is high enough, trout move into the long, shallow bay at the extreme south end of the lake, offering some very interesting fishing. The water in this bay is never more than about 1.2 meters (4 feet) deep and large trout often are clearly visible over the marl bottom. They cruise around and over a dense mat of weed that grows in the center of the bay; sedges hatch here in large numbers, and the dry-fly fishing sometimes is first rate. When the hatch is off, a scud imitation fished on a sink-tip line also can be very effective, but a very cautious approach is necessary because the fish are wary in the shallow water.

The fishing in this area is not always dependable; if the water is too low, as it often is in dry years, trout simply will not enter the bay. More dependable fishing can be found around the edge of the wide shoal at the mouth of the bay and the island just north of it. Sedges also hatch abundantly in this area and it provides consistent dry-fly action. An "electric motors only" zone keeps outboards out of this part of the lake. A wide shoal area around the long, narrow island at the northeast end of the lake also is a reliable spot for fly fishers, especially in the evening.

Construction of an elaborate resort at the north end of the lake—complete with "log chalets," conference center, swimming pool, hot tub, restaurant and lounge—has done much to spoil the esthetic qualities of the lake. Two B.C. Forest Service recreation sites also are located on the lake, and the combination of easy access, campgrounds and a resort has stimulated fishing pressure to as much as 25,000 angler days a year. Since the lake is closed to fishing from December 1 through April 30, all the pressure is concentrated during the seven-month open season, which works out to an average of 117 anglers a day—or little more than 1 hectare of water per angler. When things get that crowded, the fishing often becomes unpleasant. Nevertheless, Roche Lake remains a favorite with fly fishers patient enough to endure the crowds.

Southeast of Roche Lake lie four other lakes accessible by rough roads that require a 4x4. These include **Bulman, Ernest, Frisken** and **John Frank Lakes.**

John Frank Lake is closest to Roche; in fact, a stream connects the two. John Frank is at the same elevation as Roche and covers an area of about 20 hectares (49 acres). It is a shallow lake and winter kills with distressing frequency. However, it is heavily populated with scuds so trout grow rapidly when reintroduced after a kill, and the lake can provide exciting fishing at times. Unfortunately, its trout seldom have more than a couple of years to grow before they are wiped out by another winter kill.

Frisken Lake is located just southwest of John Frank, also at an elevation of 1,130 meters (3,707 feet) with a surface area of 29 hectares (72 acres). It too is subject to periodic winter kill, although perhaps not so often as its companion, and provides a similar fishery. Rough camping is available at the lake.

Bulman Lake lies southeast of Frisken at an elevation of 1,150 meters (3,773 feet) and is the same size as Frisken. Less susceptible to winter kill, it routinely produces trout to 4 1/2 pounds.

Ernest is the easternmost of this cluster of lakes, and perhaps the hardest to reach. A 4x4 is definitely necessary. The lake is at the same elevation as Bulman with a surface area of 25 hectares (62 acres). The fishery is similar to Bulman.

All four of these lakes are now managed under barbless-hook regulations with no bait permitted. There is a two-fish daily limit on Frisken and Ernest Lakes, and Ernest also is restricted to artificial flies only.

From the Trans-Canada Highway about 10 kilometers (6.2 miles) east of Kamloops, a branch road follows Juniper Creek southeast past the community of Barnhart Vale. From there a good secondary road, suitable for cars, runs south about 11 kilometers (7 miles) to **Campbell Lake**, which lies in open country at an elevation of 1,065 meters (3,494 feet) and covers an area of 90 hectares (222 acres). A rich, shallow lake with abundant life, Campbell is subject to heavy algae blooms during the summer months and is best fished early or late in the season. It can be a difficult lake to fish, offering little protection from strong winds. The lake is on private property and overnight camping is by permission of the owner.

Over the past decade Campbell has produced trout as large as 10 pounds, although fish of 2 to 5 pounds have been more common. Unfortunately, the lake suffered a kill during the long hot summer of 1992 and is not expected to be back in full production until at least 1994.

From Campbell and nearby **Scuitto Lake** a rough 4x4 road leads south to **Hosli Lake**, also accessible from the south off the Roche Lake road (although a 4x4 is required for this route, too). Situated at an elevation of 1,180 meters (3,871 feet), Hosli has a surface area of 20 hectares (49 acres) and contains trout to 4 1/2 pounds. Rough camping is available at the lake.

• *Northwest of Kamloops* (north of the Trans-Canada Highway and west of Highway 5 up the North Thompson River) (MAP, page 137): From North Kamloops on the west bank of the North Thompson a spur of the Lac du Bois Road reaches about 20 kilometers (12.5 miles) to **Pass Lake**. The road is adequate for cars in dry weather but can become nasty when wet. Pass is a productive lake at an elevation of 955 meters (3,133 feet) with a surface area of 30 hectares (74 acres). It yields some large trout to patient anglers, with fish of 6 pounds not unusual.

Because of its low elevation, Pass is best fished early and late in the season. It has a good early-season chironomid emergence and is a favorite of fly fishers skilled in presenting chironomid pupae imitations. Current regulations call for artificial flies with single barbless hooks and a daily limit of one fish over 20 inches. Angling effort on the lake has dropped since those regulations were imposed.

Like Island Lake in the Highland Valley, Pass has been stocked with sterilized female trout in an experimental effort to eliminate the problem of early sexual maturation. There is a small campground at the lake, but no developed facilities.

About 51 kilometers (32 miles) northwest of Kamloops and 8 kilometers (5 miles) beyond Savona, the Trans-Canada Highway crosses Deadman Creek where it flows out of the hills to join the Thompson River. A good gravel road, easily traveled by car, leaves the highway to parallel the stream through its spectacular narrow valley, rimmed with colored bluffs and "hoodoos"—strangely shaped sandstone formations. About 19 kilometers (12 miles) north of the highway is the headquarters of the Circle W Ranch, with access to **Hihium**

Lake. Truck service from the ranch carries anglers up a steep and slippery road to the lake at an elevation of 1,360 meters (4,462 feet). The lake, with a surface area of 350 hectares (865 acres), is about 6.5 kilometers (4 miles) long.

From the time I first fished it as a small boy, this lake has been one of my favorites. Its trout never have been of trophy size, but always there have been

Cabins in the pines on Owl Point, Hihium Lake.

lots of them up to 3 pounds and they come eagerly across the rocky shoals to take a fly. Hihium is one of few mountain lakes ever to have a natural population of Kamloops trout, with the fish apparently having gained access originally from the Bonaparte River via Loon Creek, Loon Lake and Hihium Creek, which flows from Hihium Lake to Loon Lake. Spawning in Hihium Creek and several small tributaries that flow into the lake, these fish maintained a natural population of wild, strong Kamloops trout until the mid-1970s, when intense angling pressure coupled with several poor spawning seasons finally made it necessary to augment the wild population with stocking.

Hihium has a maximum depth of about 18 meters (60 feet), although most of it is much shallower. It has a silty bottom with heavy aquatic vegetation and many rocky shoals, some so close to the surface that tules sprout from them. Weedbeds harbor a teeming population of scuds and late June and early July bring a sporadic but sometimes excellent sedge hatch. The phantom midge, *Chaoborus,* also is present and is taken by trout in great numbers, as are chironomids during the spring hatches. Good damselfly and dragonfly emergences occur in spring and early fall often brings flying ants. Altogether, a fly fisher at Hihium has a wealth of creatures to imitate.

The lake has several long points, some with gravel bars extending far out toward deep water, and there are a number of shallow, sheltered bays. Heavy algae blooms in July and August sometimes put a damper on the fishing, but there are nearly always some trout to be found.

The Circle W maintains remote housekeeping cabins around the lake, reached by boat from the roadhead. The lake lies on an east-west axis and sometimes is swept by strong and dangerous winds. An outboard motor is essential here, both for safety and to save time moving between distant fishing spots.

The Circle W has had three sets of owners since it was founded by Bud Walters. Bill and Bea Comeaux were the owners on my first boyhood visit when we climbed the mountainside in an old British Army ambulance. For many years afterward the ranch was operated by Pat and Harriet Kirkpatrick of Mercer Island until Harriet's untimely death. Now it is owned and operated by the Bendzak family from Seattle.

Another resort, Hihium Lake Fishing Camp, is located at the west end of the lake, accessible via Loon Lake, and a third camp has been built at the terminus of a marginal road that follows a natural gas pipeline from the Deadman Creek Valley to a point near the lake. A number of private cabins also have been built around the lake over the past couple of decades.

I have fished this lake as early as the third week of May, when there was four inches of snow on the ground and the creeks were filled with spawning trout, and sometimes as late as the third week of September when I was the last angler to leave before the cabins were closed for the winter. Of all the times I have fished there, early September is my favorite. The nights are crisp and clear then, the mornings calm and frosty, the trout strong and eager and willing to enter the shallows to feed. A scud imitation fished over the shoals can work wonders then.

Throughout the 1970s and '80s the fishing experienced a slow but steady decline, but new barbless-hook, no-bait regulations appear to have done much to restore it. The bait ban appears to have discouraged many trollers who formerly fished the lake, and boat traffic on Hihium was reported down by as much as two-thirds during the 1992 season. Anglers also reported spectacular fishing at times, and creel census figures showed a preponderance of fish in the 16- to 20-inch class, with a few as large as 8 pounds—very big fish for Hihium Lake.

Beyond the Circle W Ranch the Deadman Creek Road continues north to Vidette Lake, then doubles back sharply toward the east. A spur from the eastward connection provides access to **Fatox Lake**, a 24-hectare (59-acre) lake at an elevation of 1,130 meters (3,700 feet). Total distance from the highway is about 50 kilometers (31 miles) and a truck is necessary. Fatox contains scrap fish (chub) but also produces trout to 3 pounds or better. Rough camping is available at the lake.

Northeast of Hihium Lake and about 72 kilometers (45 miles) northwest of Kamloops lies Bonaparte Lake, a huge lake 17 kilometers (10 1/2 miles) long accessible by road from several directions, or by float plane. There are two resorts on the lake, but the attraction for fly fishers is not Bonaparte itself as much as nearby **Hammer Lake**, accessible by a sometimes slippery road about 3.2 kilometers (2 miles) southwest of Bonaparte. At an elevation of 1,250 meters (4,101 feet) and covering a surface area of 70 hectares (173 acres), Hammer is named for its shape. It has fine sedge and chironomid hatches and once was almost legendary for the huge trout that rose to feed on the adult insects. Today, trout of 4 1/2 pounds are about tops, and there are many smaller ones—but they still take floating sedges. They also share the lake with a population of chub. There are two campgrounds on the lake and other facilities are available at the Bonaparte resorts.

Many other lakes northwest of Kamloops have no road access or can be reached by road only with difficulty. Several of these have fishing camps with fly-in service from Kamloops. These include:

Akehurst Lake, about 77 kilometers (48 miles) northwest of Kamloops in Nehalliston Provincial Forest. A large lake, with a surface area of 220 hectares (543 acres), Akehurst is at an elevation of 1,390 meters (4,560 feet). Akehurst Lake Fishing Camp provides ground transportation from Kamloops and offers cabins with central plumbing, showers and prepared meals. More than a dozen nearby smaller lakes also hold trout and are fished out of this camp.

Bare Lake, about 64 kilometers (40 miles) northwest of Kamloops at an elevation of 1,433 meters (4,700 feet). The lake has a surface area of 230 hectares (568 acres), with several smaller lakes nearby. The latter include **Island Lake**, 50 hectares (124 acres), and **Secret Lake**, 55 hectares (136 acres). Bare Lake Fishing Resort provides access to these and other lakes and offers cabins, central showers and prepared meals.

Caverhill Lake, just east of Akehurst Lake about 74 kilometers (46 miles) northwest of Kamloops at an elevation of 1,400 meters (4,593 feet). About 6.5 kilometers (4 miles) long with a surface area of about 540 hectares (1,334 acres), Caverhill has an irregular shoreline with many points and bays and a large island at its northern end. Caverhill Lodge, on the southeast shore, is accessible by air or by boat from a roadhead on the lake. The lodge has cabins, central washrooms, a sauna and serves prepared meals. It also offers hike-in access to more than a dozen nearby smaller lakes, including **Bramon**, **Malcolm**, **Triangle** and **Patrick**.

Elbow Lake, immediately southwest of Bare Lake about 61 kilometers (38 miles) northwest of Kamloops at an elevation of 1,364 meters (4,475 feet). The lake, named for its shape, has a surface area of 80 hectares (198 acres). Alpine Resort on the lake has cabins, showers and prepared meals. Other lakes fished from this camp include **Moose** and **Horse Pasture**, as well as Island and Secret, also accessible from the camp at Bare Lake.

Hoopatatkwa ("Hoopy") Lake, east of Bare Lake and about 51 kilometers (32 miles) northwest of Kamloops at an elevation of 1,380 meters (4,528 feet). "Hoopy" has a surface area of 90 hectares (222 acres). The Rainbow Chain Lodge on the lake has cabins, showers and prepared meals and offers access to nine lakes.

For the most part the chemistry of these waters is not as rich as it is in lakes farther south and east, and fishing varies from season to season. Some offer fast fishing for small trout—for example, Caverhill Lake currently has a generous limit of 8 trout a day to reduce the population—while others usually offer fish in the 1- to 3-pound range with occasional larger fish. But while they may be short on giant trout, these waters do offer something that is increasingly hard to find elsewhere: The chance to fish in a near-wilderness environment.

• *Northeast of Kamloops* (north of the Trans-Canada Highway and east of Highway 5, the North Thompson route) **(MAP, page 138)**: Just north of Kamloops, the Paul Lake Road leaves Highway 5 and heads east toward Paul, Pinantan, Pemberton, Hyas and Warren Lakes, also accessible from Pritchard on the Trans-Canada Highway east of Kamloops.

Paul Lake, already extensively described, is about 18 kilometers (11 miles) east of Highway 5 at an elevation of 775 meters (2,543 feet). It is a long, rather narrow lake lying on an east-west axis with a surface area of 390 hectares (964 acres). Because of its proximity to Kamloops, it receives heavy use from a variety of recreationists and numerous homes and cabins have sprouted on its shores. The old lodge at the west end of the lake is gone, replaced by condominiums.

Nevertheless, Paul remains an attractive lake with an excellent spring hatch of *Callibaetis* mayflies and still produces occasional trout up to 6 or 7 pounds, although most are much smaller. Reinfested with redside shiners, it also offers anglers a chance to try their hand with minnow patterns tied to imitate shiners.

Pinantan Lake lies about 6.5 kilometers (4 miles) east of Paul. It has a surface area of 65 hectares (161 acres) and is located at an elevation of 871 meters (2,858) feet. It has a dark, silty bottom, and—like Paul Lake—contains a large population of redside shiners. **Little Pinantan** is a shallow, tule-rimmed pond connected to the main lake that sometimes offers exciting fishing in the evening. Trout to 1 pound may be expected. Cabins are available at a private resort.

About 5 kilometers (3 miles) east of Pinantan a dirt road, passable by cars, leads north about 11 kilometers (7 miles) to **Pemberton** and **Hyas Lakes**, both at an elevation of about 1,230 meters (4,035 feet). Pemberton has a surface area of 12.5 hectares (31 acres); nearby Hyas covers 64 hectares (158 acres). A fishing camp on Hyas serves both waters and camping is available at Pemberton. Both lakes are well suited for fly fishing, and in its very early days Hyas yielded a 16-pound Kamloops to a dry fly. Those days are gone, however, and a 5-pound trout would be a good one now.

Just a kilometer (.5 mile) west of Pemberton Lake is **Warren Lake** at an elevation of 1,275 meters (4,183 feet), but that last kilometer is a tough one and a 4x4 is necessary. The lake, covering 25 hectares (62 acres), is currently managed under regulations requiring artificial flies and barbless hooks with a daily limit of two fish. Trout to 5 1/2 pounds have been reported.

A fly caster at work on Eagle Bay, Hihium Lake.

From the Paul Lake Road Highway 5 continues north a total distance of 22.5 kilometers (14 miles) from Kamloops to the community of Heffley Creek. There the paved Heffley Creek Road leaves the highway and heads east for 8 kilometers (5 miles) to a secondary road that branches off to the north, providing access to several lakes. The road is adequate for travel by car as far as Knouff Lake, about 16 kilometers (10 miles) north of the pavement, but trucks or 4x4s are necessary to travel a spur road that branches off to the east about 8 kilometers (5 miles) north of the pavement and extends another 6 kilometers (3.75 miles) to **Community Lake**.

This lake, also sometimes known as Beaver Lake, is at an elevation of 1,395 meters (4,577 feet) and covers 40 hectares (99 acres), including several small islands. It offers good dry-fly fishing with an excellent caddis hatch and trout to 3 pounds have been reported. Camping is available at the lake.

Beyond the turnoff to Community Lake the secondary road continues north to **Knouff Lake**, also accessible via secondary road from Vinsulla on Highway 5, a distance of 13 kilometers (8 miles). Lying amid rolling hills cloaked in pine and aspen at an elevation of 1,149 meters (3,770 feet), Knouff has clear water, a gravel bottom and broad reaches of shoal water, covered with weed and broken by patches of marl. There are five small islands, four in line like a small fleet of sailing ships with living pines for masts. The lake has a surface area of 103 hectares (254 acres), a maximum depth of 24 meters (79 feet) and a mean depth of 10 meters (32 feet).

The early history of this lake already has been related. The great hatches of traveling sedges are gone, never to return, and for many years the giant trout that once rose to them were missing, too. Recently, however, big trout have returned to Knouff Lake. The Fisheries Branch cut stocking in favor of natural reproduction, but then the inlet creek dried up and there was no natural recruitment; this meant less competition for food among trout already in the lake, and they put on weight quickly. One trout of 14 pounds was reported caught in the spring of 1993 along with several in the 11- to 12-pound class. As in Peterhope Lake, however, the conditions that caused this are temporary and it may be a long time before they occur again.

There is a resort at the north end of the lake and public camping also is available. Numerous homes have been built on the lake, mostly around its south end.

Little Knouff Lake sits on a hill just to the north of Knouff, a shallow, oval-shaped lake with a marl bottom and a surface area of 40 hectares (99 acres). From time to time it has produced large trout, but usually these are extremely wary and reluctant to enter shallow water, so most fishing is limited to a small area of deeper water in the center of the lake.

From Knouff a dirt road continues north another 5 kilometers (3 miles) to **Badger Lake**. This stretch can become greasy in wet weather and probably is best suited for trucks. Badger and its smaller companion, **Spooney Lake**, connected by channel, are at an elevation of about 1,143 meters (3,750 feet). Badger has a surface area of about 60 hectares (148

acres), including two small islands, while Spooney covers about 7 hectares (17 acres). Both lie on a north-south axis and both have brushy shorelines and dark, silty bottoms. They are well populated by a wide variety of aquatic fauna and produce heavy chironomid hatches early in the season followed by a good sedge hatch that sometimes begins as early as the end of the first week of June. Both lakes have produced large trout in the past, but as in most waters the average size rises and falls in cycles. However, trout to 3 1/2 pounds usually can be expected, with some larger. There are two campgrounds on Badger, one private, the other a B.C. Forest Service recreation site.

Past the turnoff to Knouff Lake the Heffley Creek Road extends another 11 kilometers (7 miles) east to **Heffley Lake**. This long, narrow lake lies on an east-west axis at an elevation of 943 meters (3,095 feet) with a surface area of 203 hectares (501 acres). Its maximum depth is 23.5 meters (77 feet). There are two resorts and a B.C. Forest Service recreation site on the lake as well as many homes and cabins. Heffley still offers good fishing at times, however, especially during the spring mayfly and damselfly emergences, with trout to 3 pounds.

From Heffley Creek Highway 5 follows the North Thompson to Louis Creek, a total distance of 58 kilometers (36 miles) from Kamloops. There the Agate Bay Road leaves the highway and heads east 38 kilometers (23.5 miles) to **Johnson Lake**. The last 14.5 kilometers (9 miles) are steep but a car is adequate if driven with care. Johnson is a large lake, about 5.5 kilometers (3 1/2 miles) long with a surface area of 400 hectares (988 acres) at an elevation of 1,365 meters (4,478 feet). Trout to 5 pounds are available, although most are smaller. There is a fishing camp with housekeeping cabins, a store and a campground on the lake. Several smaller lakes are accessible from the road to Johnson Lake.

Little Fort-Clearwater Area

The country around the village of Little Fort (MAP, page 139) is rocky, steep and rugged. From the banks of the North Thompson the ground rises steeply to a labyrinth of ridges covered with dense thickets of pine and freckled with lakes. Highway 24, stretching west from Little Fort to Lone Butte, provides access to many of these.

Most lakes in this region were stocked much later than those farther south. Typically they grew trout rapidly and produced some fish of spectacular size, but as is usually the case the average size declined quickly as food stocks were whittled down. Many of these lakes also are interconnected by small streams in which spawning runs quickly developed, and some waters soon became overpopulated.

Although the aquatic fauna of lakes in the Little Fort area is much the same as it is in the waters around Kamloops and Merritt, the clear-water, marl-bottom lakes common farther south are mostly lacking. The majority of lakes in the hills west of Little Fort have dark or amber-colored water and their water chemistry is not as rich as that of waters to the south. Trout

A stormy sunset over Hihium Lake.

from these lakes tend to be more heavily spotted and somewhat darker in color than fish from the lakes around Kamloops and Merritt. However, this is only a sign of their adaptation to the local environment and has nothing to do with their condition; a healthy, maiden trout from these waters fights as well as any Kamloops trout.

There are so many lakes in this area it is impossible to describe them all. Most are small and located at high elevations, which makes them particularly vulnerable to rapid change, so it's especially important for anglers to obtain the latest local information. Steve Jennings' Little Fort Fly & Tackle Shop at the intersection of Highways 5 and 24 is a good place to do this.

The following list includes most of the better-known waters in the area:

Thuya Lake is accessible via the Eakin Creek Road, a distance of 20 kilometers (12 miles) from Highway 24 west of Little Fort. It is a 35-hectare (86-acre) lake at an elevation of 1,320 meters (4,330 feet); **Island Lake**, immediately adjacent, is virtually its twin, except it has a single small island. Thuya Lakes Lodge, a resort located between the two lakes, provides housekeeping cabins, central showers, prepared meals and campsites.

A number of other small waters are located nearby, includ-

Sunset scene at Bare Lake.

ing **Dot, Disappointment, Young's, Summit, Trail's End, Pearl, Robinson, Kevin, Boot, Jackpine, Randy, Scot, Jeremy** and **Two Match Lakes**. The lodge keeps boats on many of these lakes, most of which are accessible only by trail. There are also many beaver ponds in the area, some connected to lakes through a network of small streams where trout can spawn. This natural reproduction, coupled with changes in other conditions, results in rapid fluctuation of the trout populations in these lakes and they offer a wide variety of angling, from fast fishing for smaller trout in the 10-inch class to challenging angling for larger fish occasionally running up to 5 or 6 pounds. The lakes range in elevation

from 1,310 to 1,435 meters (4,300 to 4,700 feet) and usually fish well through the summer.

About 22 kilometers (13.5 miles) west of Little Fort are **Lynn** and **Latremouille Lakes**, headquarters of Aurora Lakes Resort, accessible by turning south from Highway 24. The resort, opened by Starr Brown about 1955, has since changed hands several times. It is a cozy, rustic camp perched in timber on a steep, rocky hillside overlooking 45-hectare (111-acre) Lynn Lake.

Lynn, a clear lake with extensive shallows and some patches of weed, is at an elevation of 1,240 meters (4,068 feet). It holds brook trout as well as Kamloops, with fish of either species up to 2 pounds. There is no natural spawning, so both populations are maintained by stocking. Nearby Latremouille Lake, at an elevation of 1,210 meters (3,970 feet), has a surface area of 96 hectares (237 acres) and holds Kamloops trout up to about 2 1/2 pounds.

The lodge keeps boats on some of the many other lakes in this area. These include **Laurel, Goose, Thumb, Richard, Jim** (also known as Gem), **Sedge, Dytiscid, Emar, Float, Grouse** (also known as Willowgrouse), **Boulder** and **Club Lakes.** Elevations of these waters range from just under 1,280 meters (4,200 feet) to nearly 1,340 meters (4,400 feet) and they vary in size from Dytiscid and Jim, each about 6 hectares (14 acres), to Laurel at 21 hectares (53 acres) and Emar at 30 hectares (75 acres). Most are managed as "walk-in" lakes, accessible via short hikes and best fished from a float tube or light canoe.

In addition to being the largest lake in the area, Emar is perhaps the most interesting to fish. A shallow lake with many points and bays, it routinely produces 12-inch trout with occasional fish to 3 pounds or more. It is accessible via Grouse Lake, a small, 9-hectare (22-acre), rather featureless lake that occasionally produces some very sizeable trout.

Jim Lake, scarcely more than a pothole, is reached by a 20-minute hike over rocky, rolling country. A shallow, crescent-shaped lake with a silty bottom, it produces trout in the 12-inch category. Richard Lake, only about 100 yards distant, is considerably larger at 14 hectares (34 acres). "Half shoal and half hole," it is nearly circular in shape, shallow on one side and deep on the other. The shallow portion has a marl bottom and when conditions are right it is possible to see cruising trout. This, coupled with a good sedge hatch, makes Richard an interesting lake for dry-fly anglers. It has produced trout as large as 5 pounds in the past; however, as with most of the other small lakes in this area, conditions change rapidly and it is difficult to know what to expect from one season to the next.

A short distance west of these lakes, just beyond MacDonald Summit on Highway 24, is **Janice Lake**, also known as Long Island Lake. Located just south of the highway about 32 kilometers (20 miles) from Little Fort at an elevation of 1,310 meters (4,298 feet), Janice is one of the larger lakes in the neighborhood with a surface area of 80 hectares (198 acres) including two small islands. An excellent fly-fishing lake with a good spring mayfly hatch, it has a small Forest Service recreation site on a protected bay at its eastern end and a resort, Janice Lake Lodge, at its western end. Trout in the 3-pound class are caught here, with some larger.

Another good-sized water, **Rock Island Lake**, lies about 22.5 kilometers (14 miles) northwest of Little Fort at an elevation of about 1,280 meters (4,200 feet), accessible by a rough road that can be nasty in wet weather. With a surface area of about 70 hectares (173 acres), it regularly produces trout to 2 pounds with some larger. Rock Island Fishing Camp offers housekeeping cabins and transportation from Little Fort.

Other lakes fished from this camp include **Upper and Lower Hardcastle, Crater** (sometimes known as Cone), **Donna, Wineholt, Portage** and **Ruby,** all about the same elevation and ranging in size from Wineholt at 3.3 hectares (8 acres) to Upper Hardcastle at 19 hectares (47 acres). Most of these plus **Slager Lake** (sometimes known as Sleiger) also are fished from a lodge on **Tuloon Lake** (also known as Tintlhahtan) a short distance north. Tuloon is at an elevation of about 1,250 meters (4,100) feet with a surface area of 31 hectares (76 acres). Access is via a 4x4 road to Tuloon Lake Fishing Lodge, which has cabins, central showers and serves prepared meals. These lakes offer a choice of angling experiences with trout of all sizes.

Meadow Lake, about 24 kilometers (15 miles) northwest of Little Fort via dirt road, is at an elevation of 1,380 meters (4,530 feet) with a surface area of 10 hectares (25 acres). The lake, headquarters for the Meadow Lake Fishing Camp, is reported to offer trout up to about 1 1/2 pounds. The camp has rustic cabins, central showers and serves prepared meals.

Other lakes in the vicinity, accessible either by rough 4x4 roads or trail, include **Flapjack, Lost Horse, Broken Hook, Rose, Colin, No Name, Friendly, Grizzly,** and **Tahoola,** all at elevations between 1,400 and 1,495 meters (4,600 to 4,900 feet). No Name and Friendly are the two largest, at 49 hectares (121 acres) and 46 hectares (114 acres) respectively. Many of these lakes are unusually deep, but most also have extensive shoal areas. They provide trout in a variety of sizes.

TaWeel Lake, one of the largest and best-known lakes in the region and one of the first to be stocked with trout (1928), is about 30 kilometers (19 miles) northwest of Little Fort via 4x4 road. It lies at an elevation of 1,201 meters (3,939 feet), has a surface area of 440 hectares (1,087 acres) and offers trout to 4 1/2 pounds. Two fishing camps, TaWeel Lake Fishing Lodge and Nehalliston Fishing Camp, are located on the lake. Walk-in access is available to several nearby lakes, including **Moose, Lost, Lorna, Thelma** and **Johnny.** Logging in the area could pose a threat to its future.

Farther west, toward 100 Mile House, are other worthwhile waters. One of these, **Lac des Roches,** is about 35 kilometers (22 miles) west of Little Fort on Highway 24 at an elevation of 1,129 meters (3,705 feet). A long, narrow, deep lake with a surface area of 662 hectares (1,635 ares), it contains burbot (freshwater ling), shiners and chub as well as Kamloops trout. As mentioned, the latter include some of the Gerrard Strain.

Called "L.D.R." by local anglers, Lac des Roches may have the best mayfly hatch of any lake in the region and provides good dry-fly fishing at times. Its trout run as large as 6 1/2 pounds, though most are smaller. There are two fully equipped resorts on the lake, which is paralleled by the highway for some distance.

Sheridan Lake, among the most popular of all Kamloops trout waters, lies just off Highway 24 about 16 kilometers (10 miles) east of Lone Butte. A very large lake, extending about 8 kilometers (5 miles) along its longest (northwest-southeast) axis, it has a highly irregular shape with many points and bays

Jim Unterwegner fishing Valentine Lake near 100 Mile House.

and a half dozen islands. At least 30 meters (100 feet) deep in some spots, it also has many shoal areas that are attractive to fly fishers. But the most attractive feature of Sheridan Lake is the size of its trout, with fish from 8 1/2 to 10 pounds not out of the ordinary. It also holds some large brook trout.

Sheridan is at an elevation of 1,115 meters (3,658 feet) and fishes best early and late in the season. Four resorts are located on the lake.

North of Little Fort, Highway 5 continues about 34 kilometers (21 miles) to the town of Clearwater, where a logging road extends northwest another 34 kilometers (21 miles) to **Rioux, Dubee, Coldscaur** and other lakes. Moose Camp, a fishing resort on Rioux Lake, provides facilities. The road is good except the last mile to the camp, which requires a 4x4.

Rioux and adjacent Dubee are at an elevation of 1,425 meters (4,675 feet) with a combined surface area of 30 hectares (74 acres). Coldscaur covers 35 hectares (86 acres). These lakes are part of the Canimred Creek drainage, a tributary of giant Canim Lake. They owe their trout populations to one Herbie McNeil, a Michigan native who worked as a Cariboo freight hauler before he homesteaded at the east end of Canim Lake and ran a trap line along Canimred Creek. In 1935 McNeil and his brother caught some trout in the lower creek, kept them alive in buckets of water

and hauled them above a waterfall that historically had kept trout from gaining access to the upper reaches of the creek. The trout were released, and from that initial stocking they spread throughout the drainage and into several lakes, including Rioux.

Ralph Bell, a judge in Everett, Washington, was from the same town in Michigan that had been McNeil's home. In 1946 Bell and his son, Lew, along with George Duwe and his son, Sam, traveled to the area and found wonderful fishing in Rioux and Coldscaur Lakes. But the small unnamed lake just north of Rioux still was barren of fish, so they caught some trout and released them into the lake. They named the lake Dube, a contraction of the names Duwe and Bell. Over the years common usage has added a second "e," accounting for the present name of Dubee.

The late Lew Bell recalled that they returned each year for the next decade, restocking Dubee Lake each year (there are no tributary streams suitable for spawning). Other trout caught in Rioux Lake were placed in cans full of water and carried on horseback to other barren lakes in the area, where they were released. Some of these plantings were successful and others were not, but in this way fish were introduced to the lakes now served by Moose Camp. These waters provide fishing for trout up to 4 1/2 pounds, though most are smaller.

Other Areas

From the Kootenay to the Cariboo, there are hundreds of other lakes that hold Kamloops trout. The Balfour Arm of **Kootenay Lake** itself offers a unique fishery for huge trout of the Gerrard Kamloops strain, and some are taken there on a dry fly. Under current regulations, only artificial flies may be used from June 1 to August 31. However, anyone wishing to keep trout from this lake is required to purchase a special tag that must be attached to the jaw of any trout of more than 20 inches that is kept.

The Okanagan has many outstanding lakes, including the **Dee Lake** chain off Highway 97 northeast of Winfield. These lakes, at an elevation of about 1,402 meters (4,600 feet), are accessible by car and provide excellent fly fishing at times. Dee Lake Fishing Lodge has cabins, a campground, shower house and other facilities.

In the same area is **Oyama Lake**, reached via truck road 15 kilometers (9 miles) east of the Oyama community. Noted as a good fly-fishing lake, Oyama is at an elevation of about 1,250 meters (4,100 feet) and is served by a fishing camp that offers housekeeping cabins, showers and meals. There is also public camping on the lake.

The Headwaters chain off Highway 97 about 27 kilometers (17 miles) west of Peachland provides access to **Headwaters**

Moonrise over Hihium Lake.

Lake and other small lakes nearby at an elevation of about 1,250 meters (4,100 feet). The Headwaters Fishing Camp has cabins, campsites and showers.

The country east of Kamloops has many interesting waters, including **Pinaus Lake** and its surrounding waters, **Pillar Lake**, **Arthur** and **Bolean Lakes**, **Niskonlith** and **McGillivray Lakes**, and **White Lake** near Salmon Arm. To mention only their names does little justice to them, and of course there are many more excellent waters not named here at all. But the number and variety of waters holding Kamloops trout is one of the chief attractions of the fishery, giving each angler the opportunity to assemble a personal list of favorites, adding and subtracting over the years as familiar waters decline and new discoveries take their place.

There are other waters whose names are never mentioned, except perhaps in whispers around campfires. These are legendary lakes reported to hold monstrous trout whose poundage is never measured in less than double digits. They appear on maps only as anonymous blue images lost among hundreds of their kind. Perhaps they are real and perhaps they are only imaginary, or perhaps a little of both. Whatever the truth about them, they add an extra measure of excitement to the search for the ultimate trout.

Map 1: **Lakes accessible south of Merritt**

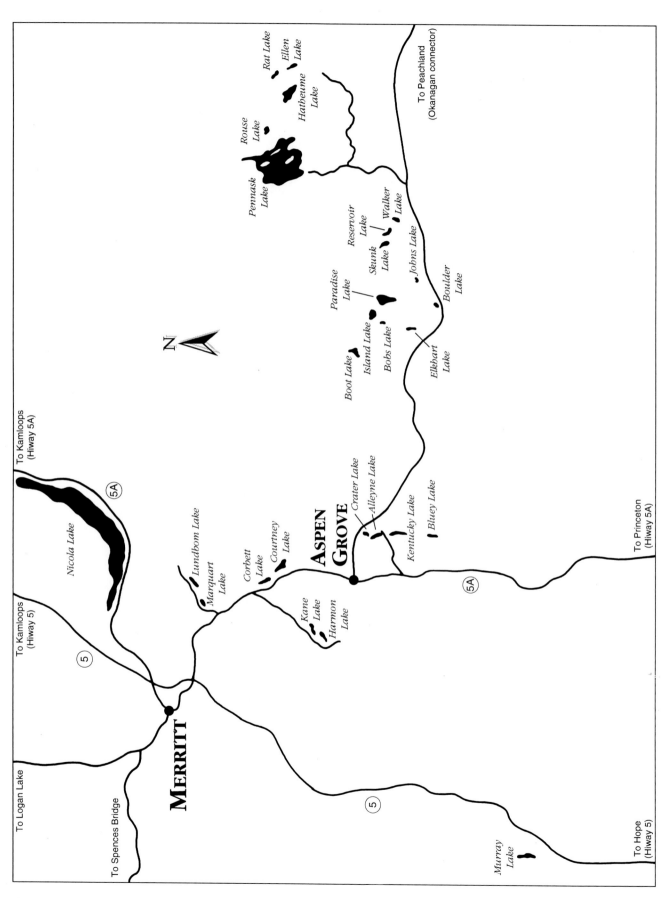

Map 2: **Lakes accessible northwest of Merritt**

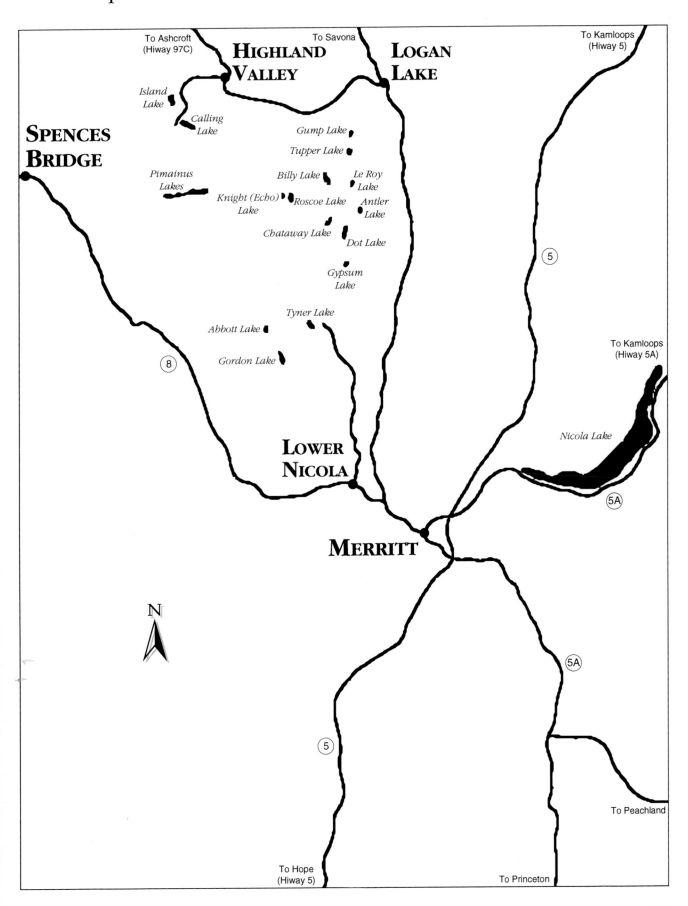

To Ashcroft (Hiway 97C)

To Savona

To Kamloops (Hiway 5)

HIGHLAND VALLEY

LOGAN LAKE

Island Lake

Calling Lake

SPENCES BRIDGE

Gump Lake

Tupper Lake

Pimainus Lakes

Billy Lake

Le Roy Lake

Knight (Echo) Lake

Roscoe Lake

Antler Lake

Chataway Lake

Dot Lake

Gypsum Lake

⑤

Tyner Lake

To Kamloops (Hiway 5A)

Abbott Lake

Gordon Lake

Nicola Lake

⑧

⑤ᴬ

LOWER NICOLA

MERRITT

⑤ᴬ

To Peachland

N

⑤

To Hope (Hiway 5)

To Princeton

Map 3: **Lakes accessible northeast of Merritt**

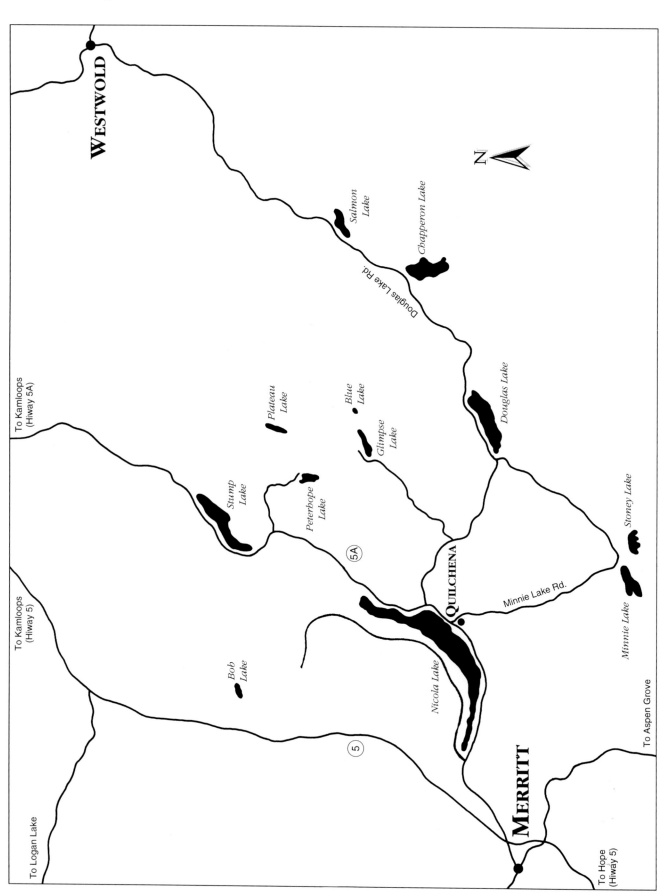

Map 4: **Lakes accessible southwest of Kamloops**

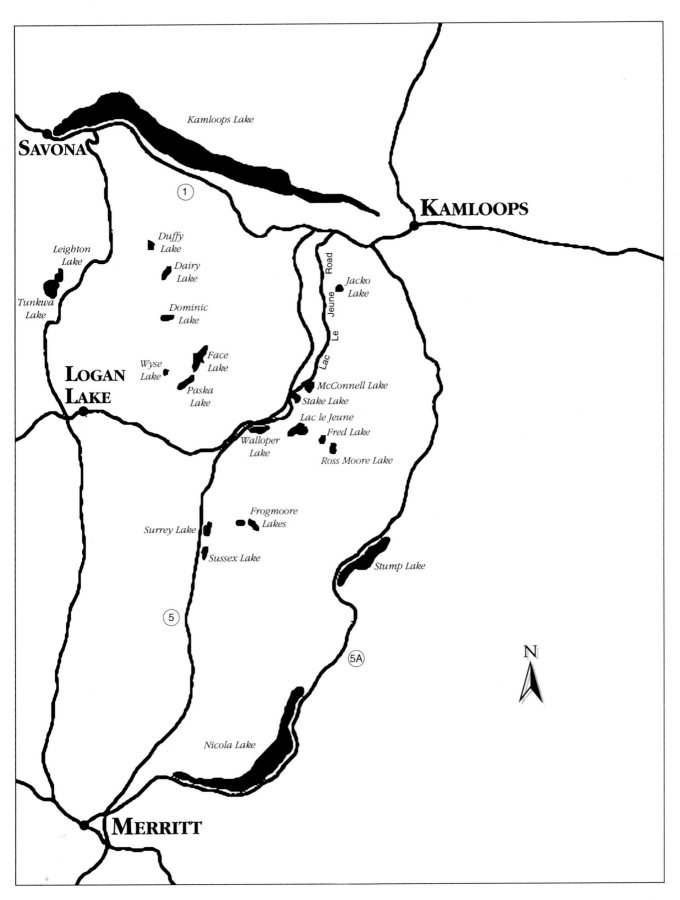

Kamloops Lake

SAVONA

KAMLOOPS

①

Leighton Lake

Duffy Lake

Dairy Lake

Jacko Lake

Tunkwa Lake

Dominic Lake

LOGAN LAKE

Wyse Lake

Face Lake

Paska Lake

McConnell Lake

Stake Lake

Lac le Jeune

Fred Lake

Walloper Lake

Ross Moore Lake

Lac Le Jeune Road

Frogmoore Lakes

Surrey Lake

Sussex Lake

Stump Lake

⑤

5A

N

Nicola Lake

MERRITT

Map 5: **Lakes accessible southeast of Kamloops**

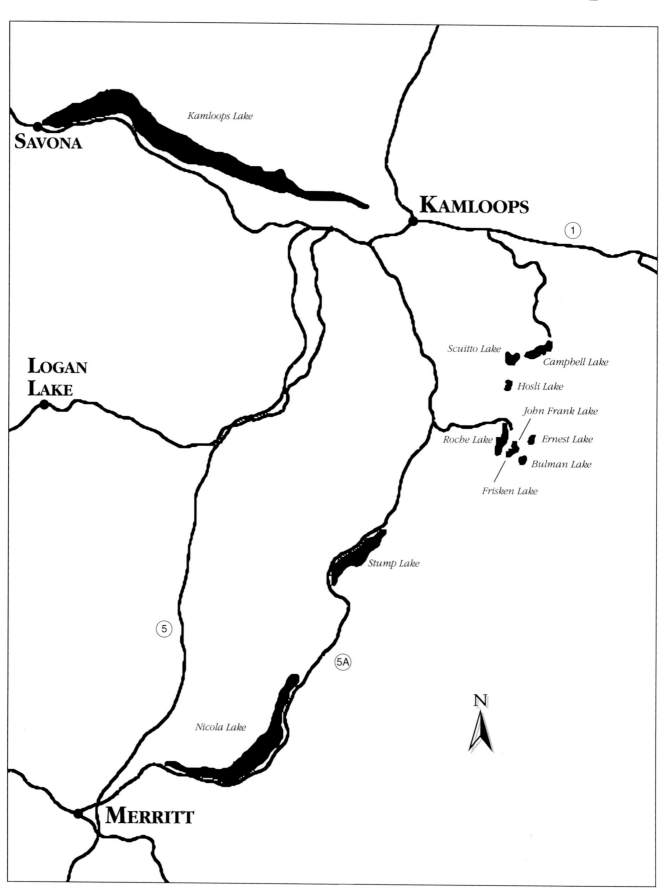

SAVONA

Kamloops Lake

KAMLOOPS

①

LOGAN
LAKE

Scuitto Lake

Campbell Lake

Hosli Lake

John Frank Lake

Ernest Lake

Roche Lake

Bulman Lake

Frisken Lake

Stump Lake

⑤

⑤A

N

Nicola Lake

MERRITT

Map 6: **Lakes accessible northwest of Kamloops**

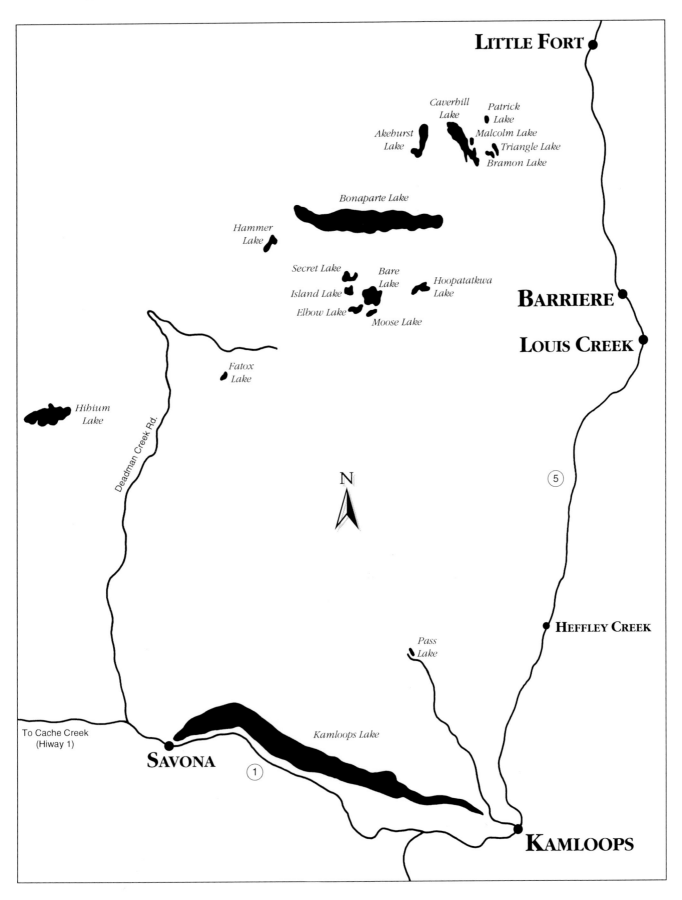

LITTLE FORT

Caverhill
Lake

Patrick
Lake

Akehurst
Lake

Malcolm Lake

Triangle Lake

Bramon Lake

Bonaparte Lake

Hammer
Lake

Secret Lake

Bare
Lake

Hoopatatkwa
Lake

Island Lake

BARRIERE

Elbow Lake

Moose Lake

LOUIS CREEK

Fatox
Lake

Deadman Creek Rd.

Hihium
Lake

N

5

HEFFLEY CREEK

Pass
Lake

To Cache Creek
(Hiway 1)

Kamloops Lake

SAVONA

1

KAMLOOPS

Map 7: **Lakes accessible northeast of Kamloops**

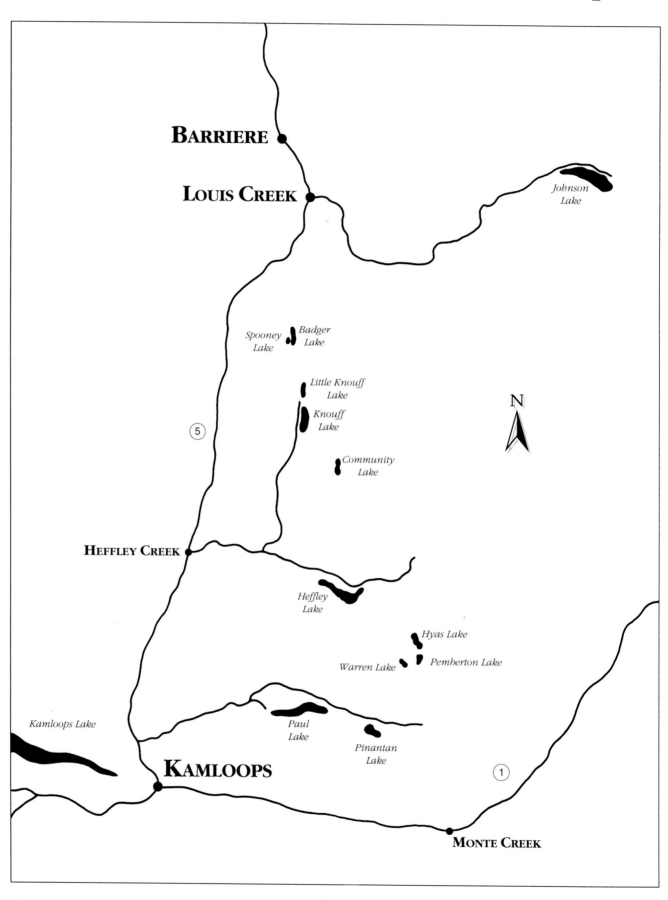

BARRIERE

LOUIS CREEK

Johnson
Lake

Spooney
Lake

Badger
Lake

Little Knouff
Lake

Knouff
Lake

(5)

Community
Lake

N

HEFFLEY CREEK

Heffley
Lake

Hyas Lake

Warren Lake

Pemberton Lake

Kamloops Lake

Paul
Lake

Pinantan
Lake

KAMLOOPS

(1)

MONTE CREEK

Map 8: **Lakes accessible from Little Fort**

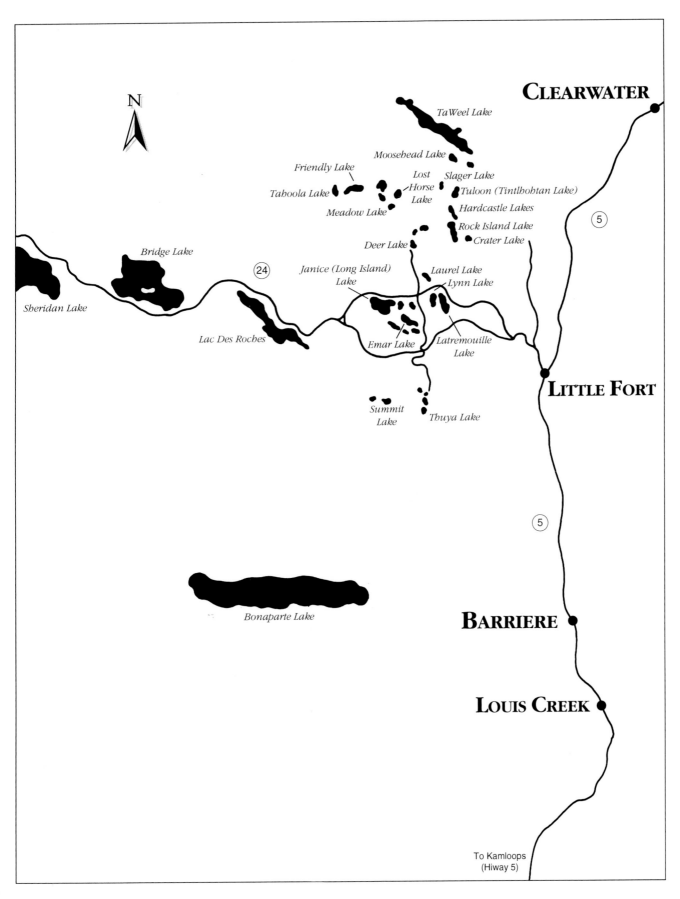

N

CLEARWATER

TaWeel Lake

Moosehead Lake

Friendly Lake

Lost
Horse
Lake

Slager Lake

Taboola Lake

Tuloon (Tintlhohtan Lake)

Meadow Lake

Hardcastle Lakes

Rock Island Lake

Crater Lake

Deer Lake

Bridge Lake

24

Janice (Long Island)
Lake

Laurel Lake

Lynn Lake

Sheridan Lake

Lac Des Roches

Emar Lake

Latremouille
Lake

LITTLE FORT

5

Summit
Lake

Thuya Lake

5

Bonaparte Lake

BARRIERE

LOUIS CREEK

To Kamloops
(Hiway 5)

BIBLIOGRAPHY

Adamson, W. A. *The Enterprising Angler;* William Morrow & Co., New York, 1945.

Almy, Gerald. *Tying & Fishing the Terrestrials;* Stackpole Books, Harrisburg, Pa., 1978.

Ashley, K. I. *Hypolimnetic Aeration of a Naturally Euthrophic Lake: Physical and Chemical Effects;* Canadian Journal of Fisheries & Aquatic Sciences, Vol. 40, No. 9, 1983.

Ashley, K. I.; Tsumura, Kanji, and Chan, Brian. *Fisheries Management of Winterkill Lakes in Southern Interior British Columbia;* N.H.R.I Symposium Series 7, Environment Canada, Saskatoon, 1992.

Behnke, Robert J. *Native Trout of Western North America;* American Fisheries Society, Bethesda, Md., 1992.

Bruhn, Karl. *Best of B.C. Lake Fishing;* Frank Amato Publications, Portland, Ore., 1992.

Carl, G. Clifford; Clemens, W. A., and Lindsey, C. C. *The Freshwater Fishes of British Columbia;* British Columbia Provincial Museum Handbook No. 5, Victoria, B.C., 1967.

Chan, Brian M.: *Flyfishing Strategies for Stillwaters;* Kamloops, B.C., 1991.

Clemens, W. A.; McHugh, J. L., and Rawson, D. S. *A Biological Survey of Okanagan Lake, B.C.;* Fisheries Research Board of Canada, Bulletin LVI.

Coker, Robert E. *Streams, Lakes, Ponds;* Chapel Hill, University of North Carolina Press, 1954.

Crossman, D. J., and Larkin, P. A. *Yearling Liberations and Change of Food as Effecting Rainbow Trout Yield in Paul Lake;* Transactions of the American Fisheries Society, Vol. 88, No. 1, January, 1959.

Davy, Alfred G. (editor). *The Gilly: A Flyfisher's Guide to British Columbia;* Kelowna, B.C., 1985.

Dibblee, G. *Effects of the Mining Industry on Fresh Water Fisheries of British Columbia;* Canadian Fish Culturist, Issue 25, October, 1959.

Dymond, J. R. *The Trout and Other Game Fishes of British Columbia;* Biological Board of Canada, Bulletin No. XXXII, 1932.

Godin, Theresa, and Tsumura, Kanji. *Rainbow Trout Broodstocks for Coarse Fish Lakes;* Habitat Conservation Fund Progress Report (1991-92), British Columbia Ministry of Environment, Lands and Parks; Fisheries Branch, Fisheries Research Section, University of British Columbia, Vancouver, 1992.

Haig-Brown, Roderick L. *A River Never Sleeps;* William Morrow & Co., New York, 1944.

Haig-Brown, Roderick L. *The Living Land;* produced by the British Columbia Natural Resources Conference, William Morrow & Co., New York, 1961.

Haig-Brown, Roderick L. *The Western Angler;* Derrydale Press, New York, 1939; 2 vols.

Haig-Brown, Roderick L. *The Western Angler,* revised edition; William Morrow & Co., New York, 1947.

Hartman, G. F. *Reproductive Biology of the Gerrard Stock Rainbow Trout;* Symposium on Salmon and Trout in Streams, University of British Columbia, February 22, 1968.

Hartman, G. F.; Northcote, T. G., and Lindsey, C. C. *Comparison of Inlet and Outlet Spawning Runs of Rainbow Trout in Loon Lake, B.C.;* Journal of the Fisheries Research Board of Canada, Vol. 19, No. 2, March, 1962.

"Huge Rainbow Trout;" British Columbia Wildlife Review, December, 1968, pp. 24-25.

Hutchison, Bruce. *Rivers of America: The Fraser;* Rinehart & Co. New York, 1950.

Inland Empire Fly Fishing Club, Spokane, Wash. *Flies of the Northwest;* Frank Amato Publications, Portland, Ore., 1986.

Johannes, R. E., and Larkin, P. A. *Competition for Food Between Redside Shiners and Rainbow Trout in Two British Columbia Lakes;* Journal of the Fisheries Research Board of Canada, Vol. 18, No. 2, March, 1961.

Kilburn, Jim. *The Caddis Larvae;* Western Fish & Game, Vol. 6, No. 2, March, 1971.

Kilburn, Jim. *The Caddis Fly;* Western Fish & Game, Vol. 6, No. 3, May, 1971.

Kilburn, Jim. *The Damselfly Nymph;* Western Fish & Wildlife, Vol. 6, No. 5, August/September, 1971.

Kilburn, Jim. *The Dragonfly;* Western Fish & Wildlife, Vol. 7, No. 2, March, 1972.

Lambert, T. W. *Fishing in British Columbia;* Horace Cox, London, 1907.

Larkin, P. A. *Introduction of the Kamloops Trout in British Columbia Lakes;* Canadian Fish Culturist, No. 16, August 16, 1954.

Larkin, P. A. *Management of Trout Lakes in British Columbia;* Tenth Annual Game Convention, Prince George, B. C., May 23-26, 1956.

Larkin, P. A., and Northcote, T. G. *Indices of Productivity in British Columbia Lakes;* Journal of the Fisheries Research Board of Canada, Vol. 13, No. 4, July, 1956.

Larkin, P. A.; Parker, R. R., and Terpenning, J. G. *Size as a Determinant of Growth Rate in Rainbow Trout;* Transactions of the American Fisheries Society, Vol. 86, 1956.

Larkin, P. A., and Smith, S. B. *Some Effects of the Introduction of the Redside Shiner on the Kamloops Trout in Paul Lake, B.C.;* Transactions of the American Fisheries Society, 1953.

McMynn, R. G. *Activities and Problems of the Fisheries Management Division;* Address to the Tenth Annual Game Convention, Prince George, B. C., May 23-26, 1956.

McPhail, J. D. *Effects on Fresh Water Fisheries of Agricultural Development in British Columbia;* Canadian Fish Culturist, Issue 25, October, 1959.

Merritt, Richard W., and Cummins, Kenneth W., eds. *An Introduction to the Aquatic Insects of North America;* Kendall/Hunt Publishing Co., Dubuque, Iowa, 1978.

Migel, J. Michael, and Wright, Leonard M., Jr., eds. *The Masters on the Nymph;* Nick Lyons Books, Doubleday & Co., Inc., New York, 1979.

Mottley, C. McC. *A Biometrical Study of the Kamloops Trout of Kootenay Lake;* Journal of the Fisheries Research Board of Canada, Vol. II, No. 4, 1936.

Mottley, C. McC. *The Classification of the Rainbow Trout of British Columbia;* Progress Reports of the Pacific Biological Station, No. 27, 1936.

Mottley, C. McC. *The Effect of Increasing the Stock in a Lake on the Size and Condition of Rainbow Trout;* Transactions of the American Fisheries Society, 1940.

Mottley, C. McC. *Fluctuations in the Intensity of the Spawning Runs of Rainbow Trout at Paul Lake;* Journal of the Fisheries Research Board of Canada, Vol. IV, No. 2, May-July, 1938.

Mottley, C. McC. *The Kamloops Trout;* Progress Reports of the Pacific Biological Station, No. 7, 1930.

Mottley, C. McC. *Loss of Weight by Rainbow Trout at Spawning Time;* Transactions of the American Fisheries Society, 1937.

Mottley, C. McC. *The Origin and Relations of the Rainbow Trout;* Transactions of the American Fisheries Society, 1934.

Mottley, C. McC. *The Production of Rainbow Trout at Paul Lake, B. C.;* Transactions of the American Fisheries Society, 1939.

Mottley, C. McC. *The Propagation of Trout in the Kamloops District, B. C.;* Transactions of the American Fisheries Society, 1932.

Mottley, C. McC. *The Spawning Migration of Rainbow Trout;* Transactions of the American Fisheries Society, 1933.

Mottley, C. McC. *Temperature and Propagation of Trout;* Progress Reports of the Pacific Biological Station, No. 8, 1931.

Mottley, C. McC. *The Trout of Streams and Small Lakes in Southern British Columbia;* Progress Reports of the Pacific Biological Station, No. 19, April, 1934.

Mottley, C. McC., and Mottley, Jean C. *The Food of Kamloops Trout;* Progress Reports of the Pacific Biological Station, No. 13, 1932.

Needham, Paul R. *Trout Streams,* revised by Carl F. Bond; Winchester Press, New York, 1969.

Northcote, T. G. *An Inventory and Evaluation of the Lakes of British Columbia, with Special Reference to Sport Fish Production,* Fifteenth British Columbia Natural Resources Conference.

Northcote, T. G. *Migratory Behavior of Juvenile Rainbow Trout in Outlet and Inlet Streams of Loon Lake, B.C.;* Journal of the Fisheries Research Board of Canada, Vol. 18, No. 2, 1962.

Pennak, Robert W. *Fresh-Water Invertebrates of the United States;* Ronald Press, New York, 1953.

"Planting Fish in the Early Days;" British Columbia Wildlife Review September, 1967, p. 21.

Prescott, G. W. *The Aquatic Plants;* Wm. C. Brown, Dubuque, Iowa, 1969.

Raymond, Steve. *Kamloops: An Angler's Study of the Kamloops Trout;* Winchester Press, New York, first edition, 1971.

Raymond, Steve. *Kamloops: An Angler's Study of the Kamloops Trout;* Frank Amato Publications, Portland, Ore., revised edition, 1980.

Rawson, Donald S. *Productivity Studies in Lakes of the Kamloops Region, B.C.;* Biological Board of Canada, Bulletin No. XLII, 1934.

Read, Stanley E. *Tommy Brayshaw, The Ardent Angler-Artist;* University of British Columbia Press, Vancouver, B.C., 1977.

Richardson, Lee. *Lee Richardson's B.C.;* Champoeg Press, Forest Grove, Ore., 1978.

Shaw, Jack. *Fly Fish the Trout Lakes;* Mitchell Press, Vancouver, B.C. 1976.

Smith, S. B. *Survival and Growth of Wild and Hatchery Trout in Corbett Lake, B.C.;* Canadian Fish Culturist, August, 1957.

Tsumura, Kanji, and Hume, Jeremy M. B. *A Comparison of Precociousness in Three Graded Size Classes of Hatchery-Reared Rainbow Trout;* British Columbia Ministry of Environment and Parks, Fisheries Branch, Fisheries Technical Circular No. 75, Vancouver, 1986.

Tsumura, Kanji, and Yesaki, Tim Y. *Alkaline Lakes Enhancement;* Habitat Conservation Fund Progress Report (1991-92), British Columbia Ministry of Environment, Lands and Parks; Fisheries Branch, Fisheries Research Section, University of British Columbia, Vancouver, 1992.

Tsumura, Kanji; Hume, Jeremy M. B., and Chan, Brian. *Effects of Size at Release in Rainbow Trout Stocked in a Winterkill Lake;* British Columbia Ministry of Environment and Parks, Recreational Fisheries Branch, Fisheries Management Report No. 88, Vancouver, 1987.

Tsumura, Kanji, and Blann, Vicki E. *Fishery Development in Barren, Winterkill Lakes;* British Columbia Ministry of Environment and Parks, Recreational Fisheries Branch, Fisheries Technical Circular No. 80, Vancouver, 1988.

Usinger, Robert L., ed. *Aquatic Insects of California;* University of California Press, Berkeley, Calif., 1956.

Whitehouse, Francis C. *Sport Fishing in Canada;* Vancouver, B.C., 1948.

Willers, Bill. *Trout Biology;* Lyons & Burford, New York, N.Y., 1991.

Williams, A. Bryan. *Fish and Game in British Columbia;* Sun Directories, Ltd., Vancouver, B.C., 1935.

INDEX

A

Abbott Lake: 106, 108, 133
Adams (fly pattern): 79
Adams Lake: 10
Adams River: 17, 84, 85
Adamson, W.A.: 16
Aeration devices: 50-51, 103, 116, 118
Aeschna: See dragonflies
Agate Bay Road: 124
Akehurst Lake: 122, 137
Akehurst Lake Fishing Camp: 122
Alder (fly pattern): 85
Alexander (fly pattern): 85
Alleyne Lake: 104, 132
Alpine Resort: 122
American Society of Ichthyologists and Herpetologists: 24
Anchors: 91, 96
Anderson's Stone Nymph (fly pattern): 80-81
Antler Lake: 106, 108, 133
Ants *(Hymenoptera)*: 56, 57, 63, 66-67
Aquatic beetles *(Coleoptera)*: 64
Aquatic earthworms *(Oligochaeta)*:58
Arthur Lake: 81, 131
Ashcroft: 41, 103, 106, 113
Ashton, Colonel: 16
Aspen Grove Store: 104
Aurora Lakes Resort: 127

B

B.C. Fishing Directory & Atlas: 102
Backswimmers *(Notonectidae)*: 57, 61, 62, 64
Badger Lake: 46, 124, 138
Baggie Shrimp (fly pattern): 71-72
Balfour: 17, 130
Bare Lake: 78-79, 122, 126-127, 137
Bare Lake Fishing Resort: 122
Barnes Lake: 106
Barnhart Vale: 120
Beaver Lake chain: 81
Beaver Lake (near Heffley Creek): See Community Lake
Bees *(Hymenoptera)*: 66
Bell, Lew: 129
Bell, Ralph: 129
Bendzak family: 121
Big Bar Lake: 17, 19
Big Bertha (fly pattern): 85
Big O.K. Lake: See Island Lake
Big Sabin Lake: See Sabin Lakes
Billy Lake: 106, 108, 133
Biological Board of Canada: 13
Black Flashabou Leech (fly pattern): 72
Black Gnat (fly pattern): 85
Black Lake: 45, 51
Black Matuka Leech (fly pattern): 72
Black O'Lindsay (fly pattern): 73, 82
Black, Spencer: 82
Blackwater River: 52
Blackwater strain rainbow trout: 52
Bleeker Lake: 51
Bloodworms: 42, 61
Blue Lake: 48, 109, 134
Bluey Lake: 104, 132
Boats: 91, 96
Bob Lake: 108, 134
Bobs Lake: 104, 132
Bolean Lake: 131

Bonaparte Lake: 121-122
Bonaparte River: 121
Boot Lake (Paradise chain): 104, 132
Boot Lake (Thuya chain): 127
Bootjack strain rainbow trout: 52
Boulder Lake (near Little Fort): 128
Boulder Lake (Paradise chain): 104, 132
Bradner, Enos: 107
Bramon Lake: 122
Brayshaw, Tommy: 16, 17, 18, 81
British Columbia Accommodations Guide: 100
British Columbia Department of Highways: 104
British Columbia Fisheries Branch: 40, 44, 46, 47, 48, 49, 51, 52, 78, 102, 104, 106, 114, 116, 119, 124; Research and Development Section, 52;
British Columbia Fisheries Research Group: 18, 45
British Columbia Fishing Camp Operators and Outfitters Association: 24, 102
British Columbia Forest Service: 22, 24, 49, 118, 119, 120, 124, 128
British Columbia Freshwater Fishing Vacations: 102
British Columbia Game Commission: 11
British Columbia Hydro: 109, 110
British Columbia Ministry of Environment, Lands and Parks: 40
British Columbia Ministry of Tourism: 100
Broken Hook Lake: 10, 128
Brown, Starr: 127
Bryan Williams' Gray-Bodied Sedge (fly pattern): 85
Bryan Williams' Green-Bodied Sedge (fly pattern): 85
Bulman Lake: 120, 136
Butcher (fly pattern): 85

C

Cache Creek: 114
Caddis flies: See sedges.
Callibaetis: See mayflies
Calling Lake: 106, 133
Calling Lake Road: 106, 108
Campbell Lake (near Kamloops): 120, 136
Campbell Lake (near Little Fort): 113
Canadian Pacific Railway: 10
Canim Lake: 129
Canim River: 17
Canimred Creek: 129
Canoes: 91
Carey, Colonel: 16, 81
Carey Special (fly pattern): 73, 74, 81, 82
Carlton, Gary: 73
Carp *(Cyprinus carpio)*: 44
Carpenter ant: 66-67
Caverhill Lake: 122, 137
Caverhill Lodge: 122
Chan, Brian: 49, 78
Chaoborus: 42, 61-62
Chara weed: 42
Chataway, George: 106

Chataway Lake: 51, 52, 106, 133
Chataway Lakes Lodge: 114
Chironomids: 42, 56, 57, 61-62, 63, 68, 77-78
Chub *(Mylocheilus caurinus)*: 44, 46, 52, 121, 122, 128
Circle W Ranch: 120-121
Claret & Mallard (fly pattern): 85
Clearwater: 114, 124, 129
Clinton: 17
Club Lake: 128
Coarse-scaled sucker *(Catostomus macrocheilus)*: 44, 52
Coast Range: 40-41
Coldscaur Lake: 129
Coldwater River: 102
Coldwater Road: 103
Colin Lake: 128
Columbia Mountains: 40
Comeaux, Bea: 121
Comeaux, Bill: 121
Community (Beaver) Lake: 124, 138
Cone Lake: See Crater Lake
Copepods: 30, 56
Coquihalla Highway: 22, 49, 102, 103
Corbett Lake: 25, 43, 46, 48, 51, 95, 103-104, 108, 109, 110-111, 132
Corbett Lake Country Inn: 101, 103-104, 109
Corixa (fly pattern): 78-79
Cornwall, 'Corny': 118
Courtney Lake: 25, 104, 132
Cranbrook: 17
Crater Lake (near Aspen Grove): 104, 132
Crater (Cone) Lake (near Little Fort): 128
Culicidae: See *Chaoborus*
Cummings Fancy (fly pattern): 85

D

Dairy Lakes: 118-119, 135
Dams: 22
Damselflies *(Zygoptera)*: 56, 57, 58-59, 63
Damselfly Adult (fly pattern): 73
Damselfly Nymph (fly pattern): 73
Daphnia: 30, 56
Day, Dr. Lloyd: 16, 81
Deadman Creek: 38-39, 120, 121
Dee Lake chain: 130
Dee Lake Fishing Lodge: 130
Diptera: See midges
Disappointment Lake: 127
Divide Lakes (Big and Little): 22
Doctor Spratley (fly pattern): 82
Dole, James D.: 14
Dolly Varden *(Salvelinus malma)*: 42
Dominic Lake: 118-119, 135
Donna Lake: 128
Dot Lake (Chataway chain): 106, 108, 133
Dot Lake (Thuya chain): 127
Douglas Lake Ranch: 22, 49, 104, 108, 109, 110, 111, 113
Douglas Lake Road: 109, 110
Dragon Lake: 46, 52, 80
Dragonflies *(Anisoptera)*: 54, 56, 57, 58-59, 63
Dragonfly Nymph (fly pattern): 73
Dry-fly fishing: 94-95

Dubee Lake: 129
Duffy Lake: 118, 135
Durkop, Tom: 17
Duwe, George: 129
Duwe, Sam: 129
Dymond, J. R.: 11, 13
Dytiscid Lake: 128
Dytiscidae: 64

E

Eagle Bay: 123
Eakin Creek Road: 126
Eastern brook trout *(Salvelinus fontinalis)*: 44, 51, 103
Echo (Knight) Lake: 106, 108, 133
Echo Lodge: 14
Egg 'n' I (fly pattern): 85
Elbow Lake: 122, 137
Elkhart Lake: 104, 132
Ellen Lake: 106, 132
Emar Lake: 128, 139
Emergence Table for aquatic insects: 63
Enallagma: See damselflies
Englishman Lake: 103
Enterprising Angler, The: 16
Ernest Lake: 48, 120, 136
Etiquette: 97-99
Eutrophic lakes: 42, 43

F

Face Lake: 118, 135
Fatox Lake: 121, 137
Field & Stream: 17
'52 Buick (fly pattern): 73
Fine-scaled sucker *(Catostomus catostomus)*: 44
Fish Lake (Lac le Jeune): 10
Fishing in British Columbia: 10
Fishing licenses: 102
Flapjack Lake: 128
Flatworms *(Turbellaria)*: 58
Flint, Colonel: 16
Float Lake: 128
Float tubes: 88, 89, 91, 97
Fly boxes: 92
Fly lines: 88-90, 95, 96, 97
Fly patterns: 68-85
Fly rods: 88, 104
Fly-line backing: 90, 97
Flying Ant (fly pattern): 80
Fort Kamloops: 10
Fraser Canyon: 16, 18
Fred Lake: 118, 135
Friendly Lake: 128, 139
Frisken Lake: 120, 136
Frogmoore Lakes: 118, 135
Fullback (fly pattern): 77

G

Gammarus limnaeus: 54, 57, 58 (also see scuds)
Geary, Dan: 111, 113
Geary, Trish: 111
Gem Lake: See Jim Lake
Geological Survey of Canada: 102
Gerrard: 11
Gerrard strain Kamloops trout: 33, 46, 112, 128, 130

Glimpse Lake: 22, 109, 115, 134
Goddard, John: 76
Goddard Sedge (fly pattern): 76
Gold-Ribbed Hare's Ear (fly pattern): 79
Golden Shrimp (fly pattern): 72
Gomphus: See dragonflies
Goofus Bug (fly pattern): 76
Goose Lake: 128
Gordon Lake: 108, 133
Gray Hackle (fly pattern): 85
Greenstone Mountain Road: 118, 119
Grizzly King (fly pattern): 84, 85
Grizzly Lake: 128
Grouse (Willowgrouse) Lake: 128
Gump Lake: 106, 133
Gypsum Lake: 108, 133

H

Habitat Conservation Fund: 49-50, 51, 52
Halfback (fly pattern): 77
Hammer Lake: 122, 137
Hardcastle Lakes: 10, 128, 139
Harmon Lake: 103, 132
Harry's Dam: 111-112
Hatcheries: 11, 46, 52, 109, 112
Hatchmaster (fly pattern): 79-80
Hatchmatcher (fly pattern): 79-80
Hatheume Lake: 48, 104, 106, 132
Headwaters Fishing Camp: 131
Headwaters Lake: 130
Heffley Creek: 124
Heffley Creek Road: 124
Heffley Lake: 51-52, 124, 138
Hemiptera: 62
Hexagenia: See mayflies
Highland Valley: 22, 103, 106, 108, 120
Highland Valley Copper: 22, 106
Highway 1 (Trans-Canada): 114, 116, 118, 119, 120, 122
Highway 5: 102, 114, 116, 118, 120, 122, 124, 126, 129
Highway 5A: 103, 104, 108, 109, 110, 113, 114, 116, 118, 119
Highway 8: 103, 106, 108
Highway 24: 124, 126, 127, 128
Highway 97: 114, 130
Highway 97C: 103, 104, 106
Hihium Creek: 121
Hihium Lake: 16, 17, 33, 62, 100, 120-121, 123, 125, 131, 137
Hihium Lake Fishing Camp: 121
Hoopatatkwa Lake: 122, 137
Hope: 22
Horse Pasture Lake: 122
Horseshoe Lake: 51
Hosli Lake: 120, 136
Hughes, Dave: 68
Humpy (fly pattern): 76
Hyalella azteci: 57-58 (also see scuds)
Hyalella knickerbockeri: 57-58 (also see scuds)
Hyas Lake: 44, 122, 138
Hymenoptera: See ants

I

Incidence Table for scuds and leeches: 63
Ischnura: See damselflies
Island Lake (Bare Lake chain): 122
Island Lake (Highland Valley): 48, 52, 106, 120, 133
Island Lake (Paradise chain): 104, 132

Island Lake (Thuya chain): 126

J

Jacko Lake: 116, 135
Jackpine Lake: 127
Janice (Long Island) Lake: 128, 139
Janice Lake Lodge: 128
Jennings, Steve: 126
Jenny Lake: 106
Jeremy Lake: 127
Jerry Lake: 106
Jewell Lake: 17
Jim Lake: 128
Jimmy Lake: 48
John Frank Lake: 120, 136
Johnny Lake: 128
Johns Lake: 104, 132
Johnson Lake: 124, 138
Jordan, Dr. David Starr: 10, 14
Juliet Creek: 103
Juniper Creek: 120

K

Kamloops, city of: 10, 22, 78, 102, 103, 114, 116, 119, 120, 121, 122, 124, 126, 131
Kamloops and District Fish & Game Club: 116
Kamloops Lake: 10, 119
Kamloops trout: Appearance of, 30, 33, 36; commercial fishing for, 11; distribution of, 10, 14, 121; evolution of, 10; feeding habits, 30-33, 36, 54-67; game qualities of, 16; growth of, 18, 29-30, 32, 36, 44-45, 46, 52; identification of, 10, 14, 24; life history, 13, 26-37, 45, 46; management of, 11, 13, 18, 22, 24, 38-52; naming of, 10; predators of, 11, 30, 36, 42-44; scale numbers of, 10, 14, 30; size of, 17; spawning, 8, 11, 18, 26, 29, 32-37, 44-45, 46, 51, 52, 121; stocking, 11, 14, 18, 44-46, 48, 52, 112-113, 120, 129;
Kane Valley Lakes: 103, 132
Kelowna: 11, 22, 81
Kentucky Lake: 104, 132
Kevin Lake: 127
Kilburn, Jim: 77
Kirkpatrick, Harriet: 121
Kirkpatrick, Pat: 121
Knight Lake: See Echo Lake
Knots: 90
Knouff Lake: 11-13, 14, 18, 44, 60, 81, 124, 138
Knouff Special (fly pattern): 73-74, 81
Knutsford: 118
Kokanee: 33, 44, 46, 114 (also see sockeye salmon)
Kootenay Lake: 10, 11, 17, 130
Kootenay River: 17

L

Lac des Roches: 46, 56, 128, 139
Lac du Bois Road: 120
Lac le Jeune: 11, 14, 16, 116, 118, 135
Lac le Jeune Resort: 118
Lac le Jeune Road: 114, 116, 118
Lady McConnel (fly pattern): 77-78
Lake Taupo: 72
Lake trout (*Salvelinus namaycush*): 44
Lambert, T.W.: 10, 11, 118
Landing nets: 92, 97

Lardeau River: 11, 33
Lardeau strain Kamloops trout: See Gerrard strain
Latremouille Lake: 127-128, 139
Laurel Lake: 128
Le Roy (Le Roi) Lake: 108, 133
Leaders: 90, 92, 96, 97
Leadwing Coachman (fly pattern): 85
Leeches (*Hirudinea*): 32, 57, 58, 63
Leighton Lake: 20, 88, 117, 119, 135
Lewinsky, Vic: 112
Lee Richardson's B.C.: 17
Limnephilus: See sedges
Ling (burbot) (*lota lota*): 44, 128
Lioness (fly pattern): 85
Little Chapperon Lake: 111-112, 113
Little Fort: 22, 103, 113, 114, 124, 127, 128, 129
Little Fort Fly & Tackle Shop: 126
Little Knouff Lake: 124, 138
Little Pinantan Lake: 122
Little River: 14, 17, 84, 85
Little Sabin Lake: See Sabin Lakes
Lodgepole Lake: 51
Logan Lake: 22, 23, 51, 103, 118
Lone Butte: 124, 128
Long Island Lake: See Janice Lake
Loon Creek: 121
Loon Lake: 121
Lorna Lake: 128
Lost Lake: 128
Lost Horse Lake: 128, 139
Louis Creek: 124
Lower Hardcastle Lake: See Hardcastle Lakes
Lower Kane Lake: See Kane Valley Lakes
Lower Nicola: 106, 108
Ludwig, Harry: 21
Lundbom Lake: 20, 22, 90, 103, 105, 107, 132
Lymnaea: See snails
Lynn Lake: 127-128, 139

M

Mab Lake Road: 108
MacDonald Summit: 128
Malcolm Lake: 122
MAPS-B.C.: 102
March Brown (fly pattern): 85
Marquart Lake: 22, 103, 132
Mayflies (*Ephemeroptera*): 56, 57, 61, 63, 64, 65, 79
McConnell Lake: 116, 135
McGillivray Lake: 131
McMahon, Dr. Bill: 16
McNeil, Herbie: 129
McVey, Peter: 103-104, 109, 112
Meadow Lake: 128, 139
Meadow Lake Fishing Camp: 128
Merritt: 11, 22, 102, 103, 104, 106, 108, 114, 124, 126
Merritt Fish & Game Club: 104
Midges (*Diptera*): See chironomids
Mikulak, Mitch: 76
Minnie Lake: 24, 62, 77, 103, 108, 111, 112, 113, 134
Minnie Lake Ranch: 109
Mitch's Sedge (fly pattern): 76
Monck Provincial Park: 108
Monte Creek: 114
Montreal (fly pattern): 85
Moose Camp: 129
Moose Lake (Elbow Lake chain): 122

Moose Lake (Ta Weel Lake chain): 128
Mottley, Dr. Charles M.: 13-14, 18, 44-45
Mountain whitefish (*Prosopium williamsoni*): 44
Muddler Minnow (fly pattern): 85
Murray Church: 15
Murray Lake: 103, 132

N

Nation, Arthur William (Bill): 8, 14, 16, 82, 84-85
Nation's Blue (fly pattern): 73, 82, 84
Nation's Fancy (fly pattern): 14, 82-83
Nation's Gray Nymph (fly pattern): 73, 84
Nation's Green Nymph (fly pattern): 73, 84
Nation's Green Sedge (fly pattern): 84
Nation's Red (fly pattern): 73, 84
Nation's Silver & Mallard (fly pattern): 84
Nation's Silvertip (fly pattern): 14, 84
Nation's Silvertip Sedge (fly pattern): 85
Nation's Special (fly pattern): 14, 85
National Marine Fisheries Service (U.S.): 77
Nehalliston Fishing Camp: 128
Nehalliston Provincial Forest: 122
Nicola: 13, 15, 108
Nicola Lake: 13, 103, 108, 113
Nicola River: 102
Niskonlith Lake: 46, 131
No Name Lake: 128
North Kamloops: 120
North Thompson River: 10, 114, 120, 124
Northern Squawfish (*Ptychocheilus oregonensis*): 44, 52, 112
Nymph fishing: 95-96

O

O.K. Lake: 106
Odonata: 58-59
Okanagan Connector: 22, 49, 103, 104
Okanagan Lake: 10, 48, 64
Oligotrophic lakes: 42
Oncorhynchus mykiss: 24
100 Mile House: 128
Outboard motors: 91-92, 98
Owl Point: 121
Oyama Lake: 130

P

Paradise Lake: 104, 132
Paska Lake: 118, 135
Paska Lake Road: 118, 119
Pass Lake: 48, 120, 137
Patrick Lake: 122
Paul Lake: 11, 12, 13, 14, 16, 18, 20, 22, 44-45, 46, 82, 84, 103, 122, 138
Paul Lake Road: 122, 123
Pazooka (fly pattern): 81
Peachland: 130
Peachland Cutoff: See Okanagan Connector
Peamouth chub: See chub
Pearl Lake: 127
Pemberton Lake: 122, 138
Pend Oreille Lake: 14
Pennask Lake: 11, 14, 46, 48, 104, 132

Pennask Lake Fishing Club: 14
Pennask Strain Kamloops trout: 46, 52, 106
Peterhope Lake: 10, 16, 48, 85, 109, 113-114, 124, 134
Peterhope Lake Fishing Camp: 114
Phantom midge: See *Chaoborus*
Pheasant-Tail Nymph (fly pattern): 79
Phillips, Len: 12
Phryganea: See sedges
Physa: See snails
Pikes Lake: 111-112
Pillar Lake: 131
Pimainus Lakes: 108, 133
Pinantan Lake: 11, 12, 14, 20, 122, 138
Pinaus Lake: 131
PKCK (fly pattern): 77
Plankton: 42
Plateau Lake: 10, 114, 116, 134
Playing and landing fish: 96-97
Pondmills: 45, 50-51
Port Coquitlam: 102
Portage Lake: 128
Powell, Dave: 77
Prankard, Dick: 82
Premier Lake: 17
Princeton: 104
Pritchard: 122
Professor (fly pattern): 85

Queen Elizabeth II: 14
Queen of the Waters (fly pattern): 85
Quesnel: 52, 80
Quilchena: 108, 109
Quiltanton Lake: 22

Rabbit Leech (fly pattern): 72-73
Rainbow Chain Lodge: 122
Rainbow trout: 10, 14, 52
Randy Lake: 127
Rat Lake: 106, 132
Redside shiner (*Richardsonius balteatus*): 18, 44, 46, 50, 52, 103, 122, 128
Reels: 90-91, 97
Reservoir Lake: 104, 132
Rhodes Favorite (fly pattern): 85
Richard Lake: 128
Richardson, Lee: 17
Rioux Lake: 129
Robinson Lake: 127
Roche Lake: 20, 21, 22, 49, 51, 64, 77, 88, 119-120, 136
Rock Lake: 106
Rock Island Fishing Camp: 128
Rock Island Lake: 128, 139
Roddy, Bill: 106, 114
Roscoe Lake: 108, 133
Rose Lake (near Kamloops): 51
Rose Lake (near Little Fort): 128
Ross Moore Lake: 118, 135
Roundworms (*Nematoda*): 58
Rouse Lake: 106, 132
Royal Coachman (fly pattern): 17, 85
Rubber rafts: 91, 93
Ruby Lake: 128

Sabin Lakes: 111-112, 113
Salmo gairdneri kamloops: 14
Salmo gairdneri: 10, 14, 24

Salmo kamloopsii: 10
Salmo: 24
Salmon: 10, 36
Salmon Arm: 114
Salmon Lake: 48, 110-111, 134
Savona: 114, 119, 120
Savona's Ferry: 10
Schmid, Werner: 71
Scot Lake: 127
Scuds (*Amphipoda*): 30, 32, 54, 56, 57-58, 63
Scuitto Lake: 120, 136
Sculpin (*Cottus*): 44
Secret Lake: 122
Sedge Adult (fly pattern): 76
Sedge Lake: 128
Sedge Pupa (fly pattern): 73-74
Sedges (*Trichoptera*): 12, 17, 22, 54, 55, 56, 57, 59-61, 63
Self-Bodied Carey (fly pattern): 81
Shaw, Jack: 78
Sheridan Lake: 128-129, 139
Shiners: See Redside shiner.
Shuswap Lake: 10, 11, 17
Silhouette Sedge (fly pattern): 84
Siphlonurus: See mayflies
Six Pack (fly pattern): 81
Skuhun Creek Road: 108
Skunk Lake: 104, 132
Slager (Sleiger) Lake: 128
Smith, Stuart B.: 46
Snails (*Gastropoda*): 32, 36, 57, 58
Sockeye salmon (*Oncorhynchus nerka*): 17, 44 (also see Kokanee)
South Thompson River: 10
Southern Interior Plateau: 10, 11, 40-41, 48, 50
Spences Bridge: 103, 108
Spooney Lake: 124, 138
Spratley, Dr. Donald A.: 82
Squawfish: See northern squawfish
Stake Lake: 51, 116, 135
Stanford University: 10
Steelhead: 10, 112
Stewart, Mary: 71
Stonewort: See *Chara*
Stoney Lake: 24, 104, 109, 111, 113, 134
Strike indicators: 88-90, 96
Stump Lake: 52, 114, 134
Stump Lake Ranch: 114
Suckers (*Catostomus*): 44, 52
Summer kill: 42, 49, 102, 119, 120
Summit Lake: 127
Suntan Shrimp (fly pattern): 72
Surrey Lake: 118, 135
Sussex Lake: 118, 135
Sympetrum: See dragonflies

TaWeel Lake: 128, 139
TaWeel Lake Fishing Lodge: 128
Tahoola Lake: 128, 139
TDC (fly pattern): 77
Teal & Green (fly pattern): 85
Teal & Red (fly pattern): 85
Teal & Silver (fly pattern): 85
Thelma Lake: 128
Thermal stratification (thermocline): 42, 46, 94
Thompson River: 10, 82, 102, 106, 120
Thompson, Dr. Richard B.: 77
Thumb Lake: 128
Thuya Lakes: 103, 126-127, 139
Thuya Lakes Lodge: 126-127

Tintlhahtan Lake: See Tuloon Lake
Tom Thumb (fly pattern): 76
Trail's End Lake: 127
Trans-Canada Highway (Highway 1): 114, 116, 118, 119, 120, 122
Traveling sedge: See sedges
Triangle Lake: 122
Tricorythodes: See mayflies
Tsumura, Kanji: 52
Tsuniah strain rainbow trout: 52
Tulip Lake: 51
Tuloon (Tintlhahtan) Lake: 128, 139
Tuloon Lake Fishing Lodge: 128
Tunkwa Lake: 20, 46, 62, 77, 119, 135
Tunkwa Lake Fishing Camp: 119
Tunkwanamid (fly pattern): 77
Tupper Lake: 108, 133
Twenty-Four Mile Lake: 22
Two Match Lake: 127
Tyner Lake: 108, 133
Tzenzaicut strain rainbow trout: 52

University of British Columbia: 52
Unterwegner, Jim: 129
Upper Hardcastle Lake: See Hardcastle Lakes
Upper Kane Lake: See Kane Valley Lakes

Valentine Lake: 50-51, 52, 129
Vidette Lake: 121
Vincent Sedge (fly pattern): 76-77
Vincent, Jack: 77
Vinsulla: 124

Walhachin: 82
Walker Lake: 104, 132
Walloper Lake: 51, 118, 135
Walters, Bud: 121
Warren Lake: 48, 122, 138
Washington Fly Fishing Club: 62
Wasps (*Hymenoptera*): 66
Water boatman (*Corixidae*): 57, 62, 64
Water bugs (*Belostomatidae*): 64
Water fleas: See *Daphnia*
Werner Shrimp (fly pattern): 70-71
Westwold: 110
Wet-fly fishing: 96
White Lake: 131
Whitefish: See mountain whitefish
Whitehouse, Francis C.: 11, 17
Willard Lake: 40-41, 106, 112-113
Williams, Arthur Bryan: 11, 17, 85
Winehold Lake: 128
Winfield: 130
Winter kill: 32, 42, 49, 50, 52, 102, 103, 106, 108, 109, 114, 118, 119, 120
Wyse Lake: 118, 135

YDC (fly pattern): 77
Yellow jackets: 67
Yoshida, Wayne: 77
Young's Lake: 127

Steve Raymond is a native of Bellingham, Washington, not far from the Kamloops trout lakes of British Columbia. He graduated from the University of Washington with a bachelor's degree in editorial journalism and after service as a Navy officer worked nearly 30 years for *The Seattle Times* as a reporter, editor and manager. During his career with the newspaper he was responsible for editing many prize-winning articles, including a series that won the 1984 Pulitzer Prize for feature writing.

Raymond has served as president of the Washington Fly Fishing Club, Seattle; vice president of the Museum of American Fly Fishing, Manchester, Vt.; secretary of the Federation of Fly Fishers, and editor of the Federation's magazine, *The Flyfisher*. In 1977 he was named the Federation's fly fisherman of the year and in 1993 received its Roderick Haig-Brown Award for literary excellence. He also appeared on the ABC television series, *The American Sportsman*.

Raymond is the author of five books on fly fishing. His first was the first edition of *Kamloops*, published in 1971. A revised edition was published in 1980. His other works include *The Year of the Angler*, (1973, 1983, 1987); *The Year of the Trout*, (1985, 1987); *Backcasts: A History of the Washington Fly Fishing Club, 1939-1989*, (1989), and *Steelhead Country* (1991). He also has contributed to numerous anthologies, including *Fishing Moments of Truth*; *The Masters on the Dry Fly*; *The Masters on the Nymph* and *Waters Swift and Still*. His articles have been published frequently in *Sports Illustrated*, *Fly Fisherman*, *Flyfishing* and other magazines.

Raymond and his wife, the former Joan Zimmerman of Seattle, live in West Seattle. They have two children, a daughter, Stephanie, and son, Randy.